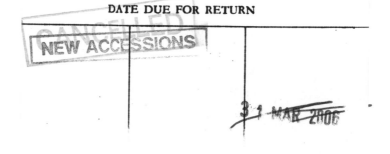

AUSTRIAN EXODUS

Edited by Edward Timms and Ritchie Robertson
AUSTRIAN STUDIES VI

AUSTRIAN EXODUS
The Creative Achievements of Refugees from National Socialism

Edited by Edward Timms and Ritchie Robertson

AUSTRIAN STUDIES VI

EDINBURGH UNIVERSITY PRESS

© Edinburgh University Press, 1995

Edinburgh University Press Ltd
22 George Square, Edinburgh

Typeset in Linotron Ehrhardt by
Koinonia Ltd, Bury, and
printed in Great Britain by
The University Press, Cambridge

A CIP record for this book is available
from the British Library.

ISBN 0 7486 0612 2

Contents

PART TWO: REVIEW ARTICLES

PART THREE: REVIEWS

Contents

List of Illustrations

Thanks are due to the following for permission to reproduce illustrations:

Figures 1, 2 and 4–8 The Estate of Joseph Otto Flatter (and the artist's son); Figure 3 Imperial War Museum; Figure 9 London News Service Ltd.

Preface

The exodus of German-speaking Jews from Nazi-dominated Europe, which reached its climax in the years 1938–9, marks a turning point in the history of the Western world. During the preceding 150 years, since Joseph II's Tolerance Patent of 1782 marked the first cautious step towards emancipation, the territories of the German-speaking world had exerted a powerful attraction for the Jewish communities of central Europe, providing challenging opportunities for entry into civil society. For upwardly mobile Jews in the process of emancipation, the prestige of German culture was so great that Berlin, Vienna, Prague and other rapidly expanding cities became the centres of a remarkable cultural efflorescence – that 'German-Jewish symbiosis' so memorably documented by Ruth Gay in *The Jews of Germany: A Historical Portrait* (New Haven and London, 1992). Although the Jews were never fully accepted by their fellow citizens, the process of assimilation was nevertheless mutually beneficial. As Austria-Hungary and the German Reich embarked on the process of modernisation, their social, economic and cultural development was greatly enhanced by the innovative contributions of their Jewish subjects. The countercurrents of anti-Semitism which emerged in the late nineteenth century were certainly profoundly disturbing; but in practice they did not significantly retard the process of assimilation, until the rise of National Socialism transformed anti-Jewish prejudice into a political system.

In Weimar Germany and the First Austrian Republic, the achievements of assimilated Jews were nevertheless outstanding, especially in fields like science, medicine and the law, music, literature and education. Even during the first five years of the Nazi regime, it was still possible to believe that there might be a future for the German-speaking Jewish communities. It was the political events of 1938–9, together with the anti-Semitic outrages which accompanied them, which finally exposed this belief as an illusion. The annexation of Austria put an end to a process of assimilation which had been steadily evolving, with occasional setbacks, for over a century. After the Anschluss, the Jews of Vienna, numbering over 200,000, were exposed to both systematic persecution and anti-Semitic abuse, and the whole community was clearly at risk. Even more damaging were the 'Kristallnacht' pogroms of November 1938, which

destroyed Jewish lives and property throughout Germany, including Austria –
now renamed the Ostmark and reduced to a province of the Greater German
Reich. By the end of 1938, it was clear that the Nazi regime was planning the
complete destruction of the Jewish communities which had made such an
extraordinary contribution to German and Austrian civilisation.

It was these events, followed by the German occupation of Prague, which
precipitated the most significant cultural exodus of modern times. The impact
of these events on Britain has been systematically documented in *Second
Chance: Two Centuries of German-speaking Jews in the United Kingdom*, edited
by Werner E. Mosse (Tübingen, 1991). During the early years of the Nazi
regime, the movement of refugees was constrained by visa restrictions
imposed by Britain, the United States and other countries of resettlement,
although an estimated 38,000 Jewish migrants did succeed in reaching
Palestine (*Second Chance*, p. 486). The celebrated survey of the refugee
problem published in 1939 by John Hope Simpson paints a bleak picture of
official attitudes in Britain, which limited immigration during the years 1933–
38 to a small annual quota. However, the crises of 1938 brought about a
fundamental change of policy. Under pressure from public opinion, the
governments of Britain and the United States lifted many of their restrictions
on immigration, and as a result these two countries became the main
beneficiaries of the exodus from Nazi-dominated Europe.

Official policy in Britain was that the majority of refugees should be
granted only transit visas, on the assumption that they would soon travel on to
other destinations, above all the United States. The fact that, in the event,
Britain gave shelter to as many as 80,000 refugees from Nazism was a kind of
historical accident. The outbreak of war prevented many of those admitted to
Britain as transmigrants from travelling on to other destinations. Official
figures record that, by autumn 1939, over 78,000 refugees from Nazism had
found sanctuary in Britain: 'Of these, adult refugees from Germany and
Austria numbered some 55,000, Czechs a further 10,000. There were some
13,000 children who had been admitted unaccompanied, and an unspecified
number of children who had come with their parents' (*Second Chance*, p. 512).
Although the British immigration authorities kept no record of religious or
racial affiliation, it has been estimated that about ninety per cent of these
refugees were of Jewish origin.

Refugees are often regarded as defenceless victims who possess few of the
skills necessary for survival in an alien environment. But the exodus from
Nazi Germany and Austria was exceptional, since it comprised a high
proportion of men, women and children from the educated middle classes,
including some of the most gifted members of the intellectual, cultural and
scientific elite. The experiences and achievements of these refugees, including
the outstanding contributions made by many of them to their countries of
resettlement, form the subject of Exile Studies, a discipline which (after
several decades of neglect) has now become an active field of research, not
only at German and Austrian centres but also at a number of universities in
the English-speaking world.

The subject was pioneered by the Society for Exile Studies in the United States, while in Germany research in this field is coordinated by the Gesellschaft für Exilforschung, in association with the Zentrum für Antisemitismus-forschung in Berlin. In Vienna, too, important projects are being undertaken by the Dokumentationsarchiv des österreichischen Widerstandes and the Exilbibliothek im Literaturhaus, supported by Austrian government funding. In Britain, by contrast, it was for many years only the Wiener Library in London, set up during the 1930s to monitor the effects of Nazism, that provided a forum for systematic research on the German-speaking Jews (supplemented by the admirable publications of the Leo Baeck Institute). The Parkes Library at the University of Southampton also includes a collection of documents relating to British support for the refugees. Since the late 1980s, however, the subject has been systematically developed at a number of other British universities, with the establishment of research groups for German and Austrian Exile Studies at the University of Aberdeen and the London Institute of Germanic Studies, followed by the Centre for German-Jewish Studies at the University of Sussex.

The experiences of refugees from National Socialism have been studied from many angles, with an emphasis on the painful experiences of social deprivation and cultural dislocation. The ordeal of internment imposed by the British government on tens of thousands of refugees from Nazism, reclassified as 'enemy aliens' during the panic which followed the fall of France, is memorably recorded in *The Internment of Aliens in Twentieth-Century Britain*, edited by David Cesarani and Tony Kushner (London, 1993). And there are many personal memoirs which record the tragic bereavements and painful readjustments suffered by the refugees. With the passage of time, however, it becomes easier to recognise not simply the fortitude with which the refugees endured such hardships, but also the extraordinary resilience with which many of them responded to their ordeal. It is this paradoxical phenomenon of creativity in exile that forms the subject of the articles collected in this volume. By focusing specifically on refugees from Austria, the book is designed to complement publications which, like *Second Chance*, deal with German-speaking migrants in general.

Austrian refugees, particularly in Britain, developed a distinctive identity with social and cultural organisations of their own, determined to defy Hitler's attempt to erase Austria from the map. Thus the work of the groups and individuals examined in *Austrian Exodus* reveals an underlying unity of purpose, despite their diversity of artistic and ideological orientation. One of the first refugees from Austria to arrive in Britain was Stefan Zweig, who found a temporary home in London and in Bath. It was here that he wrote the classic account of turn-of-the-century Vienna, his autobiography *Die Welt von gestern* (*The World of Yesterday*). Zweig is often thought of as an unpolitical writer, but his unpublished correspondence with his namesake Arnold Zweig (analysed by Jeffrey B. Berlin in the opening chapter on the 'Austrian Catastrophe') reveals a very different picture. Whether he is assessing the precarious position of the Jews in Vienna or criticising the refusal of the

Soviet Union to accept refugees, Stefan Zweig's precise insights reflect his resilient humanism, whereas the letters of Arnold Zweig, written from Palestine, tend to rely on sweeping generalisation. In this chapter, as in a number of others included in *Austrian Exodus*, the use of unpublished sources leads to a radical reassessment of established reputations.

Stefan Zweig's position was untypical, since his international reputation and secure finances made him relatively independent. By contrast, the majority of refugees from Nazism depended on support that they received from relief organisations, above all from the Jewish communities, but also from the Quakers and other charitable groups. The importance of institutional support for the integration of members of specific professions has often been emphasised. The Society for the Protection of Science and Learning played a decisive role in the resettlement of refugee scientists, while the International Psychoanalytical Association provided an effective network for its members. For the writers and artists discussed in this book, the BBC and the PEN Club were of particular importance. Less well-known, however, are the self-help organisations set up by the refugees themselves, which enabled them to sustain a creative social life under conditions of extreme adversity. Many of these organisations might by now have been forgotten, but for the personal testimony of those involved and the systematic inquiries of a new generation of researchers.

The account of 'Austrian Refugee Organisations in Great Britain' contributed by Wolfgang Muchitsch provides an invaluable framework for understanding the remarkable creativity not simply of gifted individuals but also of a wide range of political and cultural groupings. Muchitsch shows that for a period of about ten years London became the centre for highly original work, not only in theatre, cabaret and the visual arts but also in music, literature and poetry. These cultural activities had considerable political significance, not simply because they were organised along ideological lines, from Christian Socials and monarchists on one political wing to Social Democrats and Communists on the other, but also because the very existence of Austria had been obliterated by the Nazis. Politically, the Anschluss had in effect been accepted by the international community, at least until the Moscow Declaration of October 1943 proclaimed that the Allies would re-establish the Austrian Republic. Culturally, it thus became even more important for the exiles to sustain through their artistic activities the concept of a 'Free Austria'. Since there was no Austrian government in exile, the poets had to take over the role of leadership normally played by politicians. The reaffirmation of Austrian independence during the years 1938–45 was essentially the task of small groups of poets and painters, actors, musicians and cabaret performers in Hampstead, Swiss Cottage and Golders Green (paralleled by similar groups in the United States). By the end of 1943, no less than twenty-seven organisations had joined the Free Austrian Movement in London, representing more than 7,000 members.

Organisations like 'Young Austria' reaffirmed Austrian identity under the shadow of fascism. 'Young Austria' was one of the most radical of these cultural groups, with strong communist affiliations. Jörg Thunecke's chapter on 'The Problem of Political Poetry' analyses one of the most significant German-language publications of this group, the poetry anthology *Mut*, published in 1943 by an editorial collective led by the charismatic Erich Fried. Although the quality of some of the poems, especially those written in the aftermath of Stalingrad in praise of the Soviet Union and the Red Army, is impaired by a reliance on political slogans, others – like the declamatory verses of Erich Rattner – achieve a convincing balance between political commitment and aesthetic form. This leads Thunecke to challenge the view of previous researchers that the political poetry of refugees from Nazism is devoid of literary merit.

Fried was one of those doubly gifted writers whose linguistic skills enabled them to establish themselves not only through German publications but also on the English cultural scene. For such writers, the question, at the end of the war, was how to make the transition back to Germany or Austria. The complexities of this double commitment to both German and English writing form the subject of two instructive case studies. In a chapter on Fried's position after 1945, which draws on a wide range of unpublished sources, Steven W. Lawrie shows that the decisive factors were Fried's work for the BBC and his flair as a translator. At Bush House, he joined a group of fellow exiles who formed a kind of German literary academy, including Marius Goring, Bruno Adler, Martin Esslin and Ernst Jandl. Although himself a former member of the Austrian Communist Party, Fried was employed to broadcast anti-communist propaganda to the German Democratic Republic. His particular forte, however, was the translation of poetry. German publishers were initially reluctant to publish his original poetry and prose, but his breakthrough came when he produced for the BBC a widely admired translation of Dylan Thomas's *Under Milk Wood*. It was thus by 'Crossing Borders through the Ether' that Fried established his reputation as one of the leading German poets of the post-war period, although he continued to live in London until his death in 1988.

The case of Hilde Spiel is even more complex, as Konstanze Fliedl shows in a chapter on 'Linguistic Rights of Residence'. Writing with almost equal facility in English and in German, Spiel developed a kind of double identity, most memorably expressed in her play *Anna & Anna*, which enacts the creative schizophrenia of exile, juxtaposed against the putative identity left behind. After her arrival in London in 1936, she gradually came to feel at home in the English language, publishing both novels and essays in English and enjoying the warm welcome which the English PEN Club offered to writers in exile. But Spiel's reflections on language as a shared 'spiritual realm', a concept borrowed from Hofmannsthal, never obscured the recognition that a true home has to have more solid foundations. After considerable hesitation, she finally returned to Vienna in 1963, continuing in Austria the role which she had played in Britain as intermediary between the two cultures.

Since the majority of the refugees from Nazism were of Jewish origin, it is not surprising that Britain also became a focus for Zionist activities. When the young Josef Fraenkel was interned, we are told by Evelyn Adunka in her chapter on 'Austrian Zionism in Exile', he set up in the camp at Huyton a Zionist organisation with 1,000 members. In the post-war period, despite reservations about what he saw as the over-cautious strategy adopted by Chaim Weizmann to consolidate the State of Israel, Fraenkel's gifts as a journalist made him a key figure both in the international Zionist movement and in the British Section of the World Jewish Congress. In addition to his lifelong commitment to Zionism, however, Fraenkel was determined to preserve his Austro-Jewish heritage. This led him in 1967 to publish *The Jews of Austria*, a pioneering collection of essays which gives particular prominence to the achievements of assimilated Jews during the 100 years before the Anschluss.

The creativity of the exiles took many forms. In the visual arts, the most prominent figure was the artist Oskar Kokoschka, who during the 1930s painted powerful allegories on the rise of fascism and later played a leading role in the cultural organisations of the Austrian refugees. In political terms, however, a greater impact was made by the cartoons of Joseph Otto Flatter, the subject of a chapter by Dorothea McEwan on the 'Politicisation of a Portrait-Painter'. Drawing on Flatter's unpublished memoirs, she reconstructs his wartime career from the indignities of internment to the position of official war artist entrusted with the task of producing visual propaganda to be dropped in leaflet form over Nazi-occupied Europe. The economy of his artistic technique, reinforced by the ironic use of quotations and captions, enabled him to expose the hollowness of Hitler's rhetoric and the destructive consequences of his policies. For an artist whose prophetic cartoons confidently anticipated the defeat of the Hitler regime, it was gratifying to be sent to Nuremberg in 1946 to make drawings of the Nazi war criminals in the dock.

Although the main focus of this book is on the activities of refugees in Britain, the achievements of those who settled in the United States form an equally fascinating theme. The work of the Austro-American poet Felix Pollak (analysed by Gregory Mason) provides a further instance of the complex forms of creativity generated by a double linguistic gift. Pollak crossed the language barrier by setting up a poetry-reading circle at Northwestern University in Illinois, where he was employed as a librarian. Writing for little magazines, he developed a terse and laconic English poetic style reminiscent of William Carlos Williams. And during the 1960s, after moving to Madison, Wisconsin, Pollak became a key figure in the counter-culture through poetry written in protest against the Vietnam War. Like so many other Austrian exiles in the United States, however, he never lost his ambivalent attachment to Vienna. His later work, written after the onset of blindness, explores the poignant experience of returning in old age to a city replete with the memories of childhood.

The autobiographical element, which is such a recurrent feature in the writings of Austrian migrants, becomes a definitive form of creativity in the late work of Elias Canetti. In a chapter which takes issue with conventional approaches to Exile Studies, Harriet Murphy shows how Canetti's 'Passion for People', enhanced by the vividness of his narrative style, endows past experience with a timeless immediacy. Although Canetti also spent the war years in Hampstead, his uncompromising individualism places him outside the familiar parameters of group solidarity. His concept of resistance is less political than existential, dedicated to defending the integrity of the self against collective ideologies and celebrating the 'felt life' of individual relationships by means of memorable scenic re-enactments. What emerges from his autobiography is thus not the conventional picture of the rootless Jewish exile participating in a collective ordeal, but the inviolable uniqueness of interpersonal encounters.

This sequence of contributions on individual themes is complemented by three review articles which offer an overview of recent research. Assessing a wide range of recent publications on the 'Exodus from Austria', J. M. Ritchie focuses on the controversies caused by British internment policies and the more constructive role of the Pioneer Corps, as well as the remarkable contributions made by German-speaking refugees to the BBC and the world of film. He also draws attention to the development of data-banks, which now make it possible to reconstruct the achievements not simply of the cultural elite, but also of the thousands of refugees whose useful but unobtrusive careers have hitherto remained unrecorded. The ideological conflicts underlying the triumph of National Socialism form the subject of Alan Bance's account of publications dealing with 'Austria between the Wars', including the radical reassessment of cultural life in the First Republic by Klaus Amann. These publications undermine the comforting myth of Austria as (in the words of the Moscow Declaration) 'the first victim' of Nazi aggression, by demonstrating the strength of German nationalism and anti-Semitism under the Corporate State. The continuities between reactionary Austrian writing in the 1930s and the conservative restoration after 1945 are also made distressingly clear. On a more positive note, Richard Woodfield shows how the pioneering conceptions of art history associated with Alois Riegl and the 'Vienna School' were transmitted to the English-speaking world, not least through the critical reassessments undertaken by migrants like Ernst Gombrich.

Following the established policy of *Austrian Studies*, this volume concludes with a series of shorter book reviews designed to make the results of specialised research available to a wider audience. The themes of the books reviewed range from the emergence of Vienna as a political centre in the late seventeenth century to the coffeehouse wits of the First Republic, from the legends surrounding the Empress Elisabeth of Austria to the reception of controversial Austrian feminists like Elfriede Jelinek in the German-language press. Also included is an assessment of recent research on women writers' accounts of their experiences as refugees, confirming that there is scope for further work on 'authors hitherto exiled from exile studies'.

Part One

The Austrian Catastrophe

Political Reflections in the Unpublished Correspondence of Stefan Zweig and Arnold Zweig

Jeffrey B. Berlin

'The Austrian catastrophe', observed Ben Huebsch in an unpublished letter of 3 May 1938 to Arnold Zweig, 'is so great and operates so crushingly on hundreds of thousands that the loss which you and other authors suffer must be considered philosophically'. Arnold Zweig's responses to the political crises of the late 1930s were in the event anything but philosophical, to judge from his private correspondence with his Austrian namesake Stefan Zweig, which has also hitherto remained unpublished.[1] Their letters vividly record both the personal responses and the political views of the two authors, Stefan in exile in London and Arnold in Palestine. Above all, they throw light on their contrasting attitudes towards the plight of the Viennese Jews.

By 1938, Arnold and Stefan Zweig, both established authors in their fifties, had experienced many years of personal friendship as well as literary success. Their friendship was based both on personal respect and on literary appreciation of their contrasting modes of creativity. Stefan admired in Arnold's work the qualities he felt that he himself lacked: epic breadth, objectivity and concentrated use of detail.[2] But in 1938 they were also brought together by acute anxieties about their Jewish heritage in the face of the dramatic extension of Hitler's power.

Despite the political crisis, the tone of one of the earliest of Stefan's letters in this sequence is still relatively optimistic. On 20 November 1937, he writes to Arnold in Palestine, congratulating him on his fiftieth birthday and emphasising the need for solidarity: 'Bleiben wir, wie durch den Namen, auch innerlich verbunden durch den Willen, anständig zu wirken, jeder nach seiner Begabung und seinen Kräften'. However, this emotionally-charged letter also reflects the growing despair felt by German-speaking Jews since Hitler's seizure of power. Stefan's words express a vehement desire to find some way of resisting the Nazi tyranny – a task in which he believes he can count on Arnold's support. Arnold's replies, however, reveal that both politically and temperamentally there was a considerable gulf between them.

Before considering Arnold's reactions, we should first observe that although Stefan's intentions appear admirable, his opposition to Nazism in practice remained a rather private affair, articulated in his letters rather than in any public actions. Although after 1933 he continued to publish widely on literary and cultural subjects, politically Stefan Zweig maintained a cautious silence.[3] By contrast, Arnold Zweig was far more outspoken in his declarations against the Hitler regime. But he too had doubts about the most effective form in which protests against Fascism should be expressed. As Arnold wrote to Freud on 2 May 1935: 'Die Zeit ist trübe, es ist zum Glück nicht meine Aufgabe, sie aufzuhellen' (The times are dark, fortunately it is not my task to put them right).[4]

A few months earlier, Stefan and Arnold had been able to arrange a personal meeting in London, during which they had discussed the political situation. It is to this meeting that Arnold refers in a letter to Stefan dated 23 November 1937:

> Unsere Unterhaltung hat mich recht beeindruckt und ich denke öfter, als Sie glauben, an Ihre geängstigte und profetische Rede. Wir gehen zurzeit durch eine [der] dunkelsten Epochen der Menschengeschichte – wobei ich mehr an China und Spanien als an uns Beide denke.

> [Our conversation impressed me very much and I think more often than you may believe about your anxious and prophetic words. We're passing at the moment through one of the darkest periods of human history – by which I am thinking more of China and Spain than of us two personally.]

Further details about that London meeting are given in Arnold's unpublished letter of 21 November 1937 to Ben Huebsch, the American publisher of both authors.[5] This letter speaks about 'a particularly pleasant afternoon' in London with Stefan, during which they had been able to resolve certain disagreements ('während dessen wir freimütig und aufrichtig erörterten und bereinigten, was wir gegeneinander auf dem Herzen hatten (ich mehr als er)'). The nature of those disagreements is, however, not entirely clear.

While we have no reliable record of their conversation in London, certain differences of opinion do emerge from their subsequent letters, not only in their contrasting views of world events but also in their sense of personal security and emotional equilibrium. After the Anschluss, Stefan's concern focuses increasingly on the plight of his fellow Jews in continental Europe. At the same time, it becomes clear that his capacity to respond constructively to these events was inhibited by terrifying bouts of depression. Arnold's political interests, on the other hand, extended well beyond German-speaking Europe. Although genuinely concerned about the European situation, his reflections are complicated by an overriding preoccupation with developments in Palestine, his chosen place of refuge. In his letter to Stefan of 23 November 1937, he offers a differentiated account of the position of the Jews in Palestine:

> Die Lage hier ist zwar deprimierend, der Wille der Menschen, das auf falscher Grundlage begonnene Experiment durchzuhalten aber zäh und stetig. Und da man den Juden nur dieses kleine Ventil gelassen hat, bleibt wohl auch für die skeptischesten nur die Parole bessere Zeiten

vorzubereiten durch Einsicht in die begangenen Fehler. Diese verbreitet sich, wie mir scheint. Und da die moralischen Kräfte im Lande gross sind, wird das winzig gewordene Palästina wohl durchgesteuert werden.

[The situation here is admittedly depressing, but the people are maintaining a steadfast determination to carry through this experiment that began on the wrong foot. And as the Jews have been left only this small outlet, there only remains, even for the most sceptical, the motto of preparing for better times through recognising our own mistakes. This slogan seems to me to be spreading. And as the moral strength in the country is great, Palestine, even though tiny, will be steered through.]

Arnold's comments acknowledge that in Palestine the determination and willpower of Jewish settlers constitute constructive forces for change. But it becomes clear from their later exchanges that Stefan felt some resentment not so much about Arnold's preoccupation with Palestine but about his apparent lack of sympathy for the beleaguered situation of the European Jews during their hour of greatest need. A careful reading of the letters makes it possible to arrive at a just assessment of Arnold's views, also taking account of assertions made elsewhere.[6]

In a further letter, dated 30 December 1937, Stefan contrasts his European commitments with the attractions of Palestine:

eigentlich dachte ich daran, mich für Palästina als Besucher anzumelden, aber es scheint mir frivol, so weit herumzugondeln in dem einen Meere, indess jenes der Sorge unablässig ansteigt – Rumänien ist der vielleicht schwerste Schlag für das Judentum und darüberhinaus für Europa, der gedacht werden konnte; ich erwarte die Nachwirkung in Polen, Ungarn, die Folgen für Österreich ...

[I was thinking of signing myself on as a visitor to Palestine, but it seems frivolous to take such a long pleasure trip over one sea when the other, the sea of care and worry, is constantly rising – Romania is perhaps the worst blow imaginable for the Jews and for Europe itself; I am awaiting the effects on Poland and Hungary and the consequences for Austria.]

Referring again to their London encounter, Stefan emphasises his self-appointed role as an intermediary ('Vermittler').[7] He also expresses his sense of the need for more organised resistance: 'Immer mehr fühle ich die Notwendigkeit einer Organisation'.

Years earlier, Stefan had indeed attempted to gather support from colleagues and friends for the composition of a manifesto, which, as he said to Albert Einstein on 7 June 1933, 'nicht wehleidig jammert und klagt, sondern durchaus positiv, selbstbewusst und dabei mit äusserster Ruhe unsere Situation vor der Welt klarlegt' (would not be full of moans and complaints, but thoroughly positive and responsible in approach, setting out our position for the world with utmost calmness).[8] But the document found little support and, aside from a draft written by Stefan himself, never materialised as planned.[9]

From the tone of Stefan's remarks in his letter of 30 December to Arnold, we realise that even at the end of 1937 he still longs for some more concerted mode of action:

> Aber keine Einheit als die gemeinsame und gleich ohnmächtige Verzweiflung! Verzeihen Sie, dass ich, der ich Sie nur grüssen wollte, so bitter werde, aber ich war in Wien (auch bei Freud) und habe diese Stadt ganz mit dem Blick gesehen, als stünden die Feinde schon vor den Toren.

> [But our only unity is our shared impotence and despair! Forgive me for becoming so bitter, when I only wanted to send you greetings, but I was in Vienna (and also visited Freud) and looked on that city just as if the enemy were already at the gates.]

Despite Stefan's awareness of the impending crisis, we also know that he wanted to avoid a situation in which only Jews took a stand against Hitler.

Stefan felt tormented by the question of how to respond to the crisis, but the very consciousness of his dilemma may have made matters even worse. Throughout the period of Nazi domination in Europe, his outlook was characterised by indecision and perplexity. Even before Hitler's seizure of power in Germany, he had been aware of a tendency towards neuroticism. Stefan Zweig was not simply an exile from his homeland but above all a hostage to his own habits. And as the Nazis intensified their drive to rid Europe of the Jews, so too did Stefan's anxiety increase. His anguished state is already indicated in his comments of 10 April 1933 to his friend Romain Rolland, written at a time when he was wondering whether to leave his home in Salzburg: 'Bleiben und schweigen (zum Schweigen gezwungen sein) macht der Feigheit verdächtig. Fortgehen riecht noch stärker nach Feigheit' (To stay and keep silent (to be forced into silence) is to be suspected of cowardice. To go smells even more strongly of cowardice).[10]

The year 1938 intensified these feelings of alarm and indecision. By this date, Stefan had already been living for four years in the security of England. Sensing what history might bring, he had in fact taken his own fate into his own hands and willingly exiled himself from his beloved Austria. As Franz Werfel acutely observed, Stefan followed the basic principle: 'Lieber ein Jahr zu früh, als einen Tag zu spät' (Better a year too early than a day too late).[11] Arnold Zweig had also reacted promptly to the impending danger. In March 1933 he had emigrated from Germany, finally settling in Haifa, where he remained until 1948.

The pessimism and despondency felt by Stefan Zweig in exile have, of course, been emphasised in a number of previous accounts.[12] But his unpublished letters enhance our view of his situation both through their unsparing honesty and through the courage with which he challenges Arnold's views. The refreshing openness of both writers, in letters not written with one eye on publication, allows us to gain insight into their private thought-processes. Rather surprisingly, the judgements of the supposedly unpolitical Stefan Zweig come closer to the truth than those of his politically more committed namesake. Not that in acknowledging the truth there was any real consolation. After the Anschluss, Stefan observes in a letter of late April 1938:

> Es ist ungemein schwer, jetzt das Richtige zu sagen und gerade die Wahrheit vielleicht ein Seelengift.

> [It is extraordinarily hard now to say the right thing, and the truth itself is perhaps poison for the soul.]

Two months earlier, on 24 February 1938, after returning from Portugal, Stefan had written to his friend in Palestine in tones that already anticipated the disaster. He had wanted to comment on Arnold Zweig's *Einsetzung eines Königs* (*The Crowning of a King*), a work with which, apart from one or two reservations, for example about the 'contrived diction' (überkluge Diction) of the German generals, he 'completely agreed'. However, such a long letter was not possible: 'mir scheint im Augenblick alles Literarische so entsetzlich nebensächlich neben den brennenden Sorgen der letzten Wochen' (Everything literary seems to me at the moment so unimportant beside the burning anxieties of the last few weeks). Stefan's letter then continues:

> Erst Rumänien, dann Österreich, wo ich Verwandte, Freunde und zahllose Unglückliche zurücklasse: dass auch der Rest unseres Familienvermögens dort unlösbar hängt, ist nicht so arg – man wird das tausendfach für Unterstützungen brauchen.

> [First Romania, then Austria, where I have left behind relations, friends and countless unfortunates: that the remainder of our family fortune is still irretrievably stranded there is not so bad – it will be needed a thousandfold for supporting others.]

In this letter of 24 February, he also acknowledges that the impending catastrophe threatens finally to deprive him of his readership, not only in Austria but also in the wider world:

> Dass wir den letzten Boden, die letzte Wirksamkeit unserer Bücher verlieren, dass es den Leuten wirklich *gelungen* ist uns in deutscher Sprache mundtot zu machen (und sie versuchen es mit Erfolg bereits in andern Ländern) *das* ist es, was uns am tiefsten trifft.

> [The thing that really affects us most deeply is the loss of the last foothold, the last area of influence for our books, the fact that these people have *succeeded* in silencing us completely in the German language (and they are already trying, with some success, to do the same in other countries).]

While not disregarding the threat to individual lives and families, he is also concerned with the fate of books and readers. His pessimism in this letter forms a stark contrast to the remarks of Ben Huebsch, in the letter quoted at the beginning of this chapter, insisting that leading authors (like the Zweigs) were 'fortunate in having a world market'.[13]

The German threat to Austria in February 1938 leaves Stefan with the sense that he is losing his 'homeland' for the second time:

> Ich bin wirklich tiefverstört gewesen in diesen Tagen, denn ich habe ja die Austreibung *zweimal* erlebt, seit vier Jahren in der unanfechtbaren Vorahnung (mit meiner Frau, meiner Familie kämpfend und sie nicht wegreissen könnend von der 'Heimat' die längst keine mehr für mich war) und jetzt in der Realität – ...

> [I myself have been really deeply disturbed during these days, for I've experienced being driven out *twice*, four years ago with my unassailable premonition (fighting with my wife, my family, unable to tear them away from the 'homeland' which had long since ceased to be one for me), and now in reality – ...]

But the emotional power of his letters arises from his ability to identify with those left behind in Austria who are now under a direct personal threat:

> Ich muss jetzt täglich Dutzende Briefe an all die schreiben, die von mir Rat wollen wie man aus Österreich ins Ausland kommt, aber wie wirklich raten, geschweige helfen!

> [I have dozens of letters to write now every day to all those who want advice how to get abroad out of Austria; but how is one to give real advice, let alone help!]

Whereas Stefan focused directly on the immediate situation before him, Arnold tended to look beyond the European continent and the tragic turmoil which it was experiencing. On 9 March 1938 – just five days before the Anschluss – he replied to Stefan:

> Für Ihre drei Briefe danke ich herzlich, um so herzlicher, je weniger ich Ihre verzweifelte Stimmung teile. Sie haben mit allem, was Sie sagen, Recht. Dies voraus. Aber ist die Perspektive, die sich eröffnet wert, dass sich unser Gemüt verdüstert?

> [For your three letters, many thanks; the more hearty the less I share your despairing mood. Let's admit that you are right in everything you say. But does the prospect which is opening up justify such a darkening of our spirit?]

To someone of Stefan's temperament, this response must have seemed heartless, or at least far too matter-of-fact. For Arnold goes on to play down the catastrophic consequences of Nazism, directing attention instead to the dictatorial actions of Stalin in the Soviet Union:

> Ich betrachte fassungslos aber fast erheitert, was sich in Russland abspielt. Hier wird Zukunft grossen Stils aus undurchsichtigen Gründen zugrunde gerichtet. Hier bahnt sich die Thronbesteigung eines Mannes an, der sicher zu den schlauesten und subtilsten Technikern des Erfolgs gehört, die je ohne Skrupel geboren wurden. Das ist was. Das macht ganze

Schichten von Intellektuellen und Arbeitern hoffnungslos. Das hebt Millionen den Zweifel an Sinn und Wert des Sozialismus. Das beeinflusst unser aller Leben. Aber der Müll, den jeder Wind aus Deutschland herübertreiben lässt? Das Los der Austriaken, die so lange begabte Phäaken waren? Unsere Literatur? Wir? Die junge Generation?

[I view what is happening in Russia without composure, but almost with amusement. There a grandiose conception of the future is being destroyed for reasons we cannot fathom: a man is mounting the throne who is certainly one of the most cunning and subtle technicians of success who was ever born without scruples. That really is something. It deprives whole classes of intellectuals and workers of their hopes, makes millions doubt the sense and value of socialism. It influences the life of us all. But the rubbish that every wind from Germany is driving across? The fate of the Austrians, who for so long have been talented pleasure-seekers? Our literature? We ourselves? The younger generation?]

Stefan Zweig's view of the remarkable changes taking place in Russia is a topic to which the critics have devoted scant attention.[14] For Arnold's comments about Russia elicited a significant response from his Austrian friend, as we shall see.

Another striking section in Arnold's letter of 9 March appears to treat human suffering simply as if it were the 'humus' for cultural achievement:

Lieber S. Z., am Ende meiner Romane wird Berlin einen Leichenhaufen mustern: unsere Generation. Und doch sind neue nachgewachsen, mit reaktionären Süchten und Ängsten, aber doch mit viel praktischem Verstand und mehr Lebenskenntnis als wir je erwarben. Sie wird verstummen? Schön. Haben wir aber mal gehabt, zwischen 1818 und 48, zwischen 51 und 71. Und doch ist grosse schöne Kultur aus dem Humus der napoleonischen 1½ Millionen Toter gewachsen.

[Dear S. Z, at the end of my novels Berlin will muster a heap of corpses: our own generation. And yet new people have come along, with reactionary desires and fears, but still with a lot of practical sense and more knowledge of life than we ever acquired. That will be silenced? Fine. We've seen it all before, between 1818 and '48, between 1851 and '71. And yet a fine, extensive culture managed to grow out of the humus of Napoleon's 1½ million dead.]

Not surprisingly, Stefan took issue with Arnold's views. Their exchanges may be read as a debate during which, at least initially, each contestant attempted to refute the other's position.

While it is valuable to record their exchanges on current political affairs, it is also important to consider the degree to which personal factors influenced their responses. Arnold, adopting the stance of the hard-headed political realist, seems to regard Stefan's anxieties as the sign of a depressive or narcissistic temperament:

Ich fürchte, die Depression, unter der Sie leiden, kommt aus Ihnen selbst, und unsere Epoche ist nur der Anlass, sie zu entfesseln. Vieles in unserem letzten Gespräch berechtigt mich zu dieser Annahme. Der Narzissmus des Künstlers treibt Sie dazu, lieber zu leiden als analytisch zu kapitulieren und auf der Basis dessen, was wirklich ist, ein neues Dasein zu beginnen. Um von mir zu reden: ich habe 33 die deutschen Juden abgeschrieben, obwohl ich zu ihrer Verteidigung das erste starke Buch in die Läden warf. Aber, was mir an Österreich teuer und zerstörbar ist, umschreiben fünf Buchstaben: Freud.

[I fear the depression you are suffering comes from you yourself, and our epoch is only the trigger to release it. A great deal in our last discussion justifies me in making this assumption. It is the narcissism of the artist which makes you prefer to suffer than analytically to acknowledge defeat and start a new life on the basis of the real facts. To speak of myself: in 1933 I wrote off the German Jews, even though my book in their defence was the first to hit the bookstores. But what is dear to me and destructible about Austria can be expressed in five letters: Freud.]

Arnold's use of psychoanalytic terminology is hardly surprising, given that both he and Stefan were such fans of Freud. Actually, it was Arnold himself who had recently been seeing an analyst. And it must be said that Stefan's personal anxieties show a far greater sensitivity to the implications of the crisis than Arnold's historical generalisations.

The comments in Arnold's letter about having 'written off' the German Jews provoked an immediate response. In a letter dated 16 March 1938, Stefan replies:

Dank für Ihren Brief – aber wir wollen ihn lieber nicht für den Band 'Gesammelte Briefe' zum Druck bewahren, trotz seiner beschwingten Stimmung. Denn wenn Sie sagen, Sie hätten 1933 'die deutschen Juden abgestrichen', so ist das entsetzliche Leiden von Hunderttausenden doch damit nicht abgestrichen.

[Thanks for your letter – but we won't preserve it to print in the volume of 'Collected Letters', in spite of its airy mood. For when you say that in 1933 you 'wrote off the German Jews', you can't write off in that way the terrible suffering of thousands.]

Stefan's ironic comment about the 'collected letters' may be taken as an attempt to temper his own sense of outrage.[15] But Stefan strikes a very different tone when it comes to defending the Jews of Vienna against Arnold's heartless and ignorant comments:

Jeden Tag schwemmt nun eine Sturzflut auf den Tisch, dass sie mir fast die Arbeit wegreisst und ich *will* auch gar nicht dieses Elend abstreichen oder wegschieben. Nein, und auch Wien kennen Sie schlecht (vielleicht war Ihre Stimmung etwas galgenhumoristisch) – auf der Taborstrasse lebten keine 'Phäaken' sondern ein an Ostgalizien erinnerndes Kleinelend, das durch die Fülle *vordem* schon furchtbar war. Die Phäaken wohnten immer auf einer kleinen Insel – in diesem Fall um die Ringstrasse, die einzige über die der Fremde schlendert.

[Every day now a torrent submerges my desk, almost sweeping away my work, and I am *not* willing to write off this misery or set it aside. No, and Vienna too you don't really know (or maybe it was just grim humour on your part) – on the Taborstrasse [the impoverished Jewish quarter] there were no 'pleasure-seekers', but a pathetic pool of misery reminiscent of East Galicia, *already* frightful in its abundance. The sybarites always lived on a small island – in this case, round the Ringstrasse, the only one frequented by the foreigner.]

Although Stefan acknowledges his friend's admirable qualities, he is bewildered to find Arnold now espousing a position that belies his earlier sense of responsibility:

Nein, lieber Arnold Zweig, ich verstehe ja diese Aufwallung, dass man sich sagt: Genug! Und sauve qui peut! Aber Sie haben seit fünf Jahren in Ihren Aufsätzen unablässig von andern Anteilnahme an Zorn, an Hilfsnotwendigkeit gefordert und jetzt *darf* niemand Urlaub nehmen, gerade jetzt nicht, wo die ganze Front ins Wanken gekommen ist. Gerade jetzt im fürchterlichsten Augenblick!

[No, dear Arnold Zweig, I can understand this boiling over, this urge to say: enough! And sauve qui peut! But you in your essays have constantly demanded that others should participate in anger and the need for help, and now no-one *is permitted* to opt out, now least of all when the whole front is starting to waver. Not now, at this most terrible moment!]

According to Stefan, the issue involved what to him should have marked the highest of an individual's priorities: responsibility, both to oneself and to others. He even takes issue with Arnold's insinuation about his emotional state, pointing out that depression is the price that has to be paid by all those who see it as their duty to resist the political catastrophe: 'Wir stehen vor der grössten Katastrofe und jetzt oder nic ist *meiner Meinung* nach es Pflicht, beizustehen und auch die eigene Depression nicht zu fürchten ...'.

On 24 April 1938, Arnold replied, describing Stefan's letter as 'beautiful and sympathetic' (schön und teilnehmend) and commending him for facing up to the 'needs of the time' (Nöten der Zeit). He adds that he has just finished his short novel *Versunkene Tage (Lost Days)*:

In diesem Roman zeigt sich, wie schon damals, 1908, aus der österreichischen Politik ein Weltkrieg entstanden wäre, wäre die Konstellation damals durch Russlands Niederlage in Japan nicht kriegverhindernd gewesen; an den Österreichern lag es nicht. Und wenn ich nun einen

Sprung in den März 1938 mache, so können Sie sich vorstellen, wie wenig geneigt ich war, in der kampflosen Kapitulation dieses Rests einstiger habsburgischer Macht den Aufruf zu Mitleid zu sehen.

[In it I show how, even as early as 1908, a world war could have resulted from Austrian policy, had not the constellation at the time, through Russia's defeat in Japan, prevented that: it was no thanks to the Austrians. And if I now make a leap to March 1938, you can imagine how little inclined I was to see a call for sympathy in the capitulation of this remainder of what was once Habsburg power without putting up any fight.]

Insisting that he knows only too well what miscry is ('Ich weiss, was Elend ist'), Arnold emphasises the need for plain speaking, even about Palestine:

Ich bereite eben ein Buch über Palästina vor, in dem ich versuchen will, ohne eine notwendige Sache zu schädigen, die Wahrheit über sie zu sagen.

[I am preparing a book on Palestine, in which I want to try to tell the truth about it without damaging a necessary cause.]

Elaborating on conditions in Palestine, the letter continues:

Von den 400.000 Juden Palästinas leben höchstwahrscheinlich 12.000 in einigermassen gesicherten Umständen. Alle anderen haben teils durch ausserordentliche Senkung ihrer Lebenshaltung und teils durch verstecken in den Siedlungen und Kwuzoth ihr Elend unsichtbar gemacht. Dazu kommen die täglichen Morde, Überfälle, Angriffe.

[Of the 400,000 Jews in Palestine, 12,000 are most probably living in more or less assured circumstances. All the rest have managed to conceal their poverty, partly by an extraordinary drop in their living standards, partly by hiding in the settlements. And then there are the daily murders, assaults, attacks.]

His conclusion is: 'diese Menschen hier sind nicht die Opfer ihrer eigenen falschen Politik, sondern fremder Suggestionen, Neurosen und Ambitionen' (these people are the victims, not of their own mistaken ideas, but of the ideas, neuroses and ambitions of others).

Returning to his contentious remarks about Vienna, he attempts to clarify his position:

Mein Brief galt nicht den Leuten der Taborstrasse. Diesen Typus Mensch kenne ich ja seit meinen Kriegsjahren im Osten. Was mich ausser mir brachte, war die klare Erinnerung an all die klugen und kultivierten wiener Juden, deren politische Instinktlosigkeit mich seit der Niederwerfung der wiener [sic] Arbeiterregierung, d.h. seit dem Aufstieg des seligen Dollfuss, abgestossen hat.

[My letter didn't refer to the people in the Taborstrasse: I knew that type of person from my war years in Eastern Europe. What enraged me was the clear memory of all the clever and cultivated Jews of Vienna, whose lack of political instinct has repelled me ever since the overthrow of the Viennese workers' government, i.e. since the rise of the late lamented Dollfuss.]

Despite this concession, Arnold still insists that the supporters of the authoritarian regimes of Brüning and Schuschnigg (who included many members of the Jewish bourgeoisie) must bear part of the responsibility for the triumph of National Socialism:

> Immer ist Hitler die Folge irgend eines Herrn Schuschnigg oder Brüning. Dass dabei die wertvollsten Menschen, persönlich achtbarste und liebenswürdigste Leute, als erste Opfer fallen, hindert nicht die Pflicht, diese schwermütige und lähmende Pflicht, die Dinge zu verstehen und das Urteil in gelegentlichen Briefen festzuhalten. Da ich noch keinen meiner Briefe auch nur aus dem Augenwinkel mit jenem Blick betrachtet habe, der etwa einer späteren Veröffentlichung gelten könnte, muss ich die Folgen des Eindrucks tragen, den diese Briefe machen. Aber irgendwo muss ja die Unbefangenheit des Privatlebens beginnen, auch für den Schriftsteller, und gerade für ihn.

> [A Hitler is always the consequence of a Schuschnigg or a Brüning. The fact that the first victims are the most valuable, personally respected and charming people does not absolve one from the duty, the sad and crippling duty, of understanding the situation and making a judgement in occasional letters. As I have never looked on any of my letters, even from the corner of my eye, with the idea of later publication, I have to bear the consequences of the impression they may make. But the candour of private life has to begin somewhere, even for the writer, and especially for him.]

It is precisely this candour which gives this correspondence its special value.

In this same letter, Arnold claims – with some justice – that in books like *Caliban* (1927) and *Bilanz der deutschen Judenheit* (1934) he has for years been warning his readers about the destructive consequences of fascism and the dilemma of the German-speaking Jews. In this sense, he scarcely needs to offer any apology for now expressing his political disillusionment:

> Was also Ihnen, lieber Stefan Zweig, jetzt das Leben verdirbt und das Schreiben verhindert, ist mir seit geraumer Zeit ein gewohnter Umgang. Leider haben die Nazis einen grossen Teil meiner Aufsätze mit vielen anderen Manuskripten rauben können. Ich würde Ihnen sonst Proben schicken, die mich in Ihren Augen entschuldigen würden.

> [So what for you, my dear Stefan Zweig, is ruining your life and hindering your writing, has been for me the normal state of affairs for a long time now. The Nazis, alas, have been able to steal a large part of

my essays, along with many other manuscripts. Otherwise I would send you samples which would justify me in your eyes.]

Arnold insists on the need to take a global view of the political crisis:

Ich kann jetzt nur noch in grossen politischen Gruppen sehen und denken. Die Entwicklung in Spanien, die niederträchtige non intervention, die auf der anderen Seite uns hier vor den italienischen Bombenfliegern bewahrt hat, treibt mich seit Jahr und Tag ruhelos umher.

[I can now see and think only in terms of large political groupings. The developments in Spain, the despicable non-intervention, which on the other hand has preserved us here from Italian bombers, has been making me restless for at least a year.]

An undated letter written soon afterwards shows that it was only with reservations that Stefan accepted Arnold's remarks, especially his strictures on the Jews of Vienna. Turning the psychological tables on Arnold, he suggests that his political optimism is a form of 'inverted despair':

Ich hatte schon gleich verstanden, dass auch Ihr heftiger Optimismus nichts als eine umgewendete Verzweiflung war. Was in Wien geschieht hat *seines gleichen nicht* in der Geschichte des Judentums – Deutschland war ein Sammtpfötchen gegen diesen mörderischen Hieb. Nein, klagen Sie die Menschen nicht an, zu gläubig gewesen zu sein – die Wiener, die öster-reichischen Juden waren ja viel homogener in ihrer Struktur als die deutschen, sie gehörten dazu, sie hatten diese Stadt Wien geformt und mitgeschaffen.

[I had already understood right away that even your strong optimism was nothing but a inverted despair. What is happening in Vienna has *no parallel* in the history of Jewry – Germany was a velvet paw compared to that murderous blow. No, don't accuse the people of having been credulous – the Viennese, the Austrian Jews were much more homogeneous in their make-up than the Germans, they belonged there, they had shaped and helped to create that city of Vienna.]

Like Arnold, Stefan too can claim to have shown considerable foresight:

Ach, *was* habe ich gewarnt … ich wollte wenigstens mit meinen Büchern in Österreich bleiben, um nicht zu zeigen, dass ich den Untergang sehe. Aber es ist ein Verhängnis – wo Juden nicht logisch, nicht geistig durchdacht handeln sondern *sentimental* handeln sie falscher und dummer als der primitivste Bauer.

[Ah, *how* I warned everyone. … I myself wanted to stay in Austria at least with my books so as not to show that I foresaw the end. But it's fatal: where Jews don't behave logically, intelligently, but *sentimentally*, their actions are more stupid and wrong than those of the most primitive peasant.]

14

This leads Stefan to attempt to define more clearly his own position on Palestine and the Zionist movement:

> Auch Palästina war eine Sentimentalität, ein Antilogismus und Herzl, der einzige Staatsmann, sah klar, als er Uganda wollte. Palästina *kann* nicht mehr von dem verarmten und erschöpften Judentum weiter getragen und subventioniert werden ... man wird jetzt die letzten Geldreserven brauchen, um nach der *endgiltigen* Plünderung die Ausgetriebenen etwas zu stützen. Kein lebendiges Geld jetzt mehr dem toten nachwerfen!

> [Palestine too was a sentimentality, illogical, and Herzl, the only statesman, saw clearly when he wanted Uganda instead. Palestine *can* no longer be supported and subsidised by poverty-stricken and exhausted Jewry ... the last money reserves will be needed to support the *final* plundering of those who are being expelled. Good money must not be thrown any longer after bad!]

In confidence, Stefan speaks in this same undated letter to Arnold about the responsibilities of the writer:

> Ich sage Ihnen da privat meine Meinung. Sie werden – grosse Verantwortung, ungeheure sogar! – in Ihrem Palästinabuch die Ihre öffentlich sagen. Ich kann Sie als Autoren nicht beraten – bedenken Sie nur, dass man in *dieser* Stunde mit dem Judentum vorsichtig sein muss wie mit einem Schwerkranken. Es ist für viele noch eine letzte Hoffnung – oder vielleicht etwas, wovon sie noch träumen.

> [I'm giving you there my private opinion, you – what a great, enormous responsibility! – will be expressing your own in your Palestine book. I can't advise you as author – but just consider that at *this* hour one must be as gentle towards the Jews as towards a seriously-ill patient. For many it is still a last hope – or something they are dreaming of.]

For Stefan, it is the Soviet Union, rather than Palestine, which should have opened its doors to Jewish refugees:

> Mein Zorn geht gegen Russland. Wenn die Schweiz, wenn Italien, wenn Brasilien sich sperrt gegen den Elendsstrom so kann ich es billigen; diese Länder brauchen keine Ärzte, keine Regisseure, keine Ingenieure, keine Musicanten und sie sind zu klein, als dass nicht ein starker Zuzug sie umfärben würde. *Ein* Land aber brauchte jetzt bitter notwendig die grossartigen Wiener Professoren, die Chemiker, die Musiker, die Lehrer – Russland und in den 180 Millionen würden 1000 jüdische Intellektuelle nur eine Gnade sein, ein Gegengift gegen die zunehmende nationalistische Isolierung, Verdummung und Wegorientierung von Europa.

> [My anger is directed against Russia. If Switzerland, Italy, Brazil hoist the drawbridge against the flood of misery, I can understand and approve;

these countries do not need musicians, directors, engineers, and they are too small not to be affected by a big influx. But *one* country really does have bitter need of the splendid Viennese professors, chemists, musicians, teachers – Russia, among whose 180 millions a thousand Jewish intellectuals would only be a blessing, an antidote to the growing nationalist isolation, stupidity and anti-European orientation.]

Stefan had hoped that his friend Romain Rolland, one of the leading Western supporters of communism, might have used his influence to bring about a change in Soviet policy:

> Ich habe unter der Hand versucht, ich habe Rolland gebeten zu intervenieren – aber die angeblichen Totfeinde Hitlers nehmen nicht ein einziges Opfer des Hitlerismus zu sich. Die grauenhafte Angstpsychose Stalins lähmt das ganze Land. *Nie* ist eine grosse Gelegenheit stupider versäumt worden, nie eine Möglichkeit, *beiden* Teilen zu helfen, so stumpfsinnig vertan. Ich weiss nicht wer es sagte: wenn zwei Menschen lange miteinander kämpfen, so werden sie sich ähnlicher dadurch.

> [I've made private attempts, asked Rolland to intervene – but the self-proclaimed deadly enemies of Hitler take not a single victim of Hitlerism. Stalin's appalling fear psychosis is crippling the entire country. *Never* has a great opportunity been more stupidly missed, never such a chance to help *both* sides so obtusely passed up. Who was it who said: when two people fight against each other for a long time, they grow more and more to resemble one another.]

Stefan's conclusions are thus deeply pessimistic:

> Ich weiss nicht, ob Hitler heute die Verzerrung Stalins ist oder Stalin die Hitlers. Jedenfalls – dass Russland jetzt sich wie vor Pestkranken von einer Elite Europas abschliesst, *muss* zu etwas Falschem führen oder ist Zeugnis dafür, dass dort schon alles im Argen liegt. *Was* hätten die österreichischen Ärzte (eine Tradition durch vier fünf Generationen) dort geleistet! Dieser Wahnsinn hat eben *nur* mehr Methode!

> [I don't know whether today Hitler is the caricature of Stalin or Stalin that of Hitler. At all events – for Russia now to shut herself off from a European elite as from the plague, *must* lead to something wrong, or is a sign that everything there is in bad shape. *How much* might Austrian doctors (a tradition over four or five generations) have achieved there! There is *nothing but* madness in this [Soviet] method!]

Even the liberal democracies of Western Europe no longer offer any hope:

> in den Zeitungen steht nichts mehr von dem Furchtbaren, es ist nicht wie 1933, wo die Juden noch als Opfer galten und die Ausgetriebenen als Helden der Gesinnung, heute sind sie 'indesirables' und selbst die englischen liberalen Zeitungen wagen *kein Wort des Tadels* oder des

blossen Vermerks mehr – es ist dem Basilisken gelungen, das freie Wort selbst in den freien Ländern zu lähmen.

[In the papers there's no more word of terrible conditions, it's not like 1933 when the Jews still counted as victims and the exiles as heroes suffering for their convictions; today they are 'undesirables', and even the liberal English newspapers don't dare to print *a single word of reproach* or even a remark – the basilisk has succeeded in stifling free speech even in the free countries.]

For a true account of the terrible things that are happening in Vienna, one has to rely on messages from friends:

Nur mündlich erfährt man von dem Entsetzlichen, was mittlerweile geschieht und erst geschehen wird, denn Wien enthielt hundertfünfzigtausend bettelarme Juden, nur dass keine Reichen mehr sind, bei denen sie noch betteln könnten. Crepieren!

[One hears only verbally of the terror, of what is happening and is about to happen, for Vienna contained 150,000 destitute Jews and there are no more rich people from whom they could beg. They can only die!]

This series of letters can be read as a progressive dialogue which culminates on 3 June 1938 in a letter from Arnold acknowledging Stefan's superior insight:

Lieber Stefan Zweig, ja, ich nehme alles zurück. Ich verstehe noch genau, warum ich reagierte wie ich es tat. Aber ich liess mich von einer Empörung hinreissen, die der Blindheit der Menschen galt, nicht den Menschen.

[Dear Stefan Zweig, yes, I take it all back. I can see exactly why I reacted as I did. But I let myself be carried away by an indignation which was directed against people's blindness, not against the people themselves.]

Abandoning his insistence on thinking 'only in terms of large political groupings', he now endorses Stefan's principled humanism:

Wir müssen aber zuerst und immer die Menschen sehen und den Geist, nicht die Irrtümer und den Wunsch nach Heimat. Und was den Menschen in Wien geschieht, das scheint so ungeheuerlich zu sein, dass selbst der Krieg und die Okkupation in Polen, Litauen, Belgien, Rumänien daneben verblassen. Noch hören wir ja nur Andeutungen. Aber selbst sie machen mir den Kopf rot und das Herz wild.

[However, we must first and always see the human beings and the human spirit, not the errors and the homesickness. And what is happening to the people in Vienna seems so monstrous that even the war and the occupation in Poland, Lithuania, Belgium, Romania pales

beside it. We still hear only hints. But even those make my head burn
and my heart furious.]

As this epistolary dialogue shows, Arnold was flexible enough to acknowledge
his mistaken views. His reference to Vienna in this letter of 3 June once again
invokes the name of Freud, this time in a more conciliatory spirit:

> Und der rasende Rassenwühl der Schurken und Irren aus Deutschland
> erstickt jetzt unsere Freunde, Unseresgleichen. Aber die schweigende
> Welt! das stillhaltende England! Wir sind am Ende. Unsere Gesittung
> muss von Grund auch [sic] neu gebaut werden. Was werden wir noch
> zu erleben haben? ... Sie sind Freud nahe, jetzt wie von Geburt: retten
> wir Österreichs letzte Werte!

> [And the mad racism of the scoundrels and madmen from Germany is
> now stifling our friends, the people like us. But the silence of the world!
> England not stirring! We are at the end. Our morality has to be rebuilt
> from its foundations. What experiences still await us? ... You are close
> to Freud, now as from your birth: let us save Austria's ultimate values!]

The hope that Freud, symbol of all that was best in Austrian culture, might
be rescued from Vienna, was soon fulfilled. On 6 June 1938, Freud and his
family arrived as refugees in London.

After the above exchanges, it appears that the relationship between the two
authors became more firmly rooted. The following letters are written in a
calmer, more relaxed tone, although the tension of the times is ever-present.
Even when travelling outside of Europe, Stefan is still haunted by his sense of
the inescapable Jewish dilemma, as is clear from a letter to Arnold written on
19 February 1939 during an American lecture tour:

> Die jüdische Situation ist hier [in Amerika] gefährlicher als es der erste
> Blick vermuten lässt und wie seiner Zeit in Österreich sind sich die
> Juden hier dessen nicht gewahr, verwechseln ihre Übermacht in
> Newyork [sic] mit der im Lande (ähnlich wie seinerzeit in Berlin) und
> sind an Roosevelts Bleibe so gebunden wie die österreichischen Juden
> an Schuschnigg.

> [The Jewish situation here [in America] is more dangerous than it
> would seem at first glance, and as in Austria the Jews here don't know
> it, think their powerful position in New York is the same throughout
> the country (just as once in Berlin), and are as dependent on Roosevelt's
> survival as the Austrian Jews were on Schuschnigg.]

Nevertheless, Stefan also expresses in this same letter his hope that during his
lecture tour of the States he has 'done some good for our Jewish cause'
(unserer gemeinsamen jüdischen Sache genützt).

In conclusion, it is important to reflect not only on the picture which we
can gain from these letters of the political dilemmas of the late 1930s, but also

on the challenge that they offer to readers in the 1990s. They are letters which, by combining an urgent sense of political responsibility with intense emotional anguish, invite us to reflect on our own reactions to the political crises of our age. We are challenged to examine our own attitudes, as well as those of people in the 1930s who were implicated in the fascist programme of genocide, whether as perpetrators, victims or bystanders.[16] The world which we have inherited can only be understood if, acknowledging the crimes of Nazi Germany, we also commit ourselves to the task of understanding how and why these terrible events occurred.[17]

The correspondence between Stefan and Arnold Zweig thus offers more than an account of the anxieties of two Jewish writers. These documents also testify to hopes and dreams cut short by the experience of exile. In some ways, the circumstances under which they were written may remind us of the concluding line in Stefan Zweig's play *Jeremias*: 'Man kann ein Volk bezwingen, doch nie seinen Geist' (A people can be put in chains – its spirit, never).[18] Symbolically, these letters may be seen as the continuing expression of that invincible spirit, linking us to earlier generations. The survival of these letters reminds us that we should never forget the lessons of the past, for our future may be determined by our ability to remember. In his letter of 3 June 1938, three months after the Anschluss, Arnold speaks of the need to 'save Austria's ultimate values'. Stefan Zweig's response was to write *Die Welt von gestern* (*The World of Yesterday*), that act of commemoration which recreates the finest values of turn-of-the-century Vienna. Thus the correspondence does not simply shed light on the crisis years of 1937–9. It also shows that the experience of exile may become the stimulus to exceptional creativity. The lessons learnt in exile are epitomised by Arnold Zweig's anguished words of 3 June 1938: 'Our morality must be rebuilt from its foundations'.

Notes

For publication permission, I sincerely thank the Stefan Zweig Estate and its managing executors: Sonja Dobbins (London) and Lindi Preuss (Zürich); I am additionally grateful to Knut Beck, Lektor at S. Fischer Verlag (Frankfurt am Main); and to Natascha Weschenbach (Aachen); together with Knut Beck and Natascha Weschenbach I am preparing a four-volume edition of Stefan Zweig's letters, forthcoming in the S. Fischer Verlag, whom I acknowledge, with gratitude. For the Arnold Zweig letters, I thank the Aufbau-Verlag (Berlin and Weimar). I thank too the Ben Huebsch Estate (New York). Stefan's letters are deposited at the Deutsche Akademie der Künste zu Berlin; Arnold's are at the Stefan Zweig Archive at the State University College at Fredonia (New York), and Arnold's letters to Huebsch, with carbon copies of the Huebsch letters, are at the Huebsch Archive, Library of Congress (Washington, DC). To these repositories I am grateful for many courtesies extended. For favours, I also thank Donald A. Prater (Gingins) and acknowledge with pleasure A. Tilo Alt (Durham), who chaired the Arnold Zweig section of the 1992 Modern Language Association meeting (New York), where I first offered a shorter version of this paper. Any editorial emendations have been so noted by square brackets.

1. See Maritta Rost et al., *Bibliographie Arnold Zweig*, 2 vols (Berlin and Weimar, 1987); and Randolph Klawiter, *Stefan Zweig: An International Bibliography*

(Riverside, 1991). With the exception of five letters from the years 1927, 1928, 1939 and 1940, the correspondence between Arnold Zweig (1887–1968) and Stefan Zweig (1881–1942) is unpublished. The surviving documents consist of the following materials: forty-three letters, nine postcards and two notes, dated 1908 and 1919–40, from Arnold Zweig to Stefan Zweig, and seventeen letters and three postcards, dated 1933–40, from Stefan to Arnold.

2. Cf. Stefan's letter of 28 March 1930 to Romain Rolland: 'Arnold Zweig ist nicht mit mir verwandt (oder sehr weitläufig), aber ich bewundere seinen Roman sehr, und wir stehen auf bestem Fuße miteinander. Er hat alles, was mir abgeht: den Mut zu weiträumigen Werken, die mathematische Konzentration auf das Detail, die Genauigkeit und jene [Sachlichkeit], die so nötig ist' (Arnold Zweig is not related to me (or very remotely), but I admire his novel very much, and we are on the best of terms. He has everything I lack: the courage to plan extensive works, the mathematical concentration on detail, the exactitude and the objectivity which is so necessary.) In: *Romain Rolland/ Stefan Zweig: Briefwechsel 1910–1940*, ed. Waltraud Schwarze et al., vol. 2 (Berlin, 1987), p. 367.

3. See my essay 'The Struggle for Survival – From Hitler's Appointment to the Nazi Book-Burnings: Some Unpublished Stefan Zweig Letters, with an Unpublished Manifesto', *Turn-of-the-Century Vienna and its Legacy: Essays in Honor of Donald G. Daviau*, ed. J. B. Berlin, J. B. Johns and R. H. Lawson (Vienna, 1993), pp. 361–87.

4. *Sigmund Freud/ Arnold Zweig Briefwechsel*, ed. Ernst L. Freud (Frankfurt, 1984), p. 117. The translation follows *The Letters of Sigmund Freud and Arnold Zweig*, ed. Ernst L. Freud, tr. Elaine and William Robson-Scott (New York, 1970), p. 106.

5. Huebsch played a major role in the lives of both Arnold and Stefan: cf. my essays: 'Stefan Zweig and his American Publisher: Notes on an Unpublished Correspondence, with Reference to *Schachnovelle* and *Die Welt von Gestern*', *DVjs* 56 (1982), 259–76; 'An Author and His Publisher: Stefan Zweig's Unpublished Letters of 1936 to Ben Huebsch', *GRM* 37 (1987), 301–19; and 'Stefan Zweig's Unpublished Letters of 1938 to Ben Huebsch', *DVjs* 61 (1987), 325–58.

6. Cf. David R. Midgley, *Arnold Zweig: Zu Werk und Wandlung 1927–1948* (Königstein/Ts., 1980), esp. pp. 123–58; Jost Hermand, *Engagement als Lebensform: Über Arnold Zweig* (Berlin, 1992), esp. pp. 115–39; Wilhelm von Sternburg, *Arnold Zweig* (Frankfurt, 1990), esp. pp. 155–205; and George Salamon, *Arnold Zweig* (Boston, 1975). See also: *Lion Feuchtwanger/ Arnold Zweig: Briefwechsel 1933–1958*, ed. Harold von Hofe, 2 vols (Berlin and Weimar, 1984).

7. Cf. Harry Zohn, 'Stefan Zweig, the European and the Jew', *Leo Baeck Institute Year Book* (1982), pp. 323–36.

8. See my edition of 'The Unpublished Correspondence between Albert Einstein and Stefan Zweig', *Bridging the Abyss: Essays in Honor of Harry Zohn*, ed. Amy Colin and Elisabeth Strenger (Munich, 1994), pp. 337–62.

9. This draft was published for the first time in 'The Struggle for Survival' – see above, note 3.

10. *Romain Rolland/ Stefan Zweig Briefwechsel*, vol. 2 p. 507.

11. See my essay 'March 14, 1938: "Es gibt kein Österreich mehr". Some Unpublished Correspondence between Franz Werfel, Alma Mahler-Werfel and Ben Huebsch', *DVjs* 62 (1988), esp. p. 756.

12. See further, in *Turn-of-the-Century Vienna and its Legacy*: Donald A. Prater, 'Stefan Zweig and the Vienna of Yesterday', pp. 317–36; Joseph P. Strelka, 'The Paradox and Dilemma of the Humanist in Our Century', pp. 337–50; and Harry Zohn, 'Stefan Zweig's Letters from Exile', pp. 351–60. Also see Hildemar Holl and Klaus Zelewitz, 'Hausdurchsuchung 1934', *Zirkular*, Sondernummer 2 (1981), 77–95.

13. A few months after the Anschluss, Ben Huebsch sent the following still unpublished letter of 3 May 1938 to Arnold Zweig: 'The Austrian catastrophe is so great and operates so crushingly on hundreds of thousands that the loss which you and other authors suffer must be considered philosophically. You and a few others are fortunate in having a world market. Many of the friends that we have in common are ruined; others have lost life or liberty, some are already here [in America] and others are trying to come. Little did you and I think last Summer that there would never again be a possibility for us to sit comfortably together in Vienna.'

14. In article format, Sigfrid Hoefert's 'Stefan Zweigs Verbundenheit mit Rußland und der russischen Literatur' (*MAL* 14 [1981], 251–70) could not consider all aspects, but his essay remains the most instructive on this topic.

15. On the topic of his letters, see Ilse Lange's especially informative 'Zum Briefnachlaß Arnold Zweig', in *Arnold Zweig: Psyche, Politik und Literatur*, ed. David Midgley, Hans-Harald Müller and Luc Lamberechts (Bern, 1993), pp. 77–84.

16. I borrow this expression from Raul Hilberg's *Perpetrators–Victims–Bystanders: The Jewish Catastrophe 1933–1945* (New York, 1992).

17. Cf. Raul Hilberg, *The Destruction of the European Jews*, 3 vols (New York and London, 1985); see also Steven T. Katz, *The Holocaust in Historical Context*, vol. I (New York and Oxford, 1994) – volumes II and III are in preparation.

18. Stefan Zweig, *Tersites-Jeremias: Zwei Dramen*, ed. Knut Beck (Frankfurt, 1982), p. 327.

The Cultural Policy of Austrian Refugee Organisations in Great Britain

Wolfgang Muchitsch

Before March 1938, the number of Austrian refugees in Great Britain was quite small, consisting mainly of exiles who had left Austria after the Civil War of February 1934 and during the days of the Dollfuss-Schuschnigg regime. The German occupation of Austria in March 1938 started a real flood of refugees which the British Home Office tried to get under control by introducing a visa system for entry into Britain for all aliens holding Austrian and German passports. The weeks following the occupation saw many trying to leave Austria, in particular those who were immediately threatened by the Nazi regime such as its opponents of all political shades, as well as intellectuals, scientists and artists known to be anti-Nazis. A motion proposed by Colonel Josiah Wedgwood in the House of Commons generally allowing Austrian refugees to enter Britain for six months was rejected.[1] The majority of the Jewish population in Austria only started to leave the country when they were deprived of their civil and fundamental rights, their material and professional basis of existence, as well as being physically threatened. The pogroms of the 'Crystal Night' (9–10 November 1938) started a further flood of so-called 'non-Aryan' refugees, with the result that in the last year before the outbreak of the Second World War the German-speaking emigration reached its peak.

Even today, there exist no reliable estimates of the real extent of Austrian emigration to Britain. Reports of the Israelitische Kultusgemeinde of Vienna, during and immediately after the war, gave the number of refugees to Britain at around 27,000 to 31,000 Austrians, while the official British estimates were around 15,000 and those of the Austrian refugee organisations around 16,000.[2] Whatever the exact figure, it is clear that Britain, following the United States, became the second-largest centre of Austrian exile. Furthermore, Britain, as the only serious opponent of the Third Reich for a long time, became important as a centre of international resistance, giving refuge to a large number of European governments in exile, such as Belgium, the Netherlands, Luxembourg, Poland, Czechoslovakia, Yugoslavia, Greece and the Free French under de Gaulle.

About ten per cent of the total of Austrian refugees were politically active exiles, for the most part Socialists, Communists and conservatives, although the dividing line between political and 'racial' was fluid. The only officially registered political Austrian refugees in Britain were the 'Svitanics group', made up of 156 Socialists and trade unionists, and the 'Winterberg group', consisting of eighty Communists who had arrived in Britain via Czechoslovakia with the help of the Czech Refugee Trust Fund.[3] The exiles found favourable conditions for their political activities in Britain, since the political climate, particularly after the Soviet Union's entry into the war, was quite liberal, and the Austrian immigration was concentrated in a few areas such as London (Hampstead, Swiss Cottage, Golders Green, Paddington), Glasgow, Edinburgh, Liverpool, Manchester, Birmingham, Leeds, Oxford and Cambridge. Among the political exiles was no outstanding personality who had a legitimate claim to represent Austria or to lead an Austrian government in exile.

The attitude of the British government towards Austrian refugees has to be seen in relation to its attitude towards the Austrian question and the restoration of an independent Austria, which up until the Moscow Declaration of 30 October 1943 remained unclear. British officials had no objections to the formation of anti-Nazi groups, but made it clear that they would never, officially or unofficially, recognise an Austrian organisation as representing Austria. Their reason was that the various Austrian groups were unable to achieve unity among themselves; this being particularly true of the Socialists and Communists, who were open opponents. Furthermore, they claimed that these groups were not representative of the Austrian population since only a few Catholic conservatives and members of the peasantry had left the country. The British government did not see an advantage in recognising an Austrian representation in exile which in its view would have been unacceptable to people in Austria.[4]

The politico-cultural activities of Austrian refugee organisations, as a part and reflection of their general exile policy, were inseparable from their attitude towards Austria's independence and the 'Austrian nation'. The politico-cultural aims of those groups actively supporting the idea of an independent Austria can be summarised as conserving, developing and propagating an independent Austrian culture; satisfying the cultural and social demands of the Austrian refugees; deepening the understanding between the Austrian refugees and the British population; strengthening solidarity with all democratic movements; and finally cultivating relations with friends of Austria. In some respects, these aims still correspond with today's foreign cultural policy of the Republic of Austria.

The Socialists

For Austrian Social Democracy, which after the Civil War and the dissolution of the Social Democratic Party in February 1934 had been forced into illegality and exile, the occupation of March 1938 came as a further political and organisational blow, since the left-wing Revolutionary Socialists who had taken over control had neither prepared an organised illegal escape route nor tried to keep up a central organisation in Austria. Lacking a political programme, the leading Socialists went into exile without a political strategy. In some cases they succumbed to despair, in others they adopted a haphazard activism.[5] In exile, the question of Austria's independence widened the already historic gap between the Socialists and the Communists. The Socialists strictly rejected the Communist theory of an 'Austrian nation' and kept up the idea of the Anschluss, sustained by the dream of an all-German and later European revolution. Their idea was that Austria's fate was inseparable from that of Germany. It was hoped that, in Germany and the occupied countries, revolutionary crises would emerge and develop into an all-German and later European revolution resulting in a Socialist order in Europe. By more or less accepting the Anschluss and denying the idea of an 'Austrian nation', the Socialists became a rather marginal group among the Austrian exiles. According to the Socialist officials, the party leadership in exile was not allowed to make any decisions in the name of the party, which could only be represented by their comrades in Austria. Because of the focus on the remnants of what was now the 'Ostmark', the party in political representation in exile was more or less paralysed.[6] As in their view the Austrians in exile, however numerous, had no political function, the Socialists in Britain concentrated on organising their club, supporting party members and preserving the Socialist ideology. After the first casual meetings in the building of the British Trade Unions, they rented a house in Broadhurst Gardens in London, where they opened the Austrian Labour Club in 1940: 'to keep up political and social contacts, for education and discussion, to cultivate Socialist solidarity, and to organise welfare for the Socialist emigrants'.[7] According to the tradition of the 'Arbeiterheim', the Club, which financed itself, provided meeting and conference rooms, restaurant, guest rooms and a secretary's office. The Club programme included cultural and musical afternoons, as well as a choir which cultivated the tradition of the workers' songs. In order to provide information and promote education, the 'London-Information' bulletin was published twice a month until 1946, and occasionally contained poetry and short prose texts.[8] In April 1941, members of the Austrian Labour Club constituted an advisory council to act for the London exile group of Socialists – the London Bureau of the Austrian Socialists in Great Britain led by Karl Czernetz, Oscar Pollak and Franz Nozy. The London Bureau maintained close contacts with British government officials, politicians, trade unionists and journalists. It informed the Labour Party on questions relating to Austria and managed to get several of its experts into the BBC and some government offices.[9] As internationalists, the Socialists from the London Bureau opposed the Fatherland propaganda of Austrian monarchists and conservatives, as well as the newly developed nationalism of the Communists, and refused to participate in hatred of Germany (Vansittartism).[10] Their negative attitude towards Austria's independence and their persistent refusal to cooperate with other refugee organisations led to the formation of splinter groups: the Association of Austrian Social Democrats in Great Britain in February 1940, headed by former member of parliament Heinrich Allina, and the League of Austrian Socialists in Britain in autumn 1940, led by another former member of parliament, Marie Köstler. It was only in the light of the Moscow Declaration that the London Bureau abandoned its pan-German position and adopted the idea of an independent Austria in the shape of a 'Second Republic'. To forestall any Communist attempts to set up an officially recognised Austrian representation, the London Bureau, together with the Austrian Trade Unionists, the liberal Democratic Union and a few Christian Socialists, formed as early as 9 November 1943 the Austrian Representative Committee. This committee, which, just like the Communist attempt, failed to be officially recognised as an Austrian representation, saw as its main aim the drawing-up of plans for the reconstruction of post-war Austria. To spread its political ideas among the British public, the Representative Committee, together with some British friends, founded the Anglo-Austrian Democratic Society on 12 July 1944, which later became the Anglo-Austrian Society.[11]

Up to 1943, the Austrian Socialists' cultural policy reflected their pan-German and international political line. While they were anxious to improve their relations with the Labour Party, the trade unions and other Socialist parties in exile, they were politico-culturally, especially in relation to Austria, more or less inactive, since their cultural policy was more or less restricted to keeping up the traditions of a 'Red Vienna'. Artists with Socialist sympathies were persuaded not to participate in the cultural activities of other refugee organisations. Hilde Spiel, for instance, reported that Theodor Kramer, who frequently gave readings in the Austrian Centre, was after such occasions summoned before Oscar Pollak and reprimanded.[12] On the other hand, Rudolf Spitz was heavily involved in the theatre of the Austrian Centre, the Laterndl; and Erwin Weiss, as member of the Austrian Labour Club, conducted the choir of Young Austria. The London Bureau especially detested patriotic cultural activities which included Austrian folk music and folk dances, as the following diatribe shows:

'Schuhplattler' against Hitler

What was the contribution of 'Young Austria' to the international rally? They danced a 'Schuhplattler'. Many humorous and bitter words could be said about this political performance by the Communists. Just a few facts: in Austria, no-one dances a 'Schuhplattler'. This old-fashioned peasant dance forms one of the requisites of Hollywood operettas and the traditional Fatherland lie. It belongs among the spurious images of a forever gay, forever dancing Austria, which we Socialists have always opposed and which have always been so damaging to us in the world: the world had always thought Austrian democracy to be a 'Heurigen' idyll and has not taken note of Austrian Fascism – after the shootings, the yodelling continued.[13]

As a result of their change in policy in 1943–4, the Socialists started to intensify their politico-cultural activities, particularly in the Anglo-Austrian

Democratic Society, which aimed to 'further cultural relations between the two countries'.[14] As early as its first meeting, Friedrich Hertz gave a talk on cultural relations between Britain and Austria. Real politico-cultural steps were only envisaged by the Socialists in their post-war plans for the reform of the educational system in Austria.[15]

Conservative and Monarchist Exile Organisations

Right from the start, exile representatives of various monarchist, Catholic conservative and bourgeois-liberal shades became politically active. They were fairly divided, unrepresentative and politically weak, since only a few of the small number of the bourgeois emigrants, who were concentrated in Paris and later on in the United States, had come to Britain.[16] The only well-known personality who might have had a claim to represent Austria was Sir George Franckenstein, former Austrian minister to the court of St James for nearly twenty years. After the occupation, Franckenstein became a British citizen and had to be ruled out as a potential leader of an Austrian representation.

In 1939, Austrian monarchists founded the Austrian League, initially numbering nearly 200 members. This aimed to restore Austria's independence and the House of Habsburg, represented in London by Robert Habsburg (Robert of Austria). In pursuing their aims, the monarchists soon became politico-culturally active. In October 1939, Count Kurt Strachwitz initiated the short-lived *Austrian Information* to provide information and propaganda material concerning Austria, to inform the British public about cultural, economic and political matters, to register patriotic Austrians and to draw up post-war plans for the cultural, economic and constitutional reorganisation of Austria.[17]

On the initiative of monarchists and conservatives, the Austrian Circle for Arts and Science was founded. It first appeared before the public on 24 May 1939 with its programme 'Eternal Austria', including pieces of music (Mozart, Schubert, Nestroy, Raimund), poetry (Walther von der Vogelweide, Grillparzer, Lenau, Hofmannsthal) and short scenes (Schnitzler, Altenberg, Kraus, Polgar), which were performed by Austrian artists.[18]

In 1940, some of the monarchist, conservative, and liberal exiles, together with the Social Democratic splinter group of Heinrich Allina, formed the Austria Office, created to represent all Austrian exiles. As a way of informing people about its activities and ideas, the Austria Office published the monthly magazine *Free Austria* between 1940 and April 1942.[19] In its finally unsuccessful struggle for official recognition, paralleled at the same time by a similar failed attempt made by the Office Autrichien in Paris, the Austria Office intensified its politico-cultural efforts for Austria by founding the Austrian Academy in Great Britain in March 1940. Officially, the idea originated from the fact that there were among the Austrian refugees many scientists and artists who represented the national culture of their homeland. 'The Academy aims to be an Institute where lectures will be delivered on the cultural achievements nurtured and realised on Austrian soil.'[20] In contrast to its initial cultural efforts, the lectures were planned in English to attract a wider audience for the Austrian question which would be useful for obtaining official recognition. The strictly non-political character was stressed and political topics excluded from the programme. While the Austrian Academy would organise cultural lectures, the Austrian Circle for Arts and Science would arrange concerts, art exhibitions and similar activities.[21] For May and June 1940, a programme of lectures was put together which included Sir George Franckenstein on 'The Essence of Austrian Culture', Felix Braun on 'Austrian Literature', Friedrich Hertz on 'The Austrian Idea', Karl Geiringer on 'Haydn's Operas', Otto Erich Deutsch on 'Franz Schubert and England', Ernst H. Buschbeck on 'The Austrian Character of Austrian Baroque', Egon Wellesz on 'The Spirit of Austrian Music', Eric A. Blackall (Cambridge University) on 'Franz Grillparzer and the Austrian Drama', Friedrich Hayek on 'The Austrian School of Economics', and Hans Redlich on 'Anton Bruckner, the Austrian Symphonist'. Elisabeth Bergner and Stefan Zweig consented to give two special lectures in June. Four concerts, including a performance of Beethoven's Ninth Symphony conducted by Felix Weingartner, were arranged, as well as an exhibition of Austrian stage craft and stage decoration in conjunction with lectures on different aspects of 'The Theatre in Austria'.[22] Unfortunately, it is not known whether these events really took place. It has to be assumed that after the failure of the Austria Office to obtain official recognition as a kind of diplomatic representation of the Austrians accredited to the British government, and in view of the extended measures against 'enemy aliens' and the wave of internment in those months, the Austrian Academy and the Austrian Circle for Arts and Science finally stopped their activities.

In June 1940, the Austrian Youth Association (AYA) was formed within the Austria Office, attracting by December 1942 more than 600 members. The AYA was not distinctly political, but tried to cultivate the Austrian idea.[23] It aimed to educate young Austrians towards a renewed consciousness of and love for their country and to imbue them with a real and deep sense of patriotism.[24] Noteworthy were their well-attended lectures, mainly on the Austrian idea and mission, their film-shows, theatre performances, concerts and dances, as well as the occasional project of running an Austrian Institute for the purpose of supplementing the education of Austrian youth by organising lectures and courses on subjects like Austrian culture, history, philosophy, etc.[25] The premises of the AYA also accommodated the Catholic Logos group, formed to keep up Catholicism in exile, and the Austrian Women's Voluntary Workers, who became known as a result of their annual exhibitions of Austrian fine art by well-known and also by young unknown artists, in connection with their sales exhibitions of crafts and needlework.

In 1941, the Austria Office opened a British-Austrian Club in Austria House, their premises in Eaton Place (from 1943 in Bryanston Square), where lectures and artistic performances such as string quartets, piano and song concerts were organised, and which ran a Viennese Café Restaurant, 'furnished in Austrian style providing a homely atmosphere and refreshments and snacks in Viennese fashion'.[26]

As a counterbalance to the monarchist Austrian League and the Association of Austrian Social Democrats, the liberals within the Austrian Office formed the Austrian Democratic Union in August 1941, which by 1944 had attracted about 300 members, for the most part intellectuals, bankers, businessmen and lawyers. On the basis of a bourgeois liberalism and the belief in progress, the political priority of the Union was Austria's independence within the framework of a controlled, anti-monopolistic capitalism.[27] When in December 1941 the organisations of the Austria Office joined the Free Austrian Movement (FAM), their further activities coincided with those of the FAM. Finally, in autumn 1941, the few Christian Socialist exiles formed the Association of Austrian Christian Socialists in Great Britain, which was, as regards number and influence, the smallest political group and played more or less no part until 1945.

The Communists and their Popular Front Organisations

The most active and influential group of Austrian exiles in Britain, also with regard to cultural policy, were the Austrian Communists, who in 1937 had formulated the theory of the 'Austrian nation' (Alfred Klahr), which in the following years became the theoretical basis for their fight for independence, their resistance activities, their exile policy, war aims and post-war planning.[28] The Communists arrived in Britain with the purpose of promoting Austria, informing people about its recent past and demanding the restoration of a free and independent Austria. These aims were also reflected in their cultural policy, the mirror of exile policy. According to the popular front tactic (the policy of the collaboration of the working class with all those parts of the middle class and peasantry not affected by fascism), formulated at the 7th Congress of the Comintern in 1935, a mass basis was to be built up among Austrian refugees in Britain, which on the one hand would help to realise the democratic objectives, especially the independence of Austria, and on the other hand would serve as an organisation for the recruitment of sympathisers and candidates for the Party.[29]

The Communist Party group itself, with around 100 members in 1940, did not go public until the Soviet Union's entry into the war, but kept underground, since any official commitment to the KPÖ would have led to immediate internment as 'enemy aliens'. A strictly-organised lifestyle within the party was structured in party cells in the centres of exile. Between the German-Soviet Non-Aggression Pact of August 1939 and the German attack on the Soviet Union in June 1941, which the Communists defined as the 'imperialistic war', the party was politically isolated. Nevertheless, its mostly young officials, who were experienced in organisational matters, did adopt the popular front tactic of starting to unite and organise the flood of refugees, which was more or less neglected by other political groups, with the help of welfare organisations. It has to be stressed right from the start that although numerous organisations were initiated and partly controlled by Austrian Communists, these organisations did not follow an ideological Communist policy, but acted as a promoter for Austria's independence and, therefore, also attracted refugees who were far from being Communists.

The first Communists to arrive in Britain founded Austrian Self Aid, which organised the escape of and entry visas for Austrian victims of persecution, as well as offering legal advice, accommodation and opportunities to take up employment. In September 1938, the Council of Austrians in Great Britain was formed to protect the legal, social and economic interests of the refugees and to improve their official status. During the war, the Council of Austrians mainly served as an employment exchange and advice centre to integrate the refugees into the war effort.

The politically active refugees had an alternative to fascism, seeing their exile only as a transitional stage, and were, therefore, more resistant to the agonising feelings of the loss of prospects and existence, which for the majority of refugees characterised the first period of life in exile. For most refugees, the beginning of exile was marked by culture shock, which was increased by the need to learn a new language, the barriers of tradition, education and habits, the loss of material existence and the partial prohibition on employment (only domestic servants and some experts were exempted).[30] This resulted in a close bond between those who shared the same fate and led to the formation of social and cultural ghettos to resist the influences of a foreign culture. This was the breeding ground for the development of a national subculture and an Austrian culture in exile, as well as for the popular front activities of the Communists. While the other political groups mainly kept to themselves, sustained by a few supporters and British friends, the Communists founded the first Austrian Centre in Paddington in March 1939 – a vital meeting-place for thousands of refugees and an important organisational starting point for cultural activities. In July 1939, the Austrian Centre already numbered 1,500 members, and at the end of 1942 it had more than 3,500 members and seventy employees.[31] Within a short time, an extensive infrastructure was set up: a library; the reading room; the monthly magazine *Austrian News*; the *Zeitspiegel*, initially a weekly summary of news reports in German, which after its revival in September 1941 developed to become the most important weekly paper for Austrian exiles, with a circulation of 3,000 copies in forty countries; and even a restaurant, which served 600 guests daily and up to 1,000 on Sundays.[32] For homeless refugees and those without means, the Austrian Centre opened a hostel and founded the Austrian Studio for Arts and Crafts (later known as the ASTU Studio), which offered technical training, for example welding and other engineering skills, of a kind needed by middle-class refugees anxious to integrate into British life and to contribute to the war effort.[33]

In the difficult days of internment, Austrian Centre groups were created in various internment camps, which supported initiatives for educational and cultural activities, camp papers, sporting competitions, workshops, etc.; the Austrian Centre tried to support this from outside. After the ending of internment, the improvement of the material situation and the change of mood as a result of the Soviet Union's entry into the war, the Austrian Centre underwent a further upswing. In 1941, it had three premises in London (Paddington, Swiss Cottage, Finsbury Park), a large house in Glasgow and numerous provincial branches. All this was designed to satisfy the social and cultural demands of the refugees, and at the same time to support and propagate the political aims of the Austrian Centre.

One of the most important tasks of the Communists was the welfare of young Austrians, who for the most part had been separated from their families and had to struggle with the problems of exile for themselves. For instance, between 2 December 1938 and 22 August 1939, 2,262 Austrian children had been brought from Vienna to London in twenty-three 'Kindertransporte'.[34] Organising these young Austrians involved helping them to find a family substitute and the company of others of the same age, and at the same time offered the Communists an opportunity to interest young Austrians in the Communist Party.[35] On 11 March 1939, the first group of Young Austria in Great Britain was founded as the youth organisation of the Austrian Centre. Within a short time, other groups followed in London, Manchester, Liverpool, Oxford, Cambridge and other cities. At the beginning of 1941, Young Austria numbered around 600 members, and by 1943 more than 1,300.[36] At the same time, the Communists built up an illegal Kommunistischer Jugendverband (KJV). The KJV, like the Party, was organised in cells and closely linked with the leadership of Young Austria. While the KJV was mainly concerned with discussing questions such as the Austrian nation, Austrian resistance, Marxism, the history of the labour movement and analyses of the war, the unpolitical and distinctly patriotic Young Austria started a far-reaching cultural and propaganda campaign for Austria, not only among the exiles, but also aimed at the British public, with its programme: 'Young Austria wants to cultivate Austrian culture and national identity within its own ranks and wants to impart it to its host country'.[37] The choir of Young Austria conducted by Erwin Weiss, the Young Austria Players under Otto Tausig, and its folk-dance groups probably became the most successful instruments of exile propaganda. Young Austria tried to disseminate a different picture of Austria from that presented by the media, and often put Jewish youths from the Viennese working and middle classes in 'Lederhosen' and 'Dirndl', even sending them (as we have seen) to dance 'Schuhplattler'.[38] Especially noteworthy were the successes of Young Austria in various relief campaigns for the war effort (e.g. 'Austria for Britain' week), as well as its photo exhibition 'Austria shall be free' in 1943, which was shown in several cities and seen by more than 300,000 visitors.[39] Furthermore, Young Austria was represented in the International Youth Council and the World Youth Council, and together with the Austrian youth group in New York founded the Austrian World Youth Movement, uniting exile youth organisations from various countries.[40]

The German attack on the Soviet Union on 22 June 1941 brought a decisive change in policy for the Communist Party and its organisations, since the war, according to the Communists, had developed from the imperialistic one into a

European liberation war. By increasingly uniting all exile groups into a 'national front' of all Austrians, and by mobilising the Austrian refugees for the war effort, it was hoped that Austria's contribution to the fight against Nazism would be recognised. Following an appeal by the Council of Austrians on 26 July 1941, nearly all the exile organisations, except the Austrian Socialists and Christian Socialists, united on 3 December 1941 to form a work group, the Free Austrian Movement (FAM). Their common goals were the non-recognition of the occupation of Austria, the right of self-determination for the Austrian people, the mobilisation of all Austrians living in Britain for a separate Austrian fighting unit, for civil defence and war production, the alteration of the refugees' 'enemy alien' status and the strengthening of the freedom front in Austria. The declaration of the FAM was signed by a number of well-known artists in exile, such as the writers Robert Neumann and Elias Canetti, the painters Oskar Kokoschka and Siegfried Charoux, the violinist Max Rostal, and the composers and musicologists Otto Erich Deutsch and Hans Gal.[41]

By the end of 1943, twenty-seven different organisations of Austrian refugees in Britain had joined the FAM, representing more than 7,000 Austrians. While the first year of its existence was marked by the various efforts to support the war efforts, at the end of 1942 the FAM focused its attention on Austria itself and increased its patriotic line with the slogan 'Gesicht dem Land zu' ('the face towards the country'). The Moscow Declaration confirmed the policy of the FAM, which in contrast to the Socialists, and also to its bourgeois and monarchist members, who mostly left the FAM in the course of 1943, stressed the share of responsibility of the Austrian people for the war and the crimes of Nazism.[42] The formation of an Austrian National Committee as official representation immediately after the Moscow Declaration was prevented by the Socialists. Nevertheless, the FAM did try to unite all patriotic Austrians in the Free Austrian World Movement, which was formed on 11 March 1944, combining refugee organisations in the Dominions, South America and the United States, representing more than 25,000 Austrians.[43] With the gradual approach of the end of the war, the FAM increased its post-war planning for Austria and stressed the issue of the fate of refugees after the war. Like other political groups, the FAM tried to organise its British friends and sympathisers for propaganda and support for Austria; in August 1945, the Friends of Austria numbered twenty-nine branches and more than 25,000 members.[44]

Theatre in Exile

The development of the mass organisations of Austrian refugees also had politico-cultural consequences. With the formation of the first organisations, especially the Austrian Centre, to satisfy the social and cultural demands of the refugees, Austrian artists, most of whom had nothing to do with Communism, were united under the banner of Austria and given means of production and publication as well as a very receptive audience.

As early as March 1939, some exiled actors (Fritz Schrecker, Franz Bönsch and Franz Schulz) suggested the establishment of an exile theatre to the board of the Austrian Centre – the Laterndl – on the basis of the tradition of the Viennese 'Kleinkunstbühne'. On 27 June 1939, the Laterndl put on the first of a total of thirty-eight productions at the Austrian Centre in Paddington, 126 Westbourne Terrace.[45] Drawing heavily on the traditions of cabaret and agit-prop, the plays and scenes, often little vignettes or sketches by refugee authors, usually dealt with the everyday life of the refugees and offered help in coping with the exile situation. In order to help the refugees to retain a cultural identity and to reduce their feeling of loss, the performances were given in German. Franz Bönsch summarised the tasks of the Laterndl as: to take part in the fight for an independent Austria in one's own way; to offer Austrian literature a modest home; and to give hope to the uprooted and despairing as well as the confidence that the thousand-year Reich would not last very long.[46] In 1940, the period of internment forced the Laterndl to suspend its activities, although its interned actors were heavily involved in theatrical activities in various internment camps. After a short interlude in a defunct music school at 153 Finchley Road, the Laterndl found its final location in 1941 at the Austrian Centre in Swiss Cottage at 69 Eton Avenue. While in the first years the Laterndl had mainly stressed satirical 'Kleinkunst', it changed its strategy in 1942. In keeping with the increased patriotic line of the FAM and the Austrian Centre and its motto 'Gesicht dem Land zu', the Laterndl more or less devoted itself to Austrian literary productions as opposed to German plays, including Zweig, Bahr, Schnitzler, Schönherr, Nestroy and Anzengruber.

A second theatre with its roots in the Austrian Centre was founded by Peter Herz, who tried to repeat the success he had had with the Stacheldraht Cabaret in internment camps on the Isle of Man.[47] The Austrian Centre was, as he said, 'under Communist management', which he would not have minded if they had not tried to influence his programme tendentiously and to place him under their control. So he left the Austrian Centre in 1941 and set up the Blue Danube Club in the building recently vacated by the Laterndl at 153 Finchley Road, where he offered cabaret entertainment.

Daily performances were often sold out in the Laterndl up until 1945, and the Blue Danube Club until 1954. This reflects the strength of the politico-cultural demands of the Austrian refugee audience. While the above-mentioned professional stages concentrated more or less exclusively on a refugee audience, the amateur drama groups of the Austrian Centre and the Young Austria Players tried in their English revues (e.g. 'Return Ticket Vienna-London') to make Austria's culture and its fight for freedom clear to a British audience, with the help of plays, songs and dances.[48] In 1943, for instance, the theatre group from the Austrian Centre performed in front of British audiences totalling more than 10,000.[49] Besides productions of Nestroy and Raimund, as well as English revues, the Young Austria Players devoted themselves to the work of Jura Soyfer. Young Austria also had song, literature and theatre groups in its various local branches, for example in Liverpool,

Glasgow and York.[50] Although its political aims were progressive, the Austrian exile theatre tended to be culturally conservative.

Literature in Exile

One of the main tasks of refugee organisations was to conserve and popularise Austrian literature. Besides a receptive audience, the organisations offered Austrian writers in exile, who, like the actors, formed the group most affected by the change of language, a modest opportunity to publish in German. Here, the interest of conserving Austrian literature combined with the consciousness of being Austrian.[51] Hardly a single issue of the *Zeitspiegel* was published without a poem or a short prose text by an Austrian writer. The literary staff of the *Zeitspiegel* included Fritz Brügel, Erich Fried, Albert Fuchs, Joseph Kalmer, Oskar Kokoschka, Theodor Kramer, Eva Priester and Hermynia zur Mühlen.[52]

An almost unique opportunity for publication was offered by the publishing house Free Austrian Books of the Austrian Centre, which between 1942 and 1944 printed about 50,000 books and pamphlets in English and about 19,000 in German.[53] The centre produced some outstanding publications, including Jenö Kostmann, *Restive Austria* (1942); Franz C. West, *Zurück oder nicht zurück* (1942); Hilde Mareiner and Jenö Kostmann, *The Austrian Ally* (October 1942); *Zwischen Gestern und Morgen: Neue österreichische Gedichte* (1942); Anna Hornik, *This is Austria* (1942); Albert Fuchs, *Österreichs kulturelle Sendung* (1942); Wilhelm Scholz, *Ein Weg ins Leben* (1943); Juri Herman, *Viel Glück: Ein Sowjetkurzroman* (1943); J. Grünberg, *Einer für Alle, Alle für Dich* (1943); Theodor Kramer, *Verbannt aus Österreich: Gedichte* (1943); Wilhelm Scholz, *Moscow on Austria* (1943); Albert Fuchs, *Ein Sohn aus gutem Haus* (1944); Ernst Fischer, *Der österreichische Volkscharakter* (1944); Hermynia zur Mühlen, *Kleine Geschichten von großen Dichtern* (1944); Jenö Desser et al., *Die österreichischen Flüchtlinge und ihre Zukunft* (1944); and Jenö Desser, *Vom Ghetto in die Freiheit* (1945).[54] The publishing house of Young Austria, Jugend Voran, which worked together with Free Austrian Books, devoted itself especially to the work of young Austrian poets in exile such as Eva Ascher, Erich Deutsch, Erich Fried, Kitty Gans, Heinz Karpeles, Arthur Rosenthal, Hans Schmeier and Lily Spandorf, producing anthologies like *Mut: Gedichte junger Österreicher* (1943) which, despite a print-run of 5,000 copies, was soon sold out.[55]

As representatives of Austrian culture and consciousness, most writers took part in the activities of the refugee organisations. From January 1939, they were organised in the Austrian PEN (later, the Free Austrian PEN) which, thanks to its secretary Robert Neumann, was able to supply visas and residence permits and to give advice on such matters as publishers, agents and translators.[56] The Austrian PEN aimed to cultivate and promote Austrian literature and to convey Austrian culture to the British and Allied public. The strong anti-Fascist politicisation of the Austrian PEN led it to join the FAM in February 1942 and culminated in the Austrian Cultural Conference of August

1942.[57] The Austrian PEN was, furthermore, personally enmeshed with the FAM. Robert Neumann, acting president of the PEN, was a member of the executive committee of the FAM, and refers in his autobiography to his 'friends, the Communists'. The former vice-president of the Austrian Centre, Walter Hollitscher, became secretary of the PEN in 1942.[58] Austrian writers contributed decisively to the development of an Austrian consciousness by presenting a picture of the Austria of yesterday and of tomorrow, publishing articles on its cultural history and conveying a different picture of Austria to the British. The question of why so many writers were closely linked to the FAM, even though they were not Communists, and even though it was no secret that the Austrian Centre and the FAM were initiatives of the Communists, has been answered by Eva Priester. With a few exceptions, she explains, Austrian writers in Britain considered themselves to be Austrians and not Germans; they found their spiritual home in the organisation where, regardless of ideology, the commitment to Austria and the determination to contribute to its liberation was most at home: 'this was the FAM'.[59] That the pressure put on members within organisations like the KJV was sometimes too great is shown by the suicide of the young poet Hans Schmeier and the subsequent withdrawal of Erich Fried.[60]

Music in Exile

Professional refugee musicians who were less well known in Britain had great problems in settling down. In 1941, for instance, the Musicians' Refugee Committee registered 198 cases of singers, musicians, conductors and composers, of whom 147 had no work permit and 142 no means of support.[61] Although the musicians were mostly of a Jewish bourgeois background and unpolitical, an Austrian Musicians' Group (AMG) was founded within the FAM in March 1942 on the initiative of the pianist Ferdinand Rauter, the cultural secretary of the FAM Hermann Ullrich, and the musical director of the Laterndl, Georg Knepler. The AMG made its first appearance on the occasion on the 100th anniversary of the foundation of the Vienna Philharmonic on 25 May 1942.[62] It aimed at keeping the tradition of Austrian music alive and hoped 'to transplant it back into the Austrian soil after its liberation', as well as representing the interests of its members and reaching an agreement with British musicians.[63] To avoid the political influence of the FAM, the AMG left the FAM at the end of 1942 and formed the Society of Friends of the AMG (known after March 1943 as the Anglo-Austrian Music Society) in order to have a financial basis. Between September 1941 and December 1945, thirty-nine Austrian concerts were arranged in London with the participation of British musicians including Benjamin Britten, Peter Pears, Claire Born and Myra Hess, as well as Austrian exiles like the Rosé Quartet with Arnold Rosé and Friedrich Buxbaum, the pianist Peter Stadlen, the violinist Max Rostal, and the later members of the Amadeus Quartet founded in 1947, Norbert Brainin, Siegmund Nissel and Peter Schidlof.[64]

Music formed an essential part of the life of Austrian exile clubs and had a decisive influence on the cultural programme. Of particular interest was the cultivation of classical and romantic chamber music, for example Mozart, Haydn, Schubert, Beethoven and banned composers like Mahler, Mendelssohn, Schoenberg, Krenek, Gal and Wellesz, which reached a high standard, satisfying the demands of the exiles as well as the promotion of Austria among the British. Since Austrian composers were well known in Britain, it seemed superfluous for exile organisations to organise a Mozart or a Schubert concert, but the organisations, especially the Austrian Centre, did indeed do some spadework in making Gustav Mahler and contemporary Austrian composers better known in Britain. Besides the professionally-arranged Austrian concerts, hundreds of concerts were organised by amateur musicians from the musical circles of refugee organisations. The musical friends of the Austrian Centre, for instance, arranged nearly fifty concerts in 1943 in its various club premises.[65] The choir of Young Austria under Erwin Weiss became well known as a result of its numerous concerts and its participation in the rallies of the exile organisations.

The Fine Arts and Cultural Policy

To give Austrian artists the chance to present their work to a larger audience, the Austrian Centre, Young Austria, the Austrian Women's Voluntary Workers and several provincial branches organised numerous exhibitions. An outstanding role was played by the painter Oskar Kokoschka, who had close connections with the FAM and Young Austria, wrote articles for their exile papers, gave talks at their rallies and donated the proceeds from the sale of some of his pictures to them. Kokoschka, as well as the writers Stefan Zweig, Berthold Viertel and Hans Flesch-Brunningen, acted as presidents of the Freie Deutsche Kulturbund, the Free German League of Culture (which also had Communist affiliations).

The Association of Austrian Painters, Sculptors and Architects within the FAM, under the presidency of Georg Ehrlich, tried to represent the interests of its members in exile.[66] In the same way as other professional groups, the Association tried to offer its members an opportunity to break out of their isolation, encouraging discussion with colleagues and finding new points of view, which were reflected in their work. It enabled them to present their works of art to an audience and to feel the response necessary for the artist's work.

The revival of Austrian patriotism initiated by the Communists after the Soviet Union's entry into the war also led to an increase in politico-cultural activities and discussions. The first highlight was the Austrian Cultural Conference of the Austrian PEN on 29 and 30 August 1942, which was attended by representatives of the London Bureau of Austrian Socialists. The following aims of the conference were considered: (1) to unite all Austrian artists and writers living in Britain; (2) to call on them for artistic and literary events; and (3) to build up an adult education programme. Two main themes for the workshops were envisaged: Austrian culture – its national and international recognition; and the cultural duties of emigration – international cooperation and the fight against fascism.[67]

As the conference approached, an article by Jenö Kostmann in *Zeitspiegel* entitled 'Austrian cultural work – a duty to fight' initiated an intense discussion.[68] Kostmann saw the 'conservation, defence of, and propaganda for the Austrian cultural heritage' as the primary duty of exiles, redefining cultural work as a means of psychological warfare. He based his ideas on the existence of a distinct Austrian national culture and assigned exile groups a predominantly conservative cultural role. This shows that even then the innovative achievements of exile were underestimated, although at the same time exiled artists repeatedly stressed that the conservation of the cultural heritage could only be one task alongside the development of culture in exile.[69] On balance, the tendency of the cultural conservatives, who were mainly interested in cultivating national cultural treasures, tended to preponderate over individual attempts to initiate cultural reform.

About 250 members took part in the conference, with Robert Neumann in the chair. A general introduction by David Josef Bach on 'The Artist and his Time' was followed by a paper by Albert Fuchs, 'On Austrian Culture', which was published by the Austrian Centre, and in which Fuchs reviewed 1,000 years of Austrian cultural and intellectual history.[70] Reacting to the Nazi efforts to obliterate Austrian culture, Fuchs appealed to the exiles to devote themselves increasingly to the study of Austrian culture and thought. At the same time, he gave a warning not to create a new Austrian chauvinism by denigrating other nations or glorifying everything that was Austrian.[71] Fuchs's speech was followed by papers by Marie Jahoda on sociological aspects of cultural life, Ernst Buschbeck on Austrian architecture, Otto Erich Deutsch on Austrian music, Walter Hollitscher on the Viennese coffee-house tradition, Alfred Magaziner on the culture of 'Red Vienna', Friedrich Scheu on Austrian journalism, and Walter Schiff on adult education, as well as a number of other contributions.[72]

In the same month, Young Austria, which had since 1941 occasionally produced the 'Kulturblätter des Young Austria', and had also published in its paper 'Young Austria' lyrics by Fritz Brügel, Erich Fried, Eva Priester, Hans Schmeier and Arthur West, organised a cultural conference, which was attended by about 100 members.

There were three outstanding figures within the Austrian Centre and FAM who dedicated themselves to the tasks set out at the Cultural Conference of the PEN. The first was the Communist lawyer Albert Fuchs, known in exile through his autobiography *Ein Sohn aus gutem Haus*, published by the Austrian Centre.[73] Fuchs acted as secretary of the Laterndl, for which he also wrote some sketches. As an author, he dedicated himself to the work of Karl Kraus and of exiled poets, as in his anthology *Die Vertriebenen: Dichtung der Emigration* (London, 1941).[74] He particularly focused his attention on the compilation of an Austrian cultural history, an outstanding achievement which he succeeded in finishing in exile and which was published posthumously in

Vienna in 1949 under the title *Geistige Strömungen in Österreich 1867–1918*.[75] Between 1943 and 1946, as a by-product of his study on Austrian cultural history, he published more than twenty articles on Austrian writers, mostly exiled or banned by the Nazis, thus drawing a new line of tradition in Austrian literary history.[76]

The second key figure was the Austrian musicologist and composer Egon Wellesz, the greatest living authority on Byzantine music and the origins of the Christian church chants. Wellesz, who held a chair at Oxford University, arranged numerous concerts in the premises of the Austrian Centre, together with the Austrian Musicians. Even more wide-ranging were the activities of the judge, writer and musicologist Hermann Ullrich, cultural secretary of the FAM, who published between 1942 and 1946 the 'Österreichische Kultur-blätter' of the FAM, which as of May 1944 were improved in layout and entitled 'Kulturelle Schriftenreihe des FAM'.[77] Early contributions in 1942–4 (on themes like 'Stefan Zweig', 'Österreichisches Pantheon', 'Wien im Spiegel der Jahrhunderte' and 'Österreichischer Humor von Reuenthal bis zu Polgar') were designed to commemorate fragments of Austrian literature as well as individual authors. Between spring 1944 and the end of 1945, those twelve numbers were issued which Ullrich described as 'the heart' of the Schriftenreihe and which dealt with general aspects of the Austrian idea ('Österreich vor hundert Jahren', 'Österreichische Seele', 'Das Wien unserer Großeltern'), the cultural centres of Vienna and Salzburg, Austrian poetry ('Die Berühmten und die Vergessenen', 'Hofmannsthal'), music, fine arts and science. Other numbers commemorated historically important figures as well as the achievements of women in Austrian culture. The last four numbers, published as supplements of the *Zeitspiegel* at the end of 1945, covered the 175th anniversary of Beethoven's birth and the work of Grillparzer, as well as Austrian writers in exile.[78] Ullrich's staff included Felix Braun, Engelbert Broda, Leo Delitz, Otto Demus, Georg Ehrlich, Albert Fuchs, Hans Gal, Eva Priester, Egon Wellesz and Martina Wied.[79] Furthermore, Ullrich, as well as Albert Fuchs, Joseph Kalmer, Jenö Kostmann and the Czech Paul Reimann, wrote politico-cultural articles for the *Zeitspiegel*.

It was Hermann Ullrich who, together with Ernst Buschbeck and Egon Wellesz, organised the Austrian Cultural Conference of the FAM on 21 and 22 October 1944, which dealt with the cultural restoration in Austria after the war.[80] The invitation stated:

> The achievements of centuries, in literature, music, fine arts, drama, science, have created a worldwide reputation for Austrian culture; a distinctive culture that was the product of the blending of many influences from the Slavonic North, the Roman South, the Magyar East and the German West. For many years, pan-German and later Nazi propaganda sought to present Austria's culture as an integral and indistinguishable part of German culture. The Germans have tried, systematically and thoroughly, to obliterate Austria as a cultural entity in the same way as they have done politically. After Austria's liberation

and restoration to independence, every aspect of her cultural life, as well as every other field of her national life, will have to be cleansed and restored, to enable it to regain its former high level.[81]

At the conference, Albert Fuchs put forward some suggestions for the promotion of Austrian literature; these were complemented by Leo Delitz's proposals for the promotion of fine arts. Egon Wellesz drew up a plan whereby Vienna could regain its position as centre of international music. Richard Duschinsky dealt with the reconstruction of the Burgtheater as a national theatre. Herbert Herlitschka talked about the problems of cultural life in the provinces, Ernst Buschbeck about the possibility of cultural exchanges between Austria and Britain, the USSR and Czechoslovakia, and Georg Lelewer about the reform of Austrian universities and higher education.[82] In various subcommittees (universities and higher education, general cultural matters, theatre, music), the papers were discussed and permanent committees established to continue the post-war planning, which left its mark on the concepts of the FAM for the reconstruction of Austria.

In conclusion, it is clear that the politico-cultural activities of the refugee organisations, and in particular of those initiated by the Communists such as the Austrian Centre and the Free Austrian Movement, made possible a large amount of creative cultural work in exile. It must be considered as one of the most important achievements of this period that both the commitment to Austria among the refugees, and the awareness of the Austrian question among the British public, were not simply kept alive but were triumphantly reaffirmed.

Notes

The abbreviation DÖW identifies publications of the Dokumentationsarchiv des österreichischen Widerstandes in Vienna and materials in its collection.

1. Wolfgang Muchitsch, *Mit Spaten, Waffen und Worten: Die Einbindung österreichischer Flüchtlinge in die britischen Kriegsanstrengungen 1939–1945* (Vienna, 1992), pp. 7–8.
2. Wolfgang Muchitsch, 'Der Weg ins Exil', in DÖW (ed.), *Österreicher im Exil: Großbritannien 1938–1945* (Vienna, 1992), pp. 7–10.
3. Helene Maimann, *Politik im Wartesaal: Österreichische Exilpolitik in Großbritannien 1938–1945* (Vienna, 1975), pp. 13–14; Werner Röder, *Die deutschen sozialistischen Exilgruppen in Großbritannien 1940–1945: Ein Beitrag zur Geschichte des Widerstandes gegen den Nationalsozialismus* (Hanover, 1968), p. 24.
4. See Maimann, *Wartesaal*, pp. 187–91; Wolfgang Muchitsch, 'Österreichische Exilpolitik', in DÖW (ed.), *Großbritannien*, p. 154.
5. See Maimann, *Wartesaal*, pp. 35–6.
6. Ibid., p. 41.
7. Karl Ausch, 'Das London Büro der österreichischen Sozialisten', *Die Zukunft*, 10 (1971), 18.
8. See Friedrich Scheu, *Die Emigrationspresse der Sozialisten* (Vienna, 1968).
9. Karl R. Stadler, 'Das London Büro der österreichischen Sozialisten', in DÖW and Dokumentationsstelle für österreichische Literatur (ed.), *Österreicher im Exil 1934 bis 1945* (Vienna, 1977), pp. 82–3.

10. Ibid., p. 83.
11. Maimann, *Wartesaal*, p. 197.
12. Hilde Spiel, 'Keine Klage über England', *Ver Sacrum*, 1 (1972), 21.
13. 'Schuhplattler gegen Hitler', *London-Information*, 20 (1941).
14. Report on the constitution of the Anglo-Austrian Democratic Society on 5 October 1944, DÖW Library 3018/18.
15. See Maimann, *Wartesaal*, pp. 224–5.
16. Ibid., pp. 22–3.
17. Leaflet from Austrian Information, October 1939 , DÖW 9566.
18. Programme of 'Eternal Austria', 24 May 1939, DÖW 6894/1.
19. Muchitsch, 'Exilpolitik', p. 161.
20. Memorandum on the foundation of the Austrian Academy in Great Britain, March 1940, DÖW 15.639.
21. Ibid.
22. Programme of the Austrian Academy in Great Britain, May-June 1940, DÖW 15.639.
23. Muchitsch, 'Exilpolitik', p. 162.
24. See *Free Austria* (October 1941).
25. See *Free Austria* (September 1941).
26. See *Free Austria* (July 1941).
27. Maimann, *Wartesaal*, pp. 99–100.
28. Ibid., p. 31.
29. Ibid., pp. 51–2.
30. See Hilde Spiel, 'Psychologie des Exils', in DÖW (ed.), *Österreicher im Exil 1934 bis 1945*, pp. 22–37; Helene Maimann, 'Exil als Lebensform', *Jahrbuch für Zeitgeschichte* (1979), pp. 9–57; Helene Maimann, 'Sprachlosigkeit: Ein zentrales Phänomen der Exilerfahrung', in Wolfgang Frühwald and Wolfgang Schieder (eds), *Leben im Exil: Probleme der Integration deutscher Flüchtlinge im Ausland 1933–1945* (Hamburg, 1981), pp. 31–8.
31. Eva Kolmer, *Das Austrian Centre: Sieben Jahre österreichische Gemeinschaftsarbeit* (London, 1946), p. 1.
32. Ibid.
33. Ibid., p. 4.
34. Muchitsch, 'Weg ins Exil', p. 12.
35. Maimann, *Wartesaal*, p. 75.
36. Young Austria in Great Britain, Report on activities 1939–45 (n.d.), pp. 4–5, DÖW 589.
37. *Junges Österreich*, 7 (1939), 1.
38. Helene Maimann, 'Das österreichische Exil in Großbritannien', *Aufrisse*, 1 (1987), 20.
39. Young Austria in Great Britain, Report on activities 1939–45 (n.d.), pp. 4–5, DÖW 589.
40. Ibid., p. 6.
41. Declaration of Austrian Organisations in Great Britain, 1941, DÖW 2991.
42. Maimann, *Wartesaal*, p. 131.
43. See Franz West, 'Die österreichische Weltbewegung: Weder Exilregierung noch Nationalkomitee', in DÖW (ed.), *Österreicher im Exil 1934 bis 1945*, pp. 87–96.
44. *Zeitspiegel*, 32 (1945), 2.
45. See Franz Bönsch, 'Das Exiltheater "Laterndl" in London', in DÖW (ed.), *Österreicher im Exil 1934 bis 1945*, pp. 441–50; Reinhard Hippen, *Satire gegen Hitler: Kabarett im Exil* (Zurich, 1986); Hugh Rorrison, 'German Theatre and Cabaret in London 1939–45', in Günter Berghaus (ed.), *Theatre and Film in Exile: German Artists in Great Britain 1933–1945* (Oxford, 1989), pp. 47–78; Erna Wipplinger, *Das österreichische Exiltheater in Großbritannien 1938 bis 1945*, Ph. D. thesis (Vienna, 1984).

46. Bönsch, 'Laterndl', p. 441.
47. See Peter Herz, 'Die Kleinkunstbühne "Blue Danube" in London', in DÖW (ed.), *Österreicher im Exil 1934 bis 1945*, pp. 451–8; Rorrison, 'Theatre', pp. 58–9.
48. *Zeitspiegel*, 36 (1943), 7.
49. Kolmer, *Austrian Centre*, p. 27.
50. See *Jung-Österreich*, 17 (1946).
51. Eva Priester, 'Österreichische Schriftsteller in der britischen Emigration', in DÖW (ed.), *Österreicher im Exil 1934 bis 1945*, p. 437.
52. Hilde Mareiner, *'Zeitspiegel': Eine österreichische Stimme gegen Hitler* (Vienna, 1967), pp. 27–8.
53. Kolmer, *Austrian Centre*, p. 27.
54. Ibid., p. 41.
55. Priester, 'Schriftsteller', p. 439.
56. Klaus Amann, PEN *Politik. Emigration. Nationalsozialismus: Ein österreichischer Schriftstellerklub* (Vienna, 1984), p. 66.
57. Ibid., pp. 70–2; letter Robert Neumann, 20 May 1942, DÖW Library 16.993.
58. Amann, PEN, p. 71.
59. Priester, 'Schriftsteller', p. 440.
60. See Konstantin Kaiser, 'Gespräch mit Erich Fried', *Jahrbuch der Theodor Kramer Gesellschaft* (1990), pp. 80–90.
61. Report of the Musicians' Refugee Committee, January–June 1941, DÖW 8462.
62. Wolfgang Muchitsch, 'Publizistik–Kunst–Wissenschaft', in DÖW (ed.), *Groß-britannien*, p. 370.
63. *Zeitspiegel*, 1 (1943), 7.
64. List of Austrian concerts in London 1941–5 by Ferdinand Rauter (n.d.), DÖW 8462.
65. Kolmer, *Austrian Centre*, p. 27. See Georg Knepler, *Five Years of the Austrian Centre* (London, 1944).
66. Muchitsch, 'Publizistik–Kunst–Wissenschaft', p. 373.
67. Letter Robert Neumann, 20 May 1942, DÖW Library 16.993.
68. *Zeitspiegel*, 22 (1942), 8.
69. Konstantin Kaiser, 'Kulturnation, Nationalkultur: Ansätze sie im Exil neu zu bestimmen', *Aufrisse*, 1 (1987), 24–5.
70. Albert Fuchs, *Über österreichische Kultur: Vortrag gehalten auf der Kulturkonferenz des* PEN (London, 1942).
71. Ibid., pp. 6–7.
72. See *Zeitspiegel*, 36 (1942).
73. Albert Fuchs, *Ein Sohn aus gutem Haus* (London, 1944).
74. Ulrich Weinzierl, 'Albert Fuchs (1905–1946): Ein Intellektueller im Exil', in Helmut Konrad and Wolfgang Neugebauer (eds), *Arbeiterbewegung–Faschismus–Nationalsozialismus* (Vienna, 1983), pp. 322–3.
75. Albert Fuchs, *Geistige Strömungen in Österreich 1867–1918* (Vienna, 1949).
76. Weinzierl, 'Fuchs', p. 328.
77. See Hans Eberhard Goldschmidt, 'Die kulturelle Schriftenreihe des Free Austrian Movement London 1942/1946', in DÖW (ed.), *Österreicher im Exil 1934 bis 1945*, pp. 459–67; Herbert Steiner, 'Die kulturelle Tätigkeit des Free Austrian Movement in Großbritannien', in Johann Holzner et al. (eds), *Eine schwierige Heimkehr: Österreichische Literatur im Exil 1939–1945* (Innsbruck, 1991), pp. 153–68.
78. See Hermann Ullrich, 'Abschied vom Leser', *Kulturelle Schriftenreihe des* FAM (1946), p. 2.
79. Leaflet of the *Kulturelle Schriftenreihe des* FAM (n.d.), DÖW Library 3056.
80. Programme of the Austrian Cultural Conference, 21 and 22 October 1944, DÖW Library 3016/22.
81. Invitation to the Austrian Cultural Conference 1944, DÖW Library 3016/32.
82. See *Zeitspiegel*, 43 (1944).

'Doch wer den Mut verliert ist besser tot!'

Young Austria and the Problem of Political Poetry

Jörg Thunecke

Mut. Gedichte junger Oesterreicher is an anthology of poems by thirteen Austrian poets living in exile during the early 1940s, assembled by Erich Fried (1921–88).[1] The slim volume – a mere forty-eight pages – was published in London in 1943 by 'Jugend Voran' on behalf of 'Young Austria and the Austrian World Youth Movement', with a foreword in English by the English poet John Lehmann.[2] In his preface, the nominal editor Fritz Walter[3] explains the choice of title for the volume: 'Mut – das ist es, was die heutige Jugend braucht, um den Feind zu vernichten und Mut wird sie beim Aufbau einer neuen Heimat, einer besseren Welt, haben müssen' ('Courage – that's what is needed by today's young people in order to defeat the enemy, and courage they'll need to build a new homeland, a better world') (p. 2), a point reiterated in John Lehmann's foreword: 'These young authors are determined ... to build a new Austria on stronger and more hopeful foundations' (p. 3).

Mut was by no means the first anthology of exile poems published in Britain in the 1940s, though poems included in this collection differ from those contained in earlier volumes like *Die Vertriebenen. Dichtung der Emigration* (1941)[4] and *Zwischen gestern und morgen. Neue österreichische Gedichte* (1942)[5] in that they were *all* 'written by *young* poets who had spent the greater part of their youth in the Austrian Republic' (p. 3). The precise genesis of this collection is easily established, since Kitty Gans's contribution 'Entschluss' ('Decision') is marked July 1943 (p. 30), and Hans Schmeier – who contributed seven poems – committed suicide in mid-October of the same year;[6] consequently, the anthology, to which Fried himself contributed no less than twenty per cent of the poems, can confidently be dated to the summer of 1943. With the exception of Jura Soyfer (1912–39), whose poem 'Das Lied von der Erde'[7] opens the volume to honour the 'perhaps most gifted of his generation' (p. 3), who had tragically perished in Buchenwald concentration camp four years earlier, the authors are arranged in strictly alphabetical order, though not all contributions were new or specifically written for this particular anthology. In fact, three of the surviving authors, interviewed in recent years about the origin of this volume, could not even recall for sure that they had ever been asked for permission by the editors to have their poems included.[8] Perhaps the most significant point about the publication of *Mut* was its timing – just six months after the victory of the Red Army at Stalingrad, an event particularly welcomed by poets who in many cases were not only anti-Fascist but also pro-communist.

Fritz Walter, the author of the preface, points out that many of the poems included in *Mut* are about the 'life and aims of young Austrians living in freedom',[9] about their 'Stimmung, Arbeit, Kampf und Sehnsucht' (feelings, work, struggle, and longings') (p. 2), a point elaborated on by John Lehmann in his foreword: 'They are united by their love of the Austria from which they have been so cruelly separated' (p. 3). Indeed, approximately half the poems included in *Mut* deal with the struggle to defeat Nazism and the liberation of the Austrian homeland, while the other half are moved by a 'note of deep nostalgia' about Austria, 'that beautiful and historic country before it was degraded to a mere province of Hitler's Third Reich' (p. 3). Only the former texts are discussed here, poems which look towards the *future*, not the ones which reflect on the *past*. The poems dealt with here convey an air of optimism and hope, advocate – sometimes radical – changes in the socio-political system, and are often heavily tinged with propaganda elements.[10]

By no means all literature written in exile during the period 1933 to 1945 is of outstanding quality; this is common knowledge. On the contrary: the bulk of the literary output of just over a dozen years must be classed as inferior from a literary point of view, both contextually and aesthetically. Nonetheless, as has been argued elsewhere,[11] it is vital for a proper evaluation of exile literature that so-called 'minor' authors are also taken into account and analysed, in an attempt to complete the literary mosaic, and to get an overview of what exile literature amounts to in its totality. However, one has to be constantly mindful of Durzak's warning that '[n]icht die politisch-moralische Gesinnung der Exillyrik das Kriterium einer Wertung abgeben [kann], sondern die Einverwandlung dieser Gesinnung in eine ästhetische Form, die das entsprechende Dokument ... zu einem literarischen Zeugnis macht' ('The moral and political convictions expressed in exile poetry cannot be used for literary evaluation; only the transformation of these convictions into aesthetic terms can turn a document into a literary one').[12] And if this sounds defensive, as though anticipating criticism for the selection of texts by relatively unknown authors, it should be pointed out that Fritz Walter, in his preface, acknowledged some of these aesthetic problems, stating, for example, that '[m]anche Verse noch holprig [sein mögen], manche Strophe vielleicht noch unreif [sein mag]', ('some lines may be awkward, and many a verse may still be immature') (p. 2). At the same time, he emphasises that '[d]ie Autoren junge Menschen [sind], die gelernt haben und weiter lernen, denen es ein Bedürfnis war, ihre Gedanken in Verse zu fassen und die damit auch ihren Freunden und Kameraden, dem Leser etwas zu sagen haben' ('the authors are young people who have learnt a lot, and are still learning, who felt an urge to put their thoughts in verse, and thus convey a message to their friends and comrades, as well as to the reader') (p. 2).

Of the thirty-odd poems dealing with aspects of the contemporary fight against right-wing totalitarianism in Europe, especially in German-speaking lands, 'Entschluss' ('Decision') by Kitty Gans is a text which takes the approach that the issue: 'Kunst- oder Kampfwert' ('art or struggle')[13] was *not* to be interpreted dialectically, but to be understood as a call to battle. Consequently, Gans not only exhorts herself not to be deceived about the achievements of the anti-fascist struggle to date, but, by implication, she also exhorts fellow emigrants to persist in the fight against the Nazi aggressors, an appeal skilfully underpinned by the use of a pentametric caesura in the third and fourth line of the penultimate verse, focusing the reader's attention on the negative implications of a merely passive approach:

> Glaubst du, müdes Herz, dass du schlafen könntest,
> wenn die Schlacht noch nicht gewonnen ist?
> Trüge dich nicht selbst. Wenn du Rast dir gönntest,
> wär das Feigheit; mehr: Betrug und List.

> [Tired heart, do you believe that you can sleep
> as long as the battle hasn't been won?
> Do not deceive yourself. If you rest now
> cowardice it shows, and more: deceitfulness and slyness.]
>
> (p. 30)

In fact, 'Entschluss' is in many ways reminiscent of Lily Spandorf's stinging attack in the penultimate verse of 'Vision' – probably written a little earlier than Gans's poem – on those lethargic, faint-hearted and cowardly fellow emigrants, who in the past kept quiet when they should have spoken up, and refused to act when action was most urgently called for (though, as in 'Entschluss', the precise nature of such action remains vague):

> Es sind die Trägen, Zagen, Feigen,
> die, wenn sie sprechen sollten, schweigen,
> wenn sie wachen sollten – ruhn,
> und wenn sie handeln sollten – nichts tun.

> [It's the sluggards, scaredy-cats and cowards,
> who keep silent when they should raise their voice,
> who sleep when they should be awake,
> and who do nothing when they should act.]
>
> (p. 41)

Repeatedly, the poems in *Mut* under discussion here refer verbatim to *the* 'future' (the word 'Zukunft' is italicised in the texts cited below), as in the final verse of the same text by Kitty Gans ('Entschluss'), which expresses a deeply-felt urge to influence developments in Europe during the coming weeks and months, even at the risk of reopening old wounds:

> Lieber reiss ich alle Wunden auf,
> als mein Herz der *Zukunft* zu verschliessen.

Gradaus nimmt das Schicksal seinen Lauf –
alles was wir sind, muss mit ihm fliessen.

[I sooner reopen all wounds
than close my heart to the *future*,
Fate takes its imminent course –
and our whole being must flow in its wake.]

(p. 30)

More pointedly even, present and future are reviewed in the final verse of 'Trutzlied' ('Song of Defiance') by Arthur Rosenthal, a poem – *nomen est omen* – typical of the defiant attitude which characterises a good fifty per cent of the texts assembled in this volume. Despite blatant poetic weaknesses (the artificiality of the rhyme endings, and the well-worn metaphors), confirming Kaukoreit's assessment that all three anthologies of the early 1940s (*Die Vertriebenen, Zwischen gestern und morgen* and *Mut*) are 'überwiegend konventionell' ('largely conventional') from an aesthetic point of view,[14] lines like the ones cited below are undoubtedly a clarion call for freedom, promising rich rewards in the not-too-distant future for all those fighting the forces of evil (last stanza):

Wir wanken nicht mehr, wir marschieren geschweisst,
geschlossen zum neuen Gelingen!
Die *Zukunft* belohnt unsern siegreichen Geist, –
und wenn auch das Morgen die Türe uns weist:
Wir werden den Eintritt erzwingen!

[We do not waver, welded together we march
in unison towards renewed success!
The *future* will reward our victorious spirit, –
even if at dawn we are repelled:
We'll force an entry!]

(p. 38)

The language of this set of poems in *Mut* therefore mainly reflects positive aspects of exile existence, at the expense though of a 'Schrumpfung der ästhetischen Bandbreite des Gedichtes ..., bis hin zur propagandistischen Verflachung' ('a narrowing of the poetic range ..., often amounting to no more than cheap propaganda'):[15] the purposefulness and determination of many of the emigrants, especially those engaged in various cultural activities, their joint efforts, and the mutual encouragement given to each other, as well as the assuredness with which they assumed that victory in the ongoing struggle against fascism would ultimate be theirs. A similar commitment inspires their references to the darker sides of exile life – self-deception, cowardice, faint-heartedness and general lethargy, as well as shame, indignation, and even anger at the lack of effort by fellow emigrants. This finds expression in the propagandistic poem 'Wellenlänge 450' ('Wavelength 450') by Eva Aschner, deploring nostalgic radio transmissions from the 'Heimat', the old country, transmissions which at times seem to have succeeded in deceiving individual listeners, living in exile, about the true nature of the regime back home. Aschner's final stanza offers a kind of 'lyric' shock therapy to make them face reality and stir them into action:

> Du wolltest hören, was sie drüben singen –
> ja weisst du nicht, dass sie ums Leben ringen?
> Nun packt dich heisse Scham, Empörung, Wut.
> Wie kann ich helfen, die Faschisten schlagen,
> bevor das Land ertrinkt in eurem Blut?

> [You wanted to hear what they sing over there –
> don't you know that they are struggling for life?
> Now you are touched by deep shame, indignation and anger.
> What can I do to defeat the Fascists
> before the country drowns in blood?]
>
> (p. 7)

All the poems in *Mut* so far seem to convey visionary – though vague – political messages, giving expression to the hope that in the not-too-distant future Austria, and Germany for that matter, will be free from Nazi occupation. They mostly employ simplistic verse and rhyme patterns, and conventional metaphors, use relatively few propaganda devices, and are, on the whole, quite *unspecific* about some of the burning questions of the time, especially the wider political issues at stake in 1943.

At the same time, however, a good few others refer to *specific* issues under discussion at that time, above all the question of how to bring about changes in the socio-political systems of central Europe. Such poems are mainly concerned with events in the East: the war in Russia, the advances of the Red Army, and the painting of a mostly positive, though often naively unrealistic picture of the achievements and benefits of communism, and the role of the USSR under Stalin's leadership. This type of poetic propaganda is reminiscent of poems by Jura Soyfer in the Vienna *Arbeiter-Zeitung* in the 1930s.[16]

Important for our understanding of the political engagement of Austrian writers exiled in Britain is the role of the Austrian Centre and the FDKB (Free German League of Culture) in London. Erich Fried in particular, but also a number of his friends and acquaintances, were closely associated with the Austrian Centre (founded in 1939) and its cultural arm, Young Austria (YA), which, by the end of 1941, had become part of the so-called Free Austrian Movement (FAM), an organisation of twenty-seven exile groups under communist control.[17] However, while the Austrian Centre itself was politically a relatively neutral organisation, Young Austria (Junges Österreich in Groß-britannien), founded in spring 1939, was a communist-dominated organisation,[18] run by two KPÖ officials: Herbert Steiner (Honorary Secretary) and Fritz Walter (Full-time Secretary),[19] which had a fixed political programme,[20] and issued a journal called *KAM*.[21] In addition to being a regular contributor to *KAM*,[22] Erich Fried at times also worked for the 'Laterndl', an Austrian

'Kleinkunstbühne' in London, was librarian at the Austrian Centre, wrote for the journal *Young Austria*, and eventually became a member of the KPÖ (Austrian Communist Party) and its youth organisation.[23] Apart from such Austrian groupings, Fried and his friends were associated with the FDKB,[24] founded at the end of 1938, an organisation, which – despite recent disclaimers[25] – was also heavily communist-infiltrated.[26] Fried and his friends seem at times to have suffered quite a lot at the hands of an oppressive, communist-run regime at the YA, distinguished by its authoritarian leadership style, attempts at censoring members' literary contributions and influencing decision-making processes.[27] As a result, they became increasingly opposed to the rigid and dogmatic way in which such communist organisations were run[28] – quite apart from their growing doubts about Stalin's leadership.[29] It was this situation which, at the end of 1943, led Fried to break with the 'Volksfrontzirkel' of the FDKB and relinquish his KPÖ membership,[30] though he was still toeing the Communist Party line earlier that year, as reflected in some of the poems discussed below. Nearly all these texts, in particular all the poems, are written in response to political events of the time and contain propaganda elements, above all those which advocate solidarity with the USSR, the latest victim of Hitler's aggression in the summer of 1941, and predict the speedy collapse of the German armies (a common topos in anti-fascist poetry of the time).[31]

This party-political attitude took on more extreme forms in the course of 1943. Maimann refers to FAM's 'Propagierung des patriotischen Deutschland-hasses' ('propagation of hatred of Germans for patriotic reasons'),[32] and Kaukoreit talks of the 'generell deutschenfeindliche "Ehrenburg-Linie"' ('an animosity towards everything German along the "Ehrenburg" line'), according to which 'Der einzige gute Deutsche ein toter Deutscher [ist]' ('the only good German is a dead German').[33] These tendencies are clearly discernible in the two poems 'Nach Osten ...' ('Towards the East ...') by Erich Deutsch, and Erich Fried's 'Zwei Tote' ('Two Dead Men'). Both texts are distinguished by a similar topos, since in each case an unjust war of aggression is being condemned. In Deutsch's poem, a soldier's corpse symbolises – in line with the newly adopted propagandistic, pro-USSR approach – the fate awaiting the advancing German armies in the East (both citations are from the middle section of the poem):

> Ein Hirngespinst –
> die Truppe tappt vorbei,
> der Nebel liegt wie Brei
> auf den Gewehren.
> Da scheint's, als ob mit seinen leeren
> Zügen der Tote grinst.

> [A phantom –
> the troops plod past,
> the fog clings like paste
> to their rifles.
> Then a grin seems to flash
> across the dead man's expressionless face.]   (p. 14)

Similarly, the 'unlike' deaths ('ungleiche Schlaf', final stanza) of a Russian and a German soldier in Erich Fried's poem 'Zwei Tote'[34] point to the injustice of the German conquest ('Raubzug') in the East, a text written, it seems, around the time of the Battle of Stalingrad, tacitly implying that the fortunes of war will soon be reversed, and the land, seized by the German armies, be returned to her true owners (cited here are the first two verses):

> Ein Russe und ein Deutscher,
> die liegen nebeneinand;
> in die Erde verkrampft ist des Deutschen,
> weit offen des Russen Hand.

> Den Raub umklammern im Sterben
> die Diebe, ertappt bei der Tat.
> Mit offener Hand gibt den Erben,
> wer viel zu geben hat.

> [A Russian and a German,
> they are lying side by side;
> the German's hand is clutching the soil,
> the Russian's hand is open wide.

> Dying, the thieves are clutching
> their loot, caught in the act.
> With open hands passes on to his heirs
> he who has a lot to give.]
> (p. 22)

Similarly, Kitty Gans's eulogy 'Stalingrad'[35] is a structurally and linguistically rather simplistic poem, based on the contrast between a once peaceful industrial centre (verse 1), and a currently war-torn city at the point of destruction (verse 2), culminating in the praise of the heroic achievements of the Red Army, a highly problematic topos,[36] reminiscent of many slogans at the height of the Stalinist era (citation from part 2 of verse 3):

> Ewiges Denkmal der Freiheit.
> Rettende Heldentat.
> Beispiel für alle Zeiten –
> Stalingrad.

> [Eternal monument of freedom.
> Salvation by heroic deed.
> Exemplary for times immemorial –
> Stalingrad.]
> (p. 29)

Despite their aesthetic shortcomings, and despite their flawed ideology, poems like these are based on relatively solid historical foundations, in this

instance the implications of the Battle of Stalingrad in early 1943. The text
provides evidence of genuine empathy with the widespread jubilation at this
historic turning point in the military fortunes in the East, empathy which is
difficult – even with the benefit of hindsight – to extend to another of Erich
Fried's texts included in this volume, the fifteen-verse poem 'Die Bücher'
('The Books') in praise of former and present communist ideologists and
leaders. For even if one accepts Kaukoreit's thesis that this poem is the
product of a transitional period in the author's lyric oeuvre,[37] and even if one
acknowledges that it signals the beginning of Fried's disenchantment with
communism in 1943, leading to a complete break at the end of that year,[38] one
cannot ignore the fact that at least some of Stalin's criminal deeds (for
example, the show trials and purges of the 1930s) were common knowledge in
the 1940s (verse 12 of this long poem is cited below):

> Marx, Engels, Lenin, Stalin – Menschen heben
> euch auf wie Waffen, wenn ein Nachbar fällt.
> Ihr bautet Wissen uns aus Welt und Leben.
> Das Wissen lebt. Wir bauen damit die Welt.

> [Marx, Engels, Lenin, Stalin – people lift you up
> like weapons, when a neighbour perishes.
> The knowledge you imparted to us
> lives on; with it we will build our world.]
>
> (p. 25)

Of course, Fried was not the only Austrian, or German-speaking, poet in
exile who eulogised Stalin at this point in time; in fact, he had little choice in
the aftermath of Hitler's attack on the Soviet Union in the summer of 1941,
bearing in mind that the burden of the military campaign in the East was
almost solely sustained by the forces of the Red Army, which had suffered
enormous losses as a result.[39] Nonetheless, it was naive in 1943 to identify
'goodness' as one of the Soviet leader's prime qualities, as Fried would like us
to believe (verse 13), a stanza pointedly omitted by Kaukoreit in his interpretation
of this poem.[40] Consequently, this poem – at least in the light of today's
knowledge – remains an embarrassing literary product, unworthy of later poetry
by the same author:

> Von Kampf und Arbeit hart ist eure Güte ...
> vielleicht bin ich für euch heut doch zu müd.
> Mich brennt ein Tag noch, der mich lang bemühte.
> Ertrug ich doch die Glut, die euch durchglühte.

> [Your steely goodness was the result of struggle and work ...
> perhaps I'm too tired for you tonight.
> I'm still aglow with the efforts of a long day,
> having endured the fervour which burnt in you.]
>
> (p. 25)

One of the most impressive texts of the anthology is Erich Rattner's poem 'An jeden' ('To Everyone'),[41] which summarises most of the themes and topoi selected for discussion so far. Using alternating end-rhyme, this poem (lines 1–16) succinctly and pointedly reviews the immediate past of refugees currently living in exile in Britain, posing a number of rhetorical questions which prove to be highly provocative and difficult to evade:

> Sie haben dir doch etwas Haß gelassen;
> du hast auch Hirn durchs Grenzzollamt gebracht;
> du hast zwei Hände, um mit anzufassen!
> Hast du schon einmal ernstlich nachgedacht?
> Du willst mich doch nicht etwa überzeugen,
> dass du verkalkt bist – oder feig und dumm?
> dass du kaum Atem kriegst beim Treppensteigen,
> nur Brennstoff wärst fürs Krematorium –
> Du warst schon oft genug ein Angeschmierter?!
> Hast keinen Skill und keine Energie?
> Sag gleich, was willst du sein: Ein Alliierter
> oder für lebenslänglich Refugee?
> Du bist nicht fähig, einen Tank zu bauen?
> Du hast doch umgeschult und wirst trainiert [.]
> Du bist doch höchstens aus der Nazi Gauen
> und nicht aus deinem Leben emigriert!
>
> [Surely there's some hatred left in you;
> surely you've smuggled some brain cells across the border;
> surely you've got a hand to lend!
> Have you ever given the situation serious thought?
> Surely you don't want to convince me
> that you're senile – or a coward and a numbskull?
> That you're out of breath climbing stairs,
> that you're fuel for the crematorium –
> you've been cheated often enough?!
> Do you lack skills and energy?
> Say it straight out: what do you want to be? An ally
> or a refugee for life?
> Aren't you capable of constructing a tank?
> After all: you've retrained, you're receiving instruction.
> The worst thing was that you had to flee Nazi occupied territory,
> but this doesn't mean you have finished with life!]
>
> (p. 34)

Introduced by an aggressive accountancy metaphor: 'Termin ist fällig, bar zurückzuzahlen' ('Time is up for paying back in cash') (p. 34), a number of equally challenging and irrefutable statements follow the preceding series of questions, statements which closely echo the declamatory style in German socialist poetry in the 1920s and the early 1930s. According to this tradition, all

art was propaganda ('agit-prop'), a splendid weapon both for raising consciousness and for dramatising specific issues; in this instance, the call to arms against
the Fascist regime, but also, of course, a sign of the 'ästhetische Verarmung
des Gedichtes zur politischen Spruchlyrik' ('a sign of the aesthetic impoverish-
ment of poetry, reduced to a declamatory role'):[42] 'Auf, an die Arbeit, Brüder!
Ans Gewehr! / Es gibt nur eines: biegen oder brechen. Jetzt gilt nur eins: Die
Nazis oder wir' ('To work brothers! To arms! / There's only one thing left:
make or break. There's only one choice: the Nazis or us') (p. 34). Here the
reader is being addressed, and appealed to, personally, using conventional –
though highly effective – images and metaphors. For it is an all-or-nothing
situation now: either the Nazis or the refugees! The victims, once locked up
and ill-treated in Nazi concentration camps, must finally decide to fight back:
'Lass nicht nur Gottes morsche Mühlen mahlen – und Hitlers Schreckenstage
sind gezählt' ('If God's ancient mills are not allowed to grind on – / the
horrors of the Hitler regime will soon be a thing of the past') (p. 34). After all,
the individual is not alone in this struggle; many millions, from many nations,
are fighting side by side with him: 'Du stehst doch nicht allein in diesem
Kriege, / Versuchs! (der Anfang fiel uns allen schwer)' ('You are not alone in this
struggle, / Have a go! (The beginning was equally tough for all of us')') (p. 34).

At the conclusion of the first half of stanza one of 'An jeden', Rattner
employs a clever rhetorical device, switching from the second person singular
('du'), a direct personal appeal to individual fellow emigrants, to the second
person plural ('ihr'), leading to yet another rhetorical question: 'Versteht ihr
mich? – Soll ich noch klarer sprechen? / Steht jetzt noch einer auf und fragt
– wofür?' ('Do you understand me? – Must I make myself clearer yet? / Is
there anyone still asking: what's it all about?' (lines 27–8). The interrogative
adverb 'wofür', the *last* word of verse one, then leads, like a bridge, directly to
the adverbial 'dafür' (the *first* word of the following verse), which, taken in
combination with the conjunction 'daß', is repeated no fewer than eight times
in twenty-eight lines.

It is the pointed deployment of these adverbial conjunctions, the deliberate
poetic utilisation of their emphatic and declamatory qualities, which makes
the second half of Rattner's poem such an enjoyable aesthetic experience. For,
although the overall context of this part of the poem is still dominated by the
'ideology of the anti-Fascist struggle', prescribed by Communist Party organisations in exile in Britain, a distinctly personal note makes itself heard in this
text. Some new features, seemingly reflecting the author's exasperation with
prevailing political attitudes, emerge. No longer are the same old, time-worn
political clichés regurgitated, churned out *ad nauseam* in scores of other texts
during this period, including many published in this very volume. Instead,
deeply-held personal convictions are expressed in this poem. In other words,
there is something refreshingly new about this part of 'An jeden', not found
elsewhere in *Mut*, and only occasionally in the other anthologies published in
the early 1940s.[43]

Contextually, these features are, for once, enormously helped by the use of
a conventional rhyme pattern ('Kreuzreim'[44]), whose unpretentious, often

simplistic line-endings have a tremendous impact in the way that they unerringly hit the 'right' tone, while elsewhere in this part of 'An jeden' the neat use of other poetic techniques, like onomatopoeia and alliteration, rounds off the impression of an author who genuinely believes in his message. Rattner succeeds – where most others in this volume fail – in conjuring up genuine visions of a better world to come, without simultaneously joining the 'ästhetische Fluchtbewegung' ('escape into aestheticism') which many other poets of this period endorsed.[45] To put it in a nutshell: the second half of Rattner's poem 'An jeden' is 'Exillyrik' at its best, an example of how political straitjackets, and the diminution of aesthetic standards, could be avoided, refuting the commonly-held view that most lyric poetry written in exile was of inferior quality and not worth serious study:[46]

> Dafür, dass nicht mehr Bomben niederkrachen
> und Wissenschaft in Giftgas kulminiert.
> Damit wir wieder singen, wieder lachen,
> und niemand wieder hungert oder friert.
> Damit nicht Tanks und Raubarmeen ziehen
> und Gleichschritt niedertritt dein Land und Brot.
> Dass nicht mehr Völker ihre Heimat fliehen
> und in Versklavung enden, oder Tod.
> Dafür, dass wir die Ghettotore sprengen.
> Dass dieses Blackout wieder wird zu Licht.
> Dass nicht mehr Geiseln an den Galgen hängen,
> weil sie die Pflicht erfüllten, – und wir nicht.
> Dafür, dass nicht mehr Hakenkreuze wehen
> und kein KZ uns mehr gefangen hält.
> Damit ein freies Österreich bestehen
> und leben kann in einer freien Welt.

> [So that no more bombs come crashing down
> and the aim of science will not be mustard gas.
> So that we can sing and laugh again,
> and nobody needs to starve or freeze.
> So that no tanks and plundering armies come marching
> in steps across fertile lands.
> So that no more nations need flee their homeland,
> ending in slavery or death.
> So that the gates of the ghettos are thrown open.
> So that the blackout gives way to light.
> So that no more hostages are hanged at the gallows
> for having done their duty instead of us.
> So that no more swastikas are flying
> and no more concentration camps keep us captive.
> So that a free Austria may exist
> and can live in a free world.]

(p. 35)

Despite many thematic similarities, the poems in the anthology *Mut* show quite a degree of formal *and* contextual variety; and though most of the authors printed in this volume were still quite young in 1943, lacked literary experience and, undoubtedly, suffered from aesthetic immaturity, one should heed Kaukoreit's warning that 'the cited texts reveal that they have a complexity of their own which shows empathy for the conditions of exile, and which must be understood prior to any aesthetic yardsticks being applied, lest one succumbs to the common prejudice that lyric poetry written in exile (but for a few exceptions) is hopelessly imitative and, from an aesthetic point of view, unattractive'.[47] This was by no means the first time that such a warning had been sounded: a few years earlier, Wolfgang Emmerich, in response to devastating attacks on 'Exillyrik' by Manfred Durzak (who maintained that most lyric poetry written in exile is characterised by so-called 'ästhetischen Regreß' ('aesthetic regression')[48]), and Frithjof Trapp, who talked about the 'künstlerische Auszehrung' ('artistic emaciation') and 'Senkung des ästhet-ischen Niveaus' ('lowering of aesthetic standards') in exile poetry,[49] had tried to be a little more discerning. Emmerich argued that critics often made life too easy for themselves by not investigating established stereotypes more closely,[50] quoting in his support Hans Dieter Schäfer,[51] and putting forward a counter-argument: 'by now, the reverse applies to lyric poetry written in exile: it should not be evaluated by criteria like "aesthetic regression", and conse-quently not be excluded from literary developments as a whole'.[52] Such sentiments are wholeheartedly shared by this author,[53] especially since – as demonstrated in the case of Rattner's poem 'An jeden' – it was quite possible for individual authors to break out of the narrow confines imposed on writers living in exile in Britain.

In this context, mention must be made of one of the most striking features of exile poetry: the tendency to use rather conventional verse forms, notably the sonnet. As Theodore Ziolkowski pointed out some time ago, 'eine regelrechte Sonettenwut [ist] nicht nur in der Exillyrik anzutreffen, sondern [gilt] für die Lyrik der Inneren Emigration, ja des "anderen Deutschland" generell bis hin zu Gedichten, die im Widerstand und in den Konzentrationslagern ent-standen sind' ('[...] there was a proper glut of sonnets, not just in exile poetry, but also in the poetry of "inner emigration", indeed, it could even be found in the "other Germany", right down to resistance poetry, or poetry written in concentration camps').[54] Consequently, a poem like Hans Schmeier's 'Sonnett' (sic) (p. 40), and even more so his sonnet 'Widerspruch' ('Contra-diction') (p. 38), should be judged 'according to different criteria than those of aesthetic or other forms of regression'.[55] Both these sonnets are formally correct poems, consisting of fourteen lines in iambic rhyme patterns of three and two beats, arranged according to a fixed scheme, divided into octave (two quartets) and sestet (two tercets), thereby showing 'klare[n] Bauwillen' ('obvious formal intent'), one of the essential criteria of this kind of poetic form;[56] and though they cannot be ranked as highly as Erich Arendt's 'Aragonesischer Abend', or Brecht's 'Über Kleists Stück "Der Prinz von Homburg"',[57] 'Widerspruch' at least has a certain appeal. It conveys genuine emotion, which is sadly lacking in other texts by Schmeier included in *Mut*, as for example in the effete poem 'Erkenntnis' ('Realisation') (p. 39), with its self-effacing, obsequious undertone, expressing the ambivalence of someone who had already inwardly broken with Communism but, unable to come to terms with this decision, soon afterwards committed suicide:

> Zum ersten Mal seh ich mich selbst
> in Einigkeit mit andrem Leben,
> verstrickt in Maschen, die sich um mich weben,
> nicht mehr als Einzeltier, das ohne Herde läuft.

> Jetzt bin ich eins mit alledem,
> was um mich spricht und denkt;
> und auch das Tote, dem mein Geist sein Leben schenkt,
> erkenne ich als echten Teil der Welt.

> [For the first time I see myself
> in unison with life surrounding me,
> caught in a web, which is being woven around me,
> no longer a loner, running apart from the herd.

> Now I feel at one
> with all who speak and think near me;
> and even death, to whom my spirit extends,
> I recognise as a genuine part of life.]
>
> (p. 39)

By contrast, Schmeier's sonnet 'Widerspruch' has distinct poetic merits. The first two quartets clearly have an expository function, setting up a dialectical contrast between thesis and antithesis, a conflict which, in turn, is surmounted in the concluding two tercets without, however, reaching the kind of jubilant finale characteristic of many famous sonnets of the past:

> Ist uns der Weg bekannt,
> den wir bereiten,
> führt er ins gute Land,
> wer kann uns leiten?

> Nur aus Verzweiflungskraft
> wuchs uns oft Mut.
> Ein, ach, so müder Saft
> ist dieses Blut.

> Tragen der Welt Zerfall,
> und schon des Neuen Qual
> in einem Sein.

> Wir sind das Zukunftswort
> und sind ein Strauch, verdorrt
> in Wüstenein.

[Do we know the way
we are preparing,
does it lead to a good country,
who will be able to guide us?

Out of sheer despair
we gained courage.
Alas, such a viscous juice
is our blood.

The collapse of the world,
and the torments of new things to come,
we carry both in us.

We are the word of the future,
and a bush, withered
in the desert.]
(p. 39)

Writing books, above all writing poetry, must have been a matter very dear to the hearts of most authors living in exile, and not just in Britain. It was a kind of survival technique in dark times particularly for younger writers, not yet established, whose problems were quite different from those of authors recognised before being forced into exile. Under these circumstances, it is anything but surprising, as Ziolkowski has pointed out convincingly, that it was not the aesthetics but the ethics of the sonnet which makes this generation appreciate this poetic form above all else:

> Viele Menschen spürten ein geradezu existentielles Bedürfnis, sich aus dem Chaos der Hitlerjahre irgendwie durch Form geistig zu retten. Das Sonett bot sich als die Gattung an, die das Prinzip der Form schlechthin verkörperte. ... Die oft so unbeholfenen Sonette aus diesen Jahren sind ja deswegen so ergreifend, weil sie einen manchmal rührenden Glauben an die Macht der Form angesichts des Chaos und des Todes bezeugen – einen Glauben, der in klarem Kontrast steht zu dem öfters modischen Zweifeln an der Nützlichkeit der Kunst bei Schriftstellern, die nicht unmittelbar den Bedrohungen des Dritten Reiches ausgesetzt waren. Einfach dadurch, daß man ein Sonett schrieb – und solange es eine erkennbare Form aufwies, brauchte es kein Meisterwerk zu sein –, setzte man den Gedanken der Ordnung gegen das Chaos und den Zerfall.

> [Many people felt an almost existentialist need to save themselves from the chaos of the Hitler years into some sort of aesthetic haven. The sonnet offered itself as a genre epitomising formal principles. ... The sonnets written in these years, clumsy products as they often were, happen to be such moving documents because they sometimes show a touching belief in the formal aspects of the genre, especially in the face of chaos and death – a faith which contrasts sharply with the often

54

fashionable doubt expressed in the usefulness of art by writers not directly threatened by the Third Reich. Simply by writing a sonnet – there was no need for a masterpiece as long as it complied with the formal requirements – one opposed chaos and decay with a concept of order.][58]

It is this kind of profound insight into the psyche of writers working in exile which – extended to other poetic forms and techniques of lyric poetry written in exile – will help our understanding of this neglected genre, treated so disparagingly in the past, giving rise to hope that the erstwhile dualism between 'permanency of art' and 'destructive forces of history' will – at least in some instances – converge into a type of poetry satisfactory on both aesthetic and political accounts.[59]

Notes

The quotation in the title of this chapter is taken from Eva Aschner, 'Weihnachten 1941', in *Mut. Gedichte junger Oesterreicher* (London 1943), p. 7 (page references to this anthology follow the relevant citation in parentheses).

1. According to Volker Kaukoreit, *Frühe Stationen des Lyrikers Erich Fried. Werk und Biographie 1938–1966* (Darmstadt, 1991), p. 50, Erich Fried was the *de facto* editor of this volume, confirmed by Konstantin Kaiser (Vienna); Herbert Steiner, once honorary secretary of YA, was responsible for the day-to-day running of 'Jugend Voran', while Fritz Walter figured as the official editor of *Mut* (letter by Heinz Carwin of 25 January 1992).

2. John Lehmann (1907–87), English poet and author of three autobiographies *The Whispering Gallery* (1955), *I Am My Brother* (1966) and *The Ample Proposition* (1969), condensed into one book *In My Own Time: Memoirs of a Literary Life* (1969), was a friend of Jura Soyfer's and spent part of the early 1930s in Vienna as a British newspaper correspondent.

3. Fritz Walter (= Otto Brischacek): member of the illegal KPÖ (Communist Party of Austria) in Vienna, emigrated to Britain in 1938 and became secretary of the KJVÖ (Austrian Communist Youth Organisation) in London and youth representative in the KPÖ secretariat in exile; returned to Vienna in November 1945, became chairman of the FÖJ (Free Austrian Youth) (1946–53), and was also a member of the KPÖ, at times even a member of the Central Committee of the KPÖ.

4. *Die Vertriebenen. Dichtung der Emigration* (London, 1941), which contained thirty-seven poems by refugee authors from Austria *as well as* Czechoslovakia and Germany.

5. *Zwischen gestern und morgen. Neue österreichische Gedichte* (London, 1942); almost fifty per cent (i.e. twenty-six) of this volume's poems are by established authors like Theodor Kramer, Berthold Viertel and Franz Werfel, the remainder (i.e. twenty-eight) by younger and/or less well-known poets like Erich Fried, Joseph Kalmer, Eva Priester, Jura Soyfer, H. A. Vetter, Ernst Waldinger and Arthur Zanker.

6. Hans Schmeier committed suicide in London on 12 October 1943 (cf. Kaukoreit, p. 55).

7. Cf. Jura Soyfer, 'Das Lied von der Erde (Kometen-Song)', in *Das Gesamtwerk*, ed. Horst Jarka (Vienna/Munich/Zürich, 1980), p. 224 (no date!).

8. Cf. the following comment on the origin of *Mut* by Heinz Carwin (letter of 25 January 1992): 'Sicher ist nur, dass ich weder den Band noch seine Titelgebung initiiert habe ... Vielleicht wurde ich nur telephonisch, vielleicht auch persönlich

auf eine Mitarbeit hin angesprochen – ich habe es vergessen ...' ('The only thing I know for sure is that I neither suggested the publication of this volume nor its title. ... Perhaps I was consulted by phone or in person about a possible literary contribution – I simply can't remember any longer').

9. 'Die Gedichte berichten vom Leben und von den Zielen der freien österreichischen Jugend' ('These poems tell about the life and the aims of young Austrians living in freedom') (*Mut*, p. 2).

10. Cf. Manfred Durzak, 'Im Exil', in Walter Hinderer (ed.), *Geschichte der deutschen Lyrik vom Mittelalter bis zur Gegenwart* (Stuttgart, 1983), p. 503.

11. Cf. Jörg Thunecke, 'Woyzeck im Zweiten Weltkrieg: Heinrich Carwins Tragödie "Flieder" (1943) im Umkreis des Freien Deutschen Kulturbundes in London', *Jahrbuch des Dokumentationsarchivs des österreichischen Widerstandes 1990* (Vienna), 113, note 1.

12. Durzak, p. 505.

13. Ulla Hahn, 'Der Freie Deutsche Kulturbund in Großbritannien. Eine Skizze seiner Geschichte', in Lutz Winckler (ed.), *Antifaschistische Literatur* (3 vols, Kronberg/Ts., 1977), II, p. 160.

14. Kaukoreit, p. 73.

15. Durzak, p. 503.

16. Cf., for example, Jura Soyfer's poems in the Viennese *Arbeiter-Zeitung* (in Jura Soyfer, *Das Gesamtwerk*, pp. 44–157); cf. also Jörg Thunecke, 'Literatur und Propaganda: Die politische Lyrik Fritz Brainins und Jura Soyfers in der Wiener *Arbeiter-Zeitung* (1932–34)', in Herbert Arlt and Donald G. Daviau (eds), *Jura Soyfer and his Time* (Riverside, 1995) (forthcoming).

17. Cf. Kaukoreit, p. 45.

18. Cf. Helene Maimann, *Politik im Wartesaal. Österreichische Exilpolitik in Grossbritannien 1938–1945* (Vienna/Cologne/Graz, 1975), pp. 74–82; cf. idem, 'Einige Probleme der österreichischen Emigrationspolitik in Grossbritannien', in *Österreich im Exil 1934 bis 1945*, ed. Dokumentationsarchiv des österreichischen Widerstandes and Dokumentationsstelle für neuere österreichische Literatur (Vienna, 1977), pp. 73–80; cf. also the chapter 'In einem anderen Land' in Klaus Amann, *PEN – Politik Emigration Nationalsozialismus. Ein österreichischer Schriftstellerclub* (Vienna/Cologne, 1984), pp. 60–77.

19. Cf. Kaukoreit, p. 47.

20. Ibid.

21. Ibid., pp. 47–8.

22. Ibid., pp. 48, note 98.

23. Ibid., p. 51.

24. Erich Fried was an honorary member of the so-called 'Volkssfrontzirkel' of the FDKB (cf. Kaukoreit, p. 52).

25. Cf. Jörg Thunecke, '"Das Hübscheste sind die Lieder". Allan Gray's Contribution to the FDKB Revue *Mr Gulliver Goes to School*', in Günter Bergmann (ed.), *Theatre and Film in Exile. German Artists in Britain 1933–1945* (Oxford/New York/ Munich, 1989), pp. 79–97.

26. Cf. Kaukoreit, p. 52 (esp. note 120).

27. Cf. Kaukoreit, p. 54.

28. According to Fried, several young Communists had severe doubts about, and suffered deep despair at the contemporary political situation (cf. Maimann, p. 79), which was the cause – to quote just one example – of Hans Schmeier's suicide in October 1943 (cf. Kaukoreit, p. 55).

29. Cf. Erich Fried, 'Lion Feuchtwanger und Oskar Maria Graf. Begegnungen mit dem Werk von Schicksalsgenossen', in Wolfgang Müller-Funk (ed.), *Jahrmarkt der Gerechtigkeit. Studien zu Lion Feuchtwangers zeitgeschichtlichem Werk*

(Tübingen, 1987), p. 24.

30. Cf. Kaukoreit, p. 56.

31. Ibid., p. 80: 'Der Kampf an der Ostfront ist nicht mehr allein ein Kampf gegen Hitler, sondern auch die glorreiche Selbstbehauptung eines idealisierten, bewaffneten Kommunismus' ('The battle in the East is not just a battle against Hitler any longer, but also represents the glorious self-assertion of an idealised, combative type of Communism').

32. Maimann, pp. 130–2.

33. Kaukoreit, p. 84.

34. Kaukoreit, in his discussion of 'Zwei Tote' (p. 84), points out that originally Fried compared a Russian solder, killed in the East, with a dead German soldier lying next to him, not allowing them – even in death – to sleep 'the same sleep', since the evocation of victorious socialist ideals did not permit this; however, this version apparently did not meet with the approval of Communist Party officials, according to whom even in death a German soldier was not allowed to be 'a good German', and the YA official responsible for publication of *Mut* (i.e. Fritz Walter) made Fried change the last line of the poem, so that the poem eventually appeared in its current form (p. 85, notes 225 and 226).

35. This poem serves as an additional text to pinpoint the date when Erich Fried started gathering material for his anthology.

36. Cf. Kaukoreit, p. 81.

37. Ibid, p. 88.

38. Ibid.

39. Cf. Heinz Carwin's letter of 25 January 1992: 'Erich Fried. Er war blauäugig, er steckte den Kopf in den Sand, beides. Vergessen Sie aber nicht, dass diese Linkslastigkeit, von wenigen Ausnahmen ... abgesehen, auf die gesamte Intelligentsia der 30er und 40er Jahre zutraf. Eine damals lässliche Sünde. Denn vergessen Sie nicht: es war Krieg damals, ein Weltkrieg. 1943, dies auch zu Ihrer Zeitpunktfrage des Erscheinens [*Mut*], war ... ein weltgeschichtliches Schicksalsjahr. Russland entrichtete damals für uns alle einen furchtbaren Blutzoll; da kann man schon verstehen, dass Russland, Stalin und Kommunismus alle durcheinandergebracht [sic] wurden.' ('Erich Fried: he was naive and he put his head in the sand, both. But don't forget that this kind of leaning towards the Left was, with a few exceptions, prevalent among most intellectuals in the 1930s and 40s. At that time an excusable crime. For do not forget: it was wartime, the height of the Second World War. 1943, and this too is relevant to your question of when [*Mut*] was published, ... was a year of world-historical destiny. Russia, at that time, was paying a heavy toll; consequently, it is understandable that Russia, Stalin and Communism were all lumped together.')

40. Kaukoreit, pp. 85–90.

41. According to the bio-bibliographical appendix in *Mut*, Erich Rattner had published a volume of poems entitled *Zeitbild en face*, which unfortunately could not be located.

42. Cf. Jörg Thunecke, 'Jack Lindsay's Mass Declamation *On Guard For Spain* (1937) and the Speech Chorus Tradition of the Workers' Theatre Movement (1926–1936)', in Luis Costa et al. (eds), *German and International Perspectives on the Spanish Civil War: The Aesthetics of Partisanship* (Columbia, 1992), pp. 199–222, esp. pp. 201–5; cf. also Durzak, p. 503.

43. Poems by established authors like Theodor Kramer, Max Herrmann-Neisse, Berthold Viertel or Franz Werfel.

44. 'Kreuzreim' uses the following rhyme pattern: ab ab, cd cd, etc.

45. Cf. Durzak, p. 503.

46. Durzak, pp. 502–50; 'Die Lyrik', in Frithjof Trapp, *Deutsche Literatur zwischen*

den Weltkriegen. II. Literatur im Exil (Bern/Frankfurt/New York, 1983). pp. 103–38; for a different view, cf. Wolfgang Emmerich, 'Realismus und Avantgarde in der Lyrik zwischen 1935 und 1941', in Edita Koch and Frithjof Trapp (eds), *Realismuskonzeptionen der Exilliteratur zwischen 1935 und 1940/41*, Exil. Forschung, Erkenntnisse, Ergebnisse, Sonderband 1 (Frankfurt, 1987), pp. 64–75; cf. also Albrecht Schöne, *Über politische Lyrik im 20. Jahrhundert* (Göttingen, 1965), pp. 3–55.

47. Kaukoreit, pp. 75–6: 'die angeführten Texte zeigen, daß sie eine eigene, auf die Bedingungen des Exils zu beziehende Komplexität aufweisen, die erfaßt werden muß, bevor allgemeinere ästhetische Maßstäbe angelegt werden oder gar gleich dem weitverbreiteten Verdikt nachgegeben wird, daß die Lyrik des Exils (bis auf wenige zugestandene Ausnahmen) hoffnungslos "epigonal" und "ästhetisch reizlos" sei'.

48. Durzak, p. 502.

49. Trapp, pp. 104–10, esp. pp. 104 and 106.

50. Emmerich, p. 64.

51. Cf. Hans Dieter Schäfer, *Das gespaltene Bewußtsein. Über deutsche Kultur und Lebenswirklichkeit 1933–1945* (Munich/Vienna, 1981), p. 61.

52. Emmerich, p. 66: 'Für die Lyrik des Exils gilt ... vielleicht eher umgekehrt: Sie sollte nicht unter dem negativen Vorzeichen des "ästhetischen Regresses" aus der literarhistorischen Entwicklung im Ganzen ausgegrenzt werden'.

53. Cf. note 11.

54, Emmerich (p. 67) refers here to Theodore Ziolkowski, 'Form als Protest. Das Sonett in der Literatur des Exils und der Inneren Emigration', in Reinhold Grimm and Jost Hermand (eds), *Exil und innere Emigration, Third Wisconsin Workshop* (Frankfurt, 1972), p. 172.

55. Ibid., p. 68: 'nach anderen Kriterien als denen des ästhetischen oder auch sonstigen Regresses ...'.

56. Cf. Gero von Wilpert, *Sachwörterbuch der Literatur*, 7th edn (Stuttgart, 1989), pp. 864–5.

57. Examples cited by Emmerich, pp. 69–70 and 71–2.

58. Ziolkowski, pp. 171–2.

59. Cf. Durzak, p. 520.

Crossing Borders through the Ether
Erich Fried and *Under Milk Wood*
Steven W. Lawrie

Like many of his fellow exiles, the Austrian-born writer Erich Fried, who spent the war years in London, was faced with the decision whether to return to his native country after 1945. He chose to remain in Great Britain for a number of reasons. Fried and his young family would have been confronted in Austria with catastrophic conditions, and he could hardly have expected to secure any gainful employment.[1] He had left Austria at the age of seventeen and consequently lacked any vocational training or university education. The straightforward matter of survival precluded any premature thoughts of return. As the hope of reunion with friends and relatives who had remained in Germany or Austria faded,[2] so too did the desire to return. Of his closer relatives, his father had been murdered after his arrest in 1938. In early 1947, Fried's mother received a letter from the United Kingdom Search Bureau for German, Austrian and Stateless Persons from Central Europe. The letter concerned the fate of Fried's grandmother, Malvine Stein, and informed Nelly Fried euphemistically that 'she was deported to Theresienstadt on 10.9.1942 and has not yet returned'.[3] Fried himself also commented on his reasons for remaining in London, emphasising political considerations. He had recently distanced himself from the communist-led organisations in London, but his feelings were ambivalent: 'Nach und nach störten mich damals bei den Österreichern, zu denen ich dort die engsten Bindungen hatte, einige Symptome der Stalin-Ära so sehr, daß ich nicht zurückkommen wollte, um *mit* ihnen zu arbeiten. Ich hatte aber auch keine Lust, zurückzukommen, um *gegen* sie zu arbeiten'[4] ('At that time some symptoms of the Stalin era among the Austrians, with whom I was closely associated, gradually disturbed me so much that I did not want to return to work *with* them. But nor did I want to return to work *against* them').

Fried was nevertheless intent on reaching the audience of his mother tongue. He strove to do so by means of his translations and original contributions for the British re-education journals *Blick in die Welt* and *Neue Auslese*, and also vigorously sought contacts within publishing circles in Europe. He wished to publish in German-speaking countries, while remaining in London. This was a difficult point of departure for one who had still to make a name for himself in Europe. It was unrealistic of Fried to expect that his ambitions could be easily reconciled with his prolonged exile. Ultimately, Fried did achieve his aim, but this 'return' was due to his work for the BBC and in particular to his translation of Dylan Thomas's *Under Milk Wood*.

Fried's contacts with German publishers were initiated by Elisabeth Langgässer, whose financial situation was similarly dire. Unpublished correspondence from the archives of the Claassen Verlag shows how the two authors attempted to promote each other's work.[5] Fried wrote to Langgässer in April 1948, expressing the wish to appear in the *Frankfurter Hefte*.[6] He asked for help and advice, and made a similar request later that year for a letter of recommendation about his abilities as a writer and translator.[7] The same letter also makes clear that Langgässer had sought to bring her weight to bear with Suhrkamp and Rowohlt, though without success. She had more success in convincing the Claassen Verlag of Fried's merits.

Fried and Langgässer waged a campaign on two fronts. In January 1948, she wrote to Eugen Claassen from Berlin and recommended Fried in the following glowing terms:

> Hier schicke ich Ihnen als Kostprobe den kleinen Gedicht-Zyklus 'Landlos' von Erich Fried. Ich finde ihn so erstaunlich gut, daß sich eigentlich der Kommentar und jede Empfehlung erübrigt. ... Es wäre hier für mein Gefühl eine Entdeckung zu machen.[8]

> [As a taster, I enclose the short poetry cycle 'Landlos' by Erich Fried. I find it so remarkably good that comment or recommendation is really unnecessary. ... I have the feeling that a discovery is waiting to be made here.]

Claassen also received Fried's verse cycle 'Zerklagung' via Langgässer (Claassen to Fried, 13 February 1948) and simultaneously 'Die Wanderung' from Fried in London (Fried to Claassen, 23 January 1948). A long and frustrating chapter in Fried's life began. He endeavoured repeatedly to place work with the Claassen Verlag and regularly made suggestions for German translations from English but all to no avail. Fried later gave a misleading impression of these years, relating his lack of publications in Germany to his own political disillusionment and to other political developments.[9]

Initially, the work sent to Eugen Claassen elicited a positive response, with Claassen visiting Fried for discussions in London in March 1948 (Claassen to Fried, 13 February 1948). During this visit, Claassen expressed interest in Fried's prose, for not only did Fried provide two further cycles, 'Genügung' and 'Rückschritt', but he also offered Claassen first right of refusal on his collection of short stories (Fried to Claassen, c. 1 April 1948). As with Fried's lyrical production, Claassen initially gave an encouraging response (Claassen to Fried, 8 April 1948). However, after Fried had sent him examples of his prose, Claassen's reaction was less than enthusiastic.

> Mit Ihrer Geschichte 'Ausflug an die Grenze' ist es mir seltsam

ergangen. Auf den ersten Anhieb kam ich mit ihr überhaupt nicht zurecht. Ich kapierte nicht das Stilprinzip. Sie hatten zwar in Ihrem Brief versucht, mir klar zu machen, auf was es Ihnen ankommt. Die Erklärung war mir einleuchtender als der Text selbst. ... In meiner relativen Hilflosigkeit habe ich mich an andere gewandt: sie waren noch hilfloser als ich selbst. (Claassen to Fried, 11 June 1948)

[I had a strange experience with your story 'Ausflug an die Grenze'. At the first attempt, I could make nothing at all of it. I did not grasp its stylistic principle. In your letter, you did try to make your intention clear to me. Your explanation was clearer to me than the text itself. In my relatively helpless state, I turned to others: they were even more lost than I was].

Nevertheless, Claassen was genuinely interested in publishing prose by Fried, not least because this would ease the way towards poetry publications. The lack of suitable prose adversely affected the prospects for a poetry publication, as Claassen commented to Langgässer in August 1948:

Bei [Frieds] Gedichtband ist mir im Augenblick die Herausgabe schwierig, da ein geradezu grotesker Widerstand gegen Lyrik im Buchhandel existiert. Ich habe schon länger mit Fried versucht, einen Erzählband zusammenzustellen. ... Was er mir zeigte, war mißglückt. ... Wenn ich den Autor veröffentliche, möchte ich auch, daß er bekannt wird. Das ist mit Gedichten heute einfach nicht zu schaffen.[10]

[The publication of Fried's poetry volume is difficult at the moment, as there is literally a grotesque resistance to poetry around in the book trade. For some time, I have been trying with Fried to put a prose volume together. What he showed me was unsatisfactory. If I publish an author's work, I would also like him to become well known. Nowadays that simply cannot be done with poems.]

Despite his reservations, Claassen kept Fried's hope alive. Two months earlier, he had written to Fried to reassure him, accounting for the delay by explaining that bookbinders and paper manufacturers had stopped production because of the impending currency reform (Claassen to Fried, 11 June 1948). In July, Claassen repeated his assurance about publishing a volume of poetry (Claassen to Fried, 24 July 1948), but added that he was having difficulty paying the printers.

By autumn 1948, Fried had grown impatient over the delays, especially as in October he received a reply from Claassen advising him to wait and suggesting a prose publication (Claassen to Fried, 2 October 1948). At this point, Fried resigned himself to the situation and agreed to be patient (Fried to Claassen, 15 October 1948). But, after a lengthy break in the correspondence, he approached Claassen again in autumn 1951 (Fried to Claassen, 16 October 1951). He enclosed a list of planned publications, which suggests that he had in the interim been busy producing prose works. The list includes volumes of verse cycles, poems, prose pieces, translations of English poetry, essays as well as a novel in preparation and a short story, *Das Letzte*. The short story, presented to Claassen together with what later constituted the second part of the novel *Ein Soldat und ein Mädchen*, seemed to the author to be the prose work required to ease further publications, as Claassen had suggested. He described it (at a point when he was still unsure whether it should remain a short story or be expanded into a novel) as follows:

> Ich kann mir eigentlich denken, daß dieses Manuskript mehr Glück haben könnte als meine Gedichte. Es ist zwar nicht unproblematisch und würde Diskussion, wohl auch Polemik zur Folge haben, aber ich glaube, daß man diese Novelle – oder diesen Roman – erstens sicherlich lebhaft kaufen würde; nun und zweitens glaube ich auch, daß das meine erste Prosaarbeit ist, mit der ich auch künstlerisch zufrieden bin. (Fried to Claassen, 19 February 1952)

> [I can well imagine that this manuscript could have more luck than my poems. Admittedly, it is not unproblematic and would lead to discussion and probably to controversy, but I believe firstly that this short story – or this novel – would certainly sell well; and secondly I also believe that this is the first prose work by me with which I am also satisfied artistically.]

The manuscript of *Das Letzte*, sent in portions, was finally assembled in Hamburg on 15 April 1952, although more suggestions for alterations (a common practice of Fried's) were to follow. And yet, despite Fried's anticipation of success, he received a refusal. In a long letter of 14 May, Claassen detailed his objections. The first part, which contained the story of the encounter between the American Jewish soldier and the German concentration-camp guard, Helga, he found unsatisfactory as it left the impression of being merely a sketch: 'eine Skizze für einen späteren Roman'. Conscious of the dictates of the book market, he felt that the text lacked an adequate portrayal of events, a characteristic which would alienate readers. He described the stories euphemistically as being of variable quality ('von sehr verschiedenem Gewicht', Claassen to Fried, 14 May 1952). Claassen's letter was accompanied by an enclosure: the manuscript of *Das Letzte*.

Fried's disappointment led to a break of six months in the correspondence. His next letter indicates the devastating effect that Claassen's decision had had on him: 'Ihr kritischer Brief hat mir tiefen Eindruck gemacht und einige Änderungen im MS bewirkt. Es war nicht Wut, die mich schweigen ließ, sondern zunächst Depression, nachher Lebensunordnung' (Fried to Claassen, November/December 1952) ('Your critical letter made a great impression on me and led to some changes in the manuscript. It was not anger but first depression and then my disorganised lifestyle which was responsible for my silence'). The rejection of the manuscript marked the erstwhile end of Fried's endeavours both to publish with Claassen and indeed to have the novel published at all. The Rowohlt Verlag had also been suggested to Fried as a potential publisher, and the L. Schwann Verlag in Düsseldorf had shown interest (Fried to Claassen, 17 March 1952). But Fried did not look for another publisher, perhaps because he himself recognised the validity of the criticisms levelled at *Das Letzte*. In March 1954, Fried informed Claassen of his decision not to publish this work as a novel: 'Ich habe beschlossen, nicht zu versuchen "Das Letzte" als Roman zu veröffentlichen, und den ersten Teil, die Novelle, wesentlich zu vereinfachen' (Fried to Claassen, 10 March 1954).

Both literary and financial considerations may have hindered publications of Fried's own work, but Claassen was convinced of Fried's abilities as a translator. In this area, too, Fried endeavoured to establish himself with the publisher. If initially he experienced a similar lack of success, it was for different reasons. Writing to Langgässer, who had recommended Fried as a translator, Claassen indicated in 1948 that he was prepared to entrust Fried with work as a result of the excellent translations he had seen, but that he was prevented from doing so as a result of Fried's geographical whereabouts:

> Die zentrale Schwierigkeit ist nur, wie ihm das Honorar für die Übersetzungen zuleiten [sic]. Ich war darin nach der Geldumwertung eigentlich optimistisch und habe darüber schon bei der Information Control gesprochen. Dort wurde ich belehrt, daß die Hoffnung, dergleichen zu erreichen, äußerst gering ist.[11]

> [The main difficulty is just how to pass on payment to him for the translation. After the currency reform I was actually optimistic about this and I have already discussed this at Information Control. I was instructed there that hopes of achieving such things are minimal.]

Fried had the advantage of being in an English-speaking environment and of being tuned in both linguistically and culturally. Paradoxically, he was prevented from actually putting his skills into practice by the very fact that he lived in Britain. He was keen to receive commissions for translations, not least because his finances and along with them his personal circumstances had worsened (his income at this time came from labouring jobs and from work commissioned by the BBC and the re-education journals). His plea to Claassen in 1948 contains a note of despair:

> Daß die Währungsreform alles umstürzt, kann ich mir gut denken, umsomehr als auch meine Übersetzungen hier, von denen ich bisher gelebt habe, auf einen Bruchteil ihres früheren Umfangs eingeschrumpft sind. (Fried to Claassen, 31 August 1948)

> [I can fully understand the currency reform upsetting everything, the more so as my translation work here too, from which I lived until now, has shrunk to a fraction of its previous volume.]

The title which Claassen offered to Fried for translation was Richard Church's *Eight for Immortality*. He made this unsolicited offer as a result of his acquaintance with Fried's work for the re-education journals.[12] Strenuous efforts followed to make possible a translation. Claassen approached the Information Control Division and persuaded this body to make a formal request to London regarding translations done in Britain (Claassen to Fried, 23 September 1948). A letter in English, which stressed the lack of good translators into German and offered Fried a contract to translate Church's *Eight for Immortality*, was sent to Fried to support him on the British side; and negotiations were taken up with Dent, the British publisher (Claassen to Fried, 23 September and 2 October 1948). The formal request made by Claassen was, however, never granted. In November 1948, Claassen could only report in negative terms: 'Eine Entscheidung über Richard Church ist noch nicht gefallen, jedenfalls habe ich noch keine Antwort von der Control Commission' (Claassen to Fried, 11 October 1948). By January 1950, there was no longer any question of a German edition. Perhaps the delay had influenced the decision, but Claassen justified the rejection of *Eight for Immortality* once again with economic considerations and the tastes of the book-buying public (Claassen to Fried, 13 January 1950).

Just as Fried had taken to heart Claassen's comments on his prose, so too did he learn from the failure of this translation project. He sought to match his criteria in proposing translations to the tastes of the book-buying public. Charles Williams's *Descent into Hell* appeared to Fried to conform better to the tastes of German readers. In recommending the book, he emphasised the appeal of its religious theme and its avoidance of political controversy, describing it as 'klug, tiefgründig, spannend, fortlaufende Handlung, religiös (christlich) aber nicht eng konfessionell ... Keine politischen Kontroversen. Und *nicht* deprimierend!' (Fried to Claassen, 16 January 1951). However, the ever-present currency transfer problem arose again, so that Fried's fee could not be paid (Claassen to Fried, 19 October 1951).

Although decisions on whether to publish Fried's work or his translations were governed by the dictates of the market, the matter of money transfer also swayed such decisions to the writer's disadvantage. There is evidence for this assertion in at least one other instance. As early as 1948, Fried had translated an excerpt from Dylan Thomas's *Portrait of the Artist as a Young Dog*.[13] Fried drew Claassen's attention to this publication during his visit to London in the same year (Fried to Claassen, 10 March 1954). In 1954, as Fried's efforts with the Claassen Verlag ebbed, he discovered, to his dismay, that Claassen had commissioned Thomas translations by another hand without consulting Fried. In view of Claassen's admiration of his work as a translator, it can be concluded that Fried was neglected due to the problems associated with the payment of fees.

The end of his literary exile did not arrive as quickly as Fried had wished, and when it did, it was due almost exclusively to his employment with the BBC. Fried had attempted to gain access to the medium of radio as early as December 1943 in order to reach his hoped-for audience. In an undated letter to the German section at Bush House, Fried offered 'poetry for transmission to Germany'.[14] Fried's letter was passed on to the Austrian Editor, who replied in a brief note of 7 January 1944 that the poems 'have not been found suitable for ... broadcasts to Austria' (WAC, 7 January 1944). Despite this initial rejection, by summer 1945 he had had work commissioned by the BBC. His feature for the Austrian Service entitled 'Austrian Poets' (WAC, 1 August 1945) was broadcast as part of the series 'Austrians in the World', and included three of his own poems which he himself read. But his employment with the BBC throughout the years 1945–8 was no more than sporadic. It was only from 1949 onwards that his activities here increased steadily. Reportedly, the BBC had recognised his abilities by 1950 and made him a regular contributor with the Topical Unit of the German East Zone Programme (GEZP).[15] And in late summer 1952, Fried became a full-time member of staff as Programme Assistant with the GEZP (WAC, 18 February 1955). The increasing number of commissions from 1949 onwards helped alleviate Fried's dire financial situation. In 1949, he was still moving from one labouring job to another.[16] He certainly could not survive exclusively on commissions from the BBC. Based on an agreement with the Publishers' Association, payment was at the rate of approximately one guinea per minute of broadcast time and for poetry translations '2 guineas per 12 lines for the first 24 lines and one guinea per 12 lines thereafter' (WAC, 22 January 1949). Original poetry contributions in German were paid for at the higher rate of approximately one guinea per seven lines. Fried was by no means well off. However, from June 1949 onwards he contributed on a regular monthly basis to the series 'In England', for which he was required to write German verse. Paid at the higher rate, this meant a guaranteed income of on average £7 per month. For the first two broadcasts, Fried provided thirty-eight and twenty-two lines respectively (WAC, 5 August 1949), but he evidently soon recognised that, as payment depended on length, it was in his own interests to supply as many lines as possible, whether as one poem or more. But by late summer 1957 he felt secure enough to change his status to that of part-time employee with the BBC (Fried to Hilde Claassen, 23 September 1957), and in 1959 even declined a fee due to him for one poem, 'knowing the Service was poor' (WAC, 24 June 1959)!

His work for the BBC was, as his job title suggests, essentially political rather than literary. Ironically, in view of his perception of himself as a poet, it was his knowledge of politics, more exactly the politics of the left, rather than his literary ambitions which made him useful to the BBC. Although he had refused to go back to Europe to work against his former political associates, he was now doing exactly that: commenting on and criticising the excesses of Stalinism in the Soviet Zone of Occupation and later German Democratic Republic. The content of most of his broadcasts is not known,[17] but the titles are illuminating and permit tentative conclusions. The broadcast 'Pinoccio' [sic] suggests that its author discoursed on the lengthening of mendacious East German politicians' noses, as does the title 'Old Fairy Tales under Communism'. Fried's 'Sharpley Feature' was obviously critical as it was based on three articles in the *Daily Telegraph* entitled 'The Revelation of a Communist Leader'. The titles of such broadcasts as 'Red Monuments

Upkeep', 'Volksverbundene Kunst' and 'Socialist Humanism' betray a distinctly ironical note, while 'Lessing Returns' and 'Schiller in Eastern Germany' indicate that Fried contrasted the ideas of the Enlightenment and the principle of freedom with reality as he (and the West) perceived it in the GDR. Other broadcasts were quite clearly of a critical nature as their titles suggest, such as 'Two Blacks Don't Make One White', 'Security Zone', 'Sanatorium for Sick Language' and 'A Course for Eastern "Poets"', in which Socialist Realism was presumably the target. As Volker Kaukoreit has pointed out, his broadcast entitled 'Professor Kosta' referred to Oskar Kosta, whom Fried had known in London and who had been imprisoned in Czechoslovakia.[18]

Fried was taken on by the BBC following the creation in early 1949 of the new programme for the 'zone',[19] while Robert Lucas and Bruno Adler were also recruited to make the GEZP more interesting for its listeners. Richard O'Rorke writes:

> [Lucas] came up with the idea of *Der verwunderte Zeitungsleser* based on some of the more absurd items in the East German Press ... [Adler] started to produce *Die zwei Genossen* – an imaginary weekly conversation between two Party members – one naively enthusiastic and the other inclined to scepticism.[20]

The inclusion of satirical broadcasts in the GEZP evidently influenced Fried's contributions. The title 'Frau Kleinova' sounds slightly tongue-in-cheek and bears an echo of the famous satirical wartime series by Bruno Adler, *Frau Wernicke*. Again, the content of Fried's 'Comrade Stellbein and the Angel' can only be inferred, but the title does suggest a satirical approach, implying that the comrade in some way trips up either himself or the Party. These two contributions suggest an influence on Fried of other writers employed with the GEZP. If the titles of his political broadcasts are indicative of criticism of East Germany and the Stalinist regime established and maintained there, this is confirmed by a much later broadcast whose script still exists. In an extant script of 16 May 1966, Fried refers to the aftermath of Stalinism in the GDR and talks of the oppression and lack of freedom there. He attacks the persecution of the GDR dissident Robert Havemann and even uses a derogatory expression for the GDR more commonly found in the Axel Springer press: 'drüben' ('over there').[21]

Fried was conscious of the anomalous position he was in. He had become a critic of communism, even though he had worked closely with communist allies during the war. His awareness of this situation is evident in a comment which indicates beyond doubt that he was not sparing in his criticism. He describes his work as follows: 'Rundfunkpropaganda nach der deutschen Ostzone (wofür ich drüben bereits zur Vertilgung vorgemerkt bin)' (Fried to Claassen, 16 October 1951) ('Radio propaganda for the German east zone (for which I have already been marked down for extermination)'). Fried was indeed blacklisted in the GDR, and publication of his work forbidden until the appearance in 1969 of *Gedichte*.[22] Nevertheless, he had not simply switched political sides to become a Cold Warrior and thus ensure employment. His critical broadcasts may have suited the anti-communist BBC and British Government standpoint, but his criticisms of Stalinism and of the GDR were a result of his refusal to allow a political doctrine to interfere with his perception of reality – something he had learned from his experiences with the exile organisations in wartime London. During his employment with the BBC, Fried just as readily directed his attacks elsewhere. He waged a war on two fronts, both against Stalinism and against Western Cold Warriors.[23] Despite the use of the word 'Propaganda', Fried did not simply pass on the views of the BBC. He was allowed considerable freedom, as he later acknowledged: '[die] Freiheit eines Schriftstellers oder Freiheit des Oppositionellen im Rahmen des Ganzen' ('the freedom of a writer or the freedom of a member of the opposition within the overall framework').[24]

Although Fried was employed at Bush House as Political Commentator, his literary ambitions were nevertheless still strong. It was important to him that he should have time for his literary pursuits, which he carried our 'in [his] own time (Sundays, holidays) after joining BBC staff' (WAC, 6 December 1954) as well as while at work, for he had a special arrangement in his contract which allowed him to write poetry during working hours.[25] The importance to him of his career as a writer motivated the change to part-time employment in February 1958. He identified the benefits of the change as follows:

> Ich werde als freier Mitarbeiter 2 Programme in der Woche liefern, worüber ich sehr froh bin, weil ich jetzt endlich Zeit zum Schreiben haben werde. Ich kann diese Programme auch öfters im voraus machen und dann Deutschlandreisen unternehmen. (Fried to H. Claassen, 23 September 1957)

> [As a freelance employee I will provide two programmes a week. I am very happy about this because I will now at last have time to write. Often I will be able to make these programmes in advance and then make trips to Germany.]

Similarly, his decision in 1968 to leave the employment of the BBC was influenced by his work as a writer, for which he required more time.[26]

At Bush House, Fried found himself in a very stimulating environment, surrounded by other native speakers of German. Peter Fischer, who arrived there in 1956, describes the impression he had of it as a kind of German literary academy: 'wirklich eine ganze Akademie von hommes de lettres deutscher Sprache'.[27] Among Fried's colleagues at the BBC were Hans Flesch-Brunningen, Marius Goring, Bruno Adler, Robert Lucas, Martin Esslin, Enzio von Cramon and Ernst Jandl, as well as a variety of younger staff freshly imported from Germany. He also became acquainted with Rudolf Walter Leonhardt, later editor of the literary section of *Die Zeit*, who recruited Fried as a contributor to that paper in 1957.[28] Fried owed the commission of his first Shakespeare translation to Leonhardt, from whom the impetus for this came.[29] Although he knew them less well, he also encountered T. S. Eliot and Dylan Thomas.[30] Admittedly, the teetotaller Fried was not the ideal drinking companion for Thomas, and in any case the latter spent increasingly less time in London towards the end of his life. Fried was proud of his acquaintance with 'der große Dichter Dylan Thomas, den ich auch persönlich gekannt hatte' ('the great poet Dylan Thomas, whom I also knew personally').[31] But it is unlikely that he did more than meet Thomas once or twice during his intermittent visits to the capital. Nor is there any mention made of Fried in Constantine Fitzgibbon's detailed biography, *The Life of Dylan Thomas.*[32]

Besides the educated and literary atmosphere which undoubtedly suited Fried, employment with the BBC also offered him the opportunity to exploit the potential of the German Service (the Austrian Service was terminated in the 1950s) for his own literary ambitions. Although employed as Political Commentator, he also worked in the capacity of writer and translator. Commencing in June 1949, Fried's contribution of poetry for broadcast in the monthly programme 'In England' meant regular public recitals of his work to a German audience, even if this work was written 'to order'. On the occasions when Fried was responsible for the compilation of whole programmes on German literature, he ensured that he himself was well represented. 'Austrians in England IV' (July 1949) contained eleven of his own poems,[33] while his talk 'Anti-War Poetry' (January 1952) included quotations from his own cycle of poems.[34] Fried filled fifteen minutes of his 'Scriptwriter's Hour' (June 1952) with the reading of his verse cycle 'Wanderung', and a further quarter of an hour was devoted to readings from his own unpublished manuscripts (WAC, 13 June 1949). He provided translations of hymns and poems for Christmas and Easter broadcasts, and wrote his own poems on religious themes. For Good Friday 1952, he wrote 'Kreuzweg' and 'Gebet für den Zenturio' (WAC, 9 April 1952). The former describes the cross as a signpost which points the way to Jesus as a possible destination, while the latter's theme is that of forgiveness, as exemplified by the prayer of the crucified Christ for the legionary who carries off his clothes.[35] The BBC broadcast Fried's 'Weihnachtslied', which first appeared in Döblin's *Das Goldene Tor.*[36] It was used twice at Christmas 1952 in the GEZP, on 24 and 25 December, and in the feature 'December in England' on 29 December (WAC, 22 December 1952).

In literary terms, Fried's own work played a lesser role than that of his translations, of which there were many. Fried often tackled difficult works of English literature and provided translations which frequently gained him the praise of more senior members of staff. The poems which he translated were intended for inclusion in broadcasts by other members of staff. Although the majority of these translations cannot be traced, records do exist outlining *what* he translated. The list includes hymns by Henry Treece, Edmund Spenser, Nahum Tate, Isaac Watts, Clifford Dyment, Robert Southwell and Mary Ursula Bethell, and poems by John Donne, John Milton, Thomas Hardy, Walter de la Mare, Rudyard Kipling, T. S. Eliot, C. Busby Smith (i.e. John Charles Smith), Rupert Brooke, John Masefield, Roy Campbell, Norman Nicholson, George Herbert, C. Day Lewis, Sidney Keyes and Dylan Thomas. Fried was set the task of translating a wide variety of poetry of differing styles and language. He translated works as diverse as the medieval York miracle plays, traditional sixteenth- and seventeenth-century English hymns and the complicated poetic creations of Dylan Thomas.

Translation was Fried's particular forte. Judging by the praise which his translations earned him, he quickly established a reputation for his skills. C. W. Dilke of the German Service lauded Fried's translation of Masefield's 'Good Friday' and commented: 'I must say I think he has carried out an excellent job', recommending a higher fee than customary (WAC, 7 March 1951). Fried also impressed his superior with his translation of a York Christmas play. C. Gibson, German Programme Organiser, wrote: 'Mr Fried made an excellent job of first deciphering the old English of the original and then translating it into the nearest equivalent German verse' (WAC, 19 December 1951). Fried carried out work which would be a challenge to any translator. For example, his German version of an English mummery play was not a straight translation but was constructed from three English versions. Because Fried felt that the various mummery plays were 'garbled and incomplete', he 'had to take an English version, a Cornish one and one from the Isle of Wight, and telescope them into one coherent text' (WAC, 15 December 1951). His translation work prompted the publication of a collection of well-known English hymns and carols in 1966, with which he introduced many of these to Germany for the first time.[37] The extracts from York miracle plays in this publication were then broadcast in 1980 as a one-hour radio play by Radio DRS, Bern.

Given that Fried had established such a reputation, it is not surprising that, after the death of Dylan Thomas, he was presented with the challenge of translating *Under Milk Wood*. Angelika Heimann has misleadingly suggested that Fried was chosen as translator because they were personally acquainted.[38] However, the relationship between the two writers was a casual acquaintance rather than a deep friendship. Fried was the natural choice for this translation because of his wide experience with the BBC of translating texts of different literary origins and also because of his genuine interest in the work of the Welsh poet.

There is no indication of a knowledge of Thomas prior to the publication of *Deaths and Entrances* in 1946, but Fried's attention seems to have been caught by the widespread and resounding acclaim which greeted that volume.[39] He became aware of Thomas's work at the latest in 1948 with his translation of 'A Visit to Grandpa's'. He was interested enough in Thomas to attempt unpaid translations in his own time. The translation rights of 'And Death shall have No Dominion' were bought by the BBC in October 1950 (WAC, 6 December 1954), and he rewrote ten lines of this in his own time after joining the BBC (WAC, 18 February 1955). His versions of 'The Hand that Signed the Paper', 'Poem in October' and 'Fern Hill' were all written in his own time before autumn 1952, while 'Twenty-four Years' and 'In my Craft or Sullen Art' were translated after this date, but again in the poet's leisure time (WAC, 18 February 1955). Four of Fried's Thomas translations appeared later in *Texte und Zeichen*.[40] An examination of these and comparison with the originals reveals that Fried was a conscientious and meticulous translator. The only criticism which might be levelled at him concerns the translation in 'In my Craft or Sullen Art' of Thomas's 'towering dead / With their nightingales and psalms'.[41] This becomes 'die, die noch ragen im Tod, / beklagt von der Nachtigall Harm'.[42] Fried capitulates in face of the demands of the overall rhyme scheme. His solution to the problem of finding a rhyme-word is accompanied by the loss of the associations which Thomas engenders. Apart from this, Fried provides an admirable translation with only minor changes to Thomas's rhyme pattern.

Fried has described the circumstances which surrounded his translation as follows:

> [Es] kam, daß man, als der große Dichter Dylan Thomas ... mit 39 Jahren gestorben war, an mich herantrat, ob ich sein nachgelassenes Hörspiel *Under Milk Wood* übersetzen wolle. Die Topical Unit (wo ich politischer Kommentator war) könne mich aber nur für eine Woche entbehren. Wenn ich es in dieser Zeit fertigbringe, dann könnten sie das Hörspiel auf deutsch inszenieren, wenn nicht, müsse man das Projekt aufgeben. Das Stück sei aber voller Wortspiele und so gut wie unübersetzbar.[43]

> [After the great poet Dylan Thomas died at the age of thirty-nine, I was asked whether I wanted to translate his posthumously published radio play *Under Milk Wood*. But the Topical Unit (where I was Political Commentator) could only do without me for one week. If I could manage it in that time, then they could put on a production of the radio play in German, otherwise the project would have to be abandoned. The play, it was pointed out, was full of puns and as good as untranslatable.]

The urgency with which the translation was completed suited Fried well for, according to the writer himself, he had always worked at speed, and high-speed translations remained the norm for him.[44]

A greater contrast than that between Thomas and Fried is scarcely imaginable: Thomas, largely unpolitical and often outrageously drunk, and Fried the politically committed teetotaller with a tendency towards depression. Yet the two had in common the essential '[primäres] Verhältnis zum Wort' ('primal relationship to the word') of which Benn speaks.[45] Fried, with his mastery of literary styles, was well suited to act as translator of Thomas, whom he praised as 'der größte Dichter dieser letzten eineinhalb Jahrzehnte' ('the greatest poet of the last one-and-a-half decades').[46]

Fried proved that the supposedly untranslatable *Under Milk Wood* was indeed translatable. He successfully reproduced the playful and lyrical nature of much of the original with its punning and its associative and highly creative use of language. Some examples may serve to illustrate the manner in which he does justice to the original. For Thomas's 'limping invisible down to the sloeblack, slow, black, crowblack, fishingboatbobbing sea'[47] Fried writes: 'humpelt unsichtbar hinab zur schlehenschwarzen, zähen, schwarzen, krähenschwarzen fischerbootschaukelnden See'.[48] In the case of the inventive description of night: 'It is night neddying among the snuggeries of babes' (*Milk Wood*, p. 2), Fried reproduces the lines as: 'Es ist Nacht, die schnickt und schnackt ihr Iah in den Schnuckelnestern der Babies [sic]' (*Milchwald*, p. 6), whereby the sound made by a donkey ('Iah') corresponds to the verb in the English text. Fried generally remains as true to the original as possible. Where he makes changes, he does so out of necessity, such as in the case of Thomas's description of a visit to the lavatory by one of the characters: 'And Willy Nilly, rumbling, jockeys out again to the three-seated shack called the House of Commons in the back' (*Milk Wood*, p. 50). The verb 'to jockey' presents a problem for the translator. Fried overcomes this with his use of alliteration and the repetition of the separable prefix which has a comical ring to it to indicate the impending visit to the toilet in the yard: 'Und Willy Nilly stößt auf und steht auf und schlürft wieder hinaus in den Hinterhof, zum Holzhäuschen mit den drei Sitzen, genannt das Unterhaus' (*Milchwald*, p. 55). In the following extract, the use of imperial measurements of weight is awkward:

> There's the clip clop of horses on the sunhoneyed cobbles ..., gobble quack and cackle, tomtit twitter from the bird-ounced boughs, braying on Donkey Down. (*Milk Wood*, p. 49)

Fried has to find a substitute for 'ounce'. Instead he writes: 'Zeisigzwitschern von den vogelleicht gebogenen Zweigen' (*Milchwald*, p. 49), whereby the expression awakens the association of 'leicht [slightly] gebogen', a clever reproduction of Thomas's imagery. Often Fried's translations are ingenious, for example in his translation of the expression 'loony age' (*Milk Wood*, p. 65) which refers to Lord Cut-Glass. Fried's expression 'überdrehtes Alter' (*Milchwald*, p. 71) is particularly apt for this eccentric character who is obsessed with clocks and the passing of time.

Even particularly tricky challenges are overcome with skill. Thomas's adaptation of the words spoken at a marriage ceremony reads as follows:

> PREACHER: Will you take this woman Matti Richards ...
> To be your awful wedded wife? (*Milk Wood*, p. 13)

Fried retains the pun by using a word which has echoes of 'gesetzlich' but which also retains the meaning of the English text:

> PREDIGER: Willst du also diese Jungfrau Matti Richards ...
> heimführen als dein entsetzlich angetrautes Eheweib?
> (*Milchwald*, p. 17f.)

Fried overcomes the problem contained in another passage by creating a new, slightly altered version. Captain Cat, addressing the memory of his favourite whore, Rosie Probert, gives her an assurance:

> CAPTAIN CAT: I'll tell you no lies.
> The only sea I saw
> Was the seesaw sea

> With you riding on it.
> Lie down, lie easy.
> Let me shipwreck in your thighs. (*Milk Wood*, p. 70)

Fried retains the inference of sexual desire in Captain Cat's words, but emphasises the Captain's insatiability with a different pun:

> KAPITÄN CAT: Ich will dich nicht belügen
> ich sah nur ein Meer:
> das *Immermehr*,
> und *du* reitest die Wogen!
> Leg dich nieder, laß mich landen,
> laß mich scheitern in deinen Lenden.
> (*Milchwald*, p. 76; Fried's emphasis)

Other alterations are necessitated by cultural differences, such as 'milk stout' (*Milk Wood*, p. 8) which becomes 'Vollbier' (*Milchwald*, p. 13); the fourteen miles walked by the postman are metricised into 'zwanzig Kilometer' (*Milchwald*, p. 22), and Thomas's reference to Dr Crippen is explained to the German listener by the unobtrusive addition of the word 'Giftmörder' (*Milchwald*, p. 73).

On occasions, however, Fried sacrifices effect for the sake of local flavour. The German-speaking listener will be surprised to hear of the 'Scheibe kalter Brotpudding' (*Milchwald*, p. 13) under Mr Waldo's pillow; bread pudding may be consumed in Britain but Fried's translation can only puzzle a German listener. Similarly, Thomas's simile for the empty village pub after closing time which is 'quiet as a domino' (*Milk Wood*, p. 2) has associations in English with the object it is describing, where the game of dominoes is played. But with Fried's 'still wie ein Domino' (*Milchwald*, p. 6), the link between a domino and a pub is not at once apparent to a non-British listener. Equally puzzling to a German listener are the 'einundzwanzig Kreuzchen' (*Milchwald*, p. 46) at the end of a love letter from Miss Price to Mr Edwards, which might sooner call to mind a string of obituaries, but certainly not kisses. Here, Fried has overlooked the fact that his audience is not privileged to have had the same experience of Britain as himself.

At only two points does the German version seriously fall down. The first concerns Fried's translation of the Welsh 'Eisteddfodau' which he leaves in the original, adding in brackets 'de[r] große, alljährliche Sängerkrieg der Barden von Wales' (*Milchwald*, p. 25). Resorting to annotations, here in the form of parenthesis, is a sign of defeat. The other weak point is a straightforward error of comprehension. In describing the sweets bought by the local children, Thomas talks of 'brandyballs, winegums, hundreds and thousands, liquorice sweet as sick ...' (*Milk Wood*, p. 60). Fried translates 'hundreds and thousands' as a numeral (*Milchwald*, p. 66) and not, as would have been correct, as '(kunter)bunte Streusel'. However, these criticisms do not detract from the overall merits of Fried's translation, which reflects accurately the different levels of language employed: everyday speech, humorous or grotesque elements and the highly lyrical descriptive passages of the two narrators.

Unter dem Milchwald was first broadcast by the BBC German Service on 10 March 1954 (Fried to Claassen, 10 March 1954).[49] This broadcast was not altogether satisfactory from a technical point of view, so that there is some doubt as to its impact.[50] *Unter dem Milchwald* reached a larger audience when transmitted by the radio stations within Germany. The NWDR (later NDR) led the way,[51] broadcasting the radio play on 20 September 1954 and again two months later on 8 December.[52] According to Fried, other stations followed suit: 'Diese Übersetzung wurde in Deutschland ein ungeheurer Erfolg. Sie ging über alle Rundfunksender und praktisch über alle Bühnen der Bundesrepublik und Westberlins'[53] ('This translation became a huge success in Germany. Every radio station and practically every theatre in the Federal Republic and West Berlin put it on'). Judging by the frequency of performance by NDR alone, Fried's rendition of the radio play was enormously popular with its listeners.[54]

The première of the stage version of *Under Milk Wood* took place at the Edinburgh Festival in 1956 and provided the idea for a German stage performance.[55] Using a mammoth cast of seventy actors,[56] this was put on by Boreslaw Barlog at the Berlin Schiller Theater in 1956,[57] again with Fried's text. An opera version by Walter Steffen followed in 1973 which retained Fried's text,[58] and a successful television film was made of it.[59] His translation is still performed today, and whatever objections critics may raise about individual performances, they generally agree on the excellence of the German text. A review of the 1989–90 performance at the Schauspielhaus in Hamburg contains praise for Fried which is not untypical: 'Die Überraschung der Hamburger *Milchwald*-Renaissance: Die Sprache von Thomas, in Erich Frieds kongenialer Übersetzung, hat kaum etwas von ihrem Elan eingebüßt'[60] ('The surprising thing about the Hamburg *Under Milk Wood* renaissance is this: Dylan Thomas's language, in Erich Fried's ideally matched translation, has lost scarcely anything of its élan').

Fried's escape from the obscurity of exile is attributable to his abilities as translator. His translation *Unter dem Milchwald* marked the turning point in his career. It attracted the attention of both the German public and German publishers. It led to further translations and ultimately to publication of his own work. He has described the effects of this overnight fame:

> Ich war mit einem Schlag als Übersetzer schwerübersetzbarer Texte bekannt und erhielt mehr interessante Angebote als ich annehmen konnte. … Ich mußte nur die literarisch interessantesten Angebote annehmen. Das half auch meinem Ruf als Autor meiner eigenen Prosatexte und Gedichte.[61]

> [All of a sudden I was known as a translator of difficult texts and I received more interesting offers than I could accept. I needed to accept only the offers which were of the greatest literary interest. That also helped my own reputation as the author of prose and poems.]

Fried's name now became familiar, but via the airwaves and not via prose publications as Eugen Claassen had suggested. The avalanche of translations led ultimately to *Ein Sommernachtstraum* (May 1963, Bremen), which in turn marked the beginning of his career as Shakespeare translator. His activities with the BBC provided a link to German radio, and from the late 1960s he gained access to a German public via NDR. His work for NDR involved new translations of three works by Dylan Thomas: *Return Journey*, *The Doctor and the Devils* and *Bank Holiday* (*Rückreise, Der Doktor und die Teufel* and *Erinnerung an einen Feiertag*).[62]

These contacts then led to the broadcast of three of his own radio plays.[63] *Izanagi und Izanami* (1960) is a reworking of an ancient Japanese legend about the two gods who created the world. Fried had learned from his translation *Unter dem Milchwald*. Like Thomas, Fried uses poetic language to evoke images in his listeners and also includes songs. He uses the device of the two narrators from *Unter dem Milchwald* (here these are 'Der Weitersager' and 'Die Lautespielerin') to ensure continuity and clarity and explain the action. Thomas's influence is indicated in the subtitle given to *Izanagi und Izanami*, in which Fried pays tribute to the Welsh poet. *Under Milk Wood* bears the subtitle *A Play for Voices*; the title of Fried's first radio drama is followed by the words *Ein Spiel für Sprechstimmen, Gesang und Musik*. In *Under Milk Wood*, Thomas overcomes the 'blindness' of radio by including the blind character Captain Cat, whose descriptions of village life are based on his sense of sound, as is the reception of the play by its listeners. In Fried's second radio play, *Die Expedition* (1962), the two explorers are, like Captain Cat, also blind, with the result that their comments to one another centre on aural perceptions. *Eifersucht* (1966) was Fried's last radio play. It consists of a monologue by the main character, Lilo, who has committed suicide because of an imagined rival.

In 1957, after a break of three years, the Claassen Verlag wrote quite unexpectedly to Fried in London and asked whether he still had manuscripts of unpublished poetry which the publisher might view (H. Claassen to Fried, 6 March 1957). This renewed contact resulted in the publication of *Gedichte* (1958), *Ein Soldat und ein Mädchen* (1960) and *Reich der Steine* (1963). Claassen's sudden interest in him awakened Fried's curiosity about the reasons for this. The Claassen Verlag wrote back citing the success of his translation of Thomas's play: 'Wir erinnerten uns, Ihre sehr schöne Übersetzung *Unter dem Milchwald* gelesen zu haben' (H. Claassen to Fried, 12 April 1957). In the post-war period, Erich Fried had initially hoped to further his career as a writer by securing publications in Germany, but ultimately be crossed the border between the obscurity of exile and a career as a translator and writer through the ether.

Notes

1. See Helene Maimann, *Politik im Wartesaal: Österreichische Exilpolitik in Großbritannien 1938–1945* (Vienna, Cologne, Graz, 1975), pp. 229f.
2. As early as 1944, the *FDKB Sozial Abteilung* (sic) was engaged in investigations as to

the whereabouts of relatives in Europe; see *Freie Deutsche Kultur*, February 1942, p. 10. Fried talks at one point of '[s]eine vergasten Angehörigen'; see '"Die Wieder-künftigen": Zum Streit um die deutsche Geschichte', in Michael Lewin (ed.), *Gedanken in und an Deutschland* (Vienna and Zürich, 1988), pp. 227–42 (p. 233).

3. See Gerhard Lampe, '*Ich will mich erinnern an alles was man vergißt': Erich Fried, Biographie und Werk* (Cologne, 1989), p. 67.

4. Erich Fried, 'Die Freiheit zu sehen, wo man bleibt', in Michael Lewin (ed.), *Nicht verdrängen – Nicht gewöhnen: Texte zum Thema Österreich* (Vienna, 1987), pp. 15–22 (p. 16).

5. In all, fifteen letters exist from Langgässer to Fried. Two of these are dated 28 February 1942 and 7 September 1942. See 'Verzeichnis der von Herrn Erich Fried 18.8.1958 mit Begleitbrief vom 18. August 1958 erhaltenen Briefe', Claassen-Archiv, Deutsches Literaturarchiv, Marbach/Neckar (DLA). References for letters from the Claassen-Archiv appear in the main text.

6. Letter of 30 April 1948 from Erich Fried to Elisabeth Langgässer, in File (A: Langgässer) Erich Fried, Langgässer, Elisabeth, 1948 (70.3395/1–3), DLA.

7. Letter (undated; after 27 August 1948) from Erich Fried to Elisabeth Langgässer, ibid.

8. Letter of 8 January 1948 from Elisabeth Langgässer to Eugen Claassen, in Eugen Claassen, *In Büchern denken: Briefwechsel mit Autoren und Übersetzern* (Hamburg and Düsseldorf, 1970), p. 299.

9. Erich Fried, *Von Bis nach Seit: Gedichte 1945–58* (Vienna, 1985), p. 5f.

10. Letter of 31 August 1948 from Eugen Claassen to Elisabeth Langgässer, in Claassen, *In Büchern denken*, p. 300f.

11. Ibid.

12. Fried had translated 'Richard Church, T. S. Eliot', in *Neue Auslese*, vol. III, 1948, no. 5, pp. 69–76.

13. Dylan Thomas, 'A Visit to Grandpa's' ('Besuch beim Großvater', translated by Erich Fried), in *Neue Auslese*, vol. III, 1948, no. 6, pp. 74–80.

14. Letter from Erich Fried to the BBC German Section, Bush House. The letter is undated. Fried gives his age as twenty-three years, but this would mean the letter was written after 6 May 1944. The handwritten note to the Austrian editor is dated '5.i.44'. See BBC Written Archives Centre, Caversham (BBC WAC). For reasons of economy, references for documents in the BBC WAC appear together with the date in the main text as 'WAC'.

15. Lampe, *Biographie und Werk*, p. 91. The BBC files contain no indication of this. The date of the first broadcast for the German Soviet Zone Programme is listed as 23.8.1951 (WAC, late August 1951). This suggests that Fried was intially involved in the capacity of assistant and only later made his own broadcasts.

16. Lampe, *Biographie und Werk*, p. 87.

17. The BBC Archive contains scripts in English, including one by Fried, but it was not BBC policy to retain scripts in foreign languages. If Fried himself collected his scripts, which is likely, then they are to be found in the literary estate in the Österreichische Nationalbibliothek in Vienna (currently inaccessible). The titles of all broadcasts mentioned in the main text are listed in the BBC WAC.

18. Volker Kaukoreit, *Frühe Stationen des Lyrikers Erich Fried* (Darmstadt, 1991), p. 219.

19. Richard O'Rorke, 'Der Deutsche Dienst der BBC 1948–75: Vom Krieg zum Frieden', in Gundula Cannon (ed.), '*Hier ist England' – 'Live aus London': Das deutsche Programm der British Broadcasting Corporation 1938–1988* (BBC External Services, London, 1988), pp. 37–45 (p. 38).

20. Ibid., p. 39.

21. See Lampe, *Biographie und Werk*, pp. 94–8.

22. Erich Fried, *Gedichte, Poesiealbum 22*, ed. Bernd Jentzsch (East Berlin, 1969).
23. Erich Fried, 'Vorbeugemord', in Lewin, *Gedanken*, pp. 74–103 (p. 75).
24. Erich Fried, 'Abschied von der BBC', ibid., pp. 31–3 (p. 33).
25. 'Es erinnert sich Erich Fried', in Cannon, *'Hier ist England'*, pp. 148–9 (p. 148).
26. Ibid., p. 149.
27. 'Es erinnert sich Peter Fischer', in Cannon, *'Hier ist England'*, p. 63.
28. 'Es erinnert sich Rudolf Walter Leonhardt', in Cannon, *'Hier ist England'*, p. 138.
29. 'Es erinnert sich Erich Fried', in Cannon, *'Hier ist England'*, p. 149.
30. Fried persuaded T. S. Eliot to write an introduction to Charles Williams's *Descent into Hell*, which Fried hoped to translate. See Fried to H. Claassen, 30 July 1957. He mentions having been with Thomas in a London pub; see Erich Fried, 'Der Doktor und die Teufel: Zu einem historischen Drama von Dylan Thomas', in *FAZ*, 1.4.1959, no. 75, p. 7.
31. 'Es erinnert sich Erich Fried', in Cannon, *'Hier ist England'*, pp. 148–9 (p. 148).
32. Constantine Fitzgibbon, *The Life of Dylan Thomas* (London, 1965; London, 1975).
33. 'July 1927', 'Ballade vom Feuerschlagen', 'Begräbnis meines Vaters', 'Wiener Glockenspiel – 1943', 'Kreuzweg', 'Flora Nostra', 'Wir', 'Ergänzung', 'Die Prüfung' and 'Das Wort' (only ten are listed); see WAC, 22 July 1949.
34. 'Zur Zeit der Kriege', 'Lied der schlechten Hirten', 'Der Erschossene' and 'Wir sind ein Tun aus Ton'; WAC, 30 November 1952.
35. See Fried, *Von Bis nach Seit*, p. 23, p. 37.
36. *Das Goldene Tor*, vol. III, 1948, p. 163f.
37. Fried, *Der Stern der tat sie lenken* (Munich, 1966).
38. Angelika Heimann, *'Bless thee! Thou art translated.' Erich Fried als Übersetzer moderner englischsprachiger Lyrik* (Amsterdam, 1987), p. 37.
39. This assertion is sustained by Fried's translation of 'The Hand that Signed the Paper'. It includes the final stanza of the 1952 *Collected Poems* version. Fried did not work from the pre-war version (*New Verse*, XVIII, pp. 15–16, December 1935), which has only three stanzas. Cf. WAC, 6 December 1954.
40. 'Fern Hill', 'Gedicht im Oktober', 'Meine Arbeit oder trübe Kunst' and 'Und dem Tod soll kein Reich mehr bleiben', *Texte und Zeichen*, vol. I, 1955, no. 4, pp. 462–8.
41. Dylan Thomas, *The Poems* (London, 1971; London, 1990), p. 196f.
42. *Texte und Zeichen*, vol. I, 1955, no. 4, p. 467.
43. 'Es erinnert sich Erich Fried', in Cannon, *'Hier ist England'*, pp. 148–9 (p. 148).
44. His later Shakespeare translations were also dictated at great speed. Personal interview (unpublished) between S. W. Lawrie and Anne Duden, London, 18.12.90.
45. Gottfried Benn, 'Probleme der Lyrik', in *Gesammelte Werke in vier Bänden* (Wiesbaden, 1959), 4 vols, vol. I, pp. 494–532 (p. 510).
46. Erich Fried, 'Englische Streiflichter', in *Schweizer Rundschau*, vol. LIV, February/March 1955, no. 11/12, pp. 651–6 (p. 652).
47. Dylan Thomas, *Under Milk Wood: A Play for Voices* (London, 1954; London, 1961), p. 1 (abbreviated in the main text as *Milk Wood*).
48. Erich Fried, *Unter dem Milchwald* (Heidelberg, 1954; Frankfurt am Main, 1984), p. 5 (abbreviated in the main text as *Milchwald*).
49. A further broadcast by the Austrian Service followed on 19.3.1954 and again in the German Service on 7.4.1954. See Volker Kaukoreit, *Frühe Stationen*, p. 497.
50. See Eleanor Ransome, 'Es erinnert sich Eleanor Ransome', in Cannon, *'Hier ist England'*, pp. 145–8 (p. 146).
51. See Klaus Wagner, 'Der Milchwald als Oper', in *FAZ*, no. 110, 12.5.1973, p. 2.
52. NDR Hörspielredaktion-Archiv, card-index.
53. 'Es erinnert sich Erich Fried', in Cannon, *'Hier ist England'*, pp. 148–9 (p. 149).
54. It was broadcast by NWDR on the following dates: 20.9.1954; 8.12.1954; 7.4.1958;

5.8.1958; 22.12.1961; 4.7.1964; 28.5.1966; 1.3.1980; 10.4.1986. See NDR Hörspiel-redaktion-Archiv, card-index. The Südwestfunk broadcast it on 21.9.1954. See Volker Kaukoreit, *Frühe Stationen*, p. 497.

55. See Klaus Wagner, 'Der Milchwald als Oper'.

56. Mechthild Lange, 'Die Debütantin überzeugte mehr: Zwei Neuinszenierungen im Deutschen Schauspielhaus Hamburg', in *Frankfurter Rundschau*, no. 1, 2.1.1990, p. 8.

57. Dietmar Placzek, 'Wenn es Tag wird in Llareggyb', in *Süddeutsche Zeitung*, vol. XXIX, no. 112, 16.5.1973, p. 13.

58. Ibid.

59. *Das Hörspiel im Sommer 1963* (NDR), ed. Heinz Schwitzke and Franz Hiesel, p. 3.

60. Karin Kathrein, 'Zwischen Heiligen, Säufern und vielen lustigen Vögeln', in *Die Welt*, no. 294, 18.12.1989, p. 19.

61. 'Es erinnert sich Erich Fried', in Cannon, *'Hier ist England'*, pp. 148–9 (p. 149).

63. Broadcast on 20.2.1958, 15.4.1959, 20.2.1958: NDR Hörspielredaktion-Archiv, card-index.

63. *Izanagi und Izanami*, NDR Hörspielredaktion-Archiv, File 973. *Die Expedition* (initial working title *Die Reisenden*), ibid., File 1058. *Eifersucht* (the working title was *Die Nebenfrau; Indizienbeweise* was the internal NDR title, while the play was actually broadcast as *Eifersucht*), ibid., File 1241.

Hilde Spiel's Linguistic Rights of Residence

Konstanze Fliedl
(translated by Francis James Finlay)

Just Visiting (comme on visite des amis)

When Stella Rotenberg, a twenty-three-year-old Viennese medical student, emigrated via Holland to England following the annexation of Austria by Hitler, she found herself in a country whose language she did not speak. She was soon able to make herself understood, but she resolved 'nicht mehr als unbedingt nötig mit der englischen Sprache zu tun zu haben, in der irrsinnigen Hoffnung, daß mir um so mehr von der deutschen Sprache verbleiben würde, je weniger ich von der englischen erlernte' ('to have recourse to English no more than is absolutely necessary in the insane hope that the less English I learned, the more of my German I would retain').[1] One of the tragic fates which befell writers in exile was the recognition that their German vocabulary was being steadily eroded by the lack of contact with the spoken language, thus undermining and unsettling their sense of belonging to their mother tongue.[2] Many authors have described how their reservoir of German gradually grew cold and froze over. Hilde Spiel, for example, told of the recurring nightmare which she experienced during the war years in England, 'in dem ich meinte, nach Wien versetzt zu sein – eine Feindin in meinem Vaterland, mit englischem Geld in der Tasche, mit englischen Worten auf der Zunge, indes meine Muttersprache mir in der Kehle gefror' ('in which I imagined being removed to Vienna – an enemy in my native country, with English money in my pocket, with English words on my tongue, while my native language froze in my throat').[3] Authors who continued to write in German had to contend with their medium becoming embalmed in the museum of the past. Moreover, the possibilities for an author exiled in Britain who continued to publish in the German language were extremely limited, with the result that the exiles were under a particularly great pressure to assimilate their language.[4] Those writers who did make the switch into the foreign language, however, were unable to avoid the feeling that they did not possess a complete and recognisable linguistic identity. Robert Neumann, the president of the Austrian PEN-in-Exile, is a good example. Neumann started to write in English as an émigré in Britain and achieved a tour de force in linguistic accommodation with the publication, in 1942, of his novel *Scene in Passing*. The *Times Literary Supplement* was suitably impressed, declaring that 'nobody would suspect on the evidence of this book that he knew scarcely a word of English only a short time ago.'[5] Neumann, for his part, regarded his second language as a nomadic, homeless kind of Anglo-Saxon idiom:

> [*Scene in Passing* war] in einer Sprache geschrieben, die Nichtengländer für englisch halten, Engländer für 'irgendwoher von den Äußeren Hebriden vielleicht' oder amerikanisch, Amerikaner ebenfalls für amerikanisch 'aber nicht dorther, wo ich zu Hause bin – Amerika ist ein großes Land!'[6]

> [*Scene in Passing* was written in a language which non-native-speakers of English consider to be English; the English believe to be 'from some place or other like the Outer Hebrides, perhaps', or American; the Americans likewise think it American 'but not from where I come from – America is a big country!']

Although a good many authors ventured into the foreign language, the greatest success was reserved for those who published biographical, political or historical works, while the English-language publications of creative writers whose mother tongue was German subsequently disappeared from both Anglo-Saxon and German literary histories.[7] The fact that a writer could never be quite at home in a foreign language and literary tradition, or could not at least share the same uncomplicated sense of linguistic belonging enjoyed by the native speaker, meant that the new 'Gastrecht' or 'hospitality' offered in the linguistic 'house' was an uneasy and conditional one: 'Jede Sprache ist Teil der Gesamtwirklichkeit, auf die man wohlgegründetes Besitzrecht haben muß, wenn man guten Gewissens und sicheren Schrittes in den Sprachraum eintreten soll' ('Every language is part of the overall reality for which one must have well-established rights of ownership if one is to set foot on the linguistic terrain with a clear conscience').[8] It was this dilemma which determined the linguistic and thematic concerns of the works of authors in exile, and the influence which they were to achieve.

In Hilde Spiel's novel *The Darkened Room*, Fleming, who has emigrated to the USA, declares that a 'writer without a language is no less ridiculous than a banker without capital'.[9] The conversation had also touched on the financial predicament of the exiles, which accounts for Fleming's choice of the derogatory financial simile. For a writer, however, the loss of 'the house of language' ('das Haus der Sprache') could be a painful and disorientating experience: 'schmerzlicher ... als der Entzug der vertrauten Umgebung' ('more painful than the deprivation of one's familiar environment').[10] It is to this extent that Hilde Spiel's biography embodies Karl Kraus's metaphor:[11] for her, the problem of the 'linguistic rights of residence' ('Wohnrecht') was of an existential nature.[12] Spiel's novel is itself an example of the problems facing writers whose works were published in two linguistically separate markets. *Lisas Zimmer* made its initial appearance in 1961, in English, four years before the German edition. Moreover, the novel was set in émigré circles in New York, which clearly predestined it for a largely American readership, and its critical reception was initially cool.[13] In many respects, this reception provides a typical illustration of the effects of exile on author and reading public alike, notwithstanding the fact that Hilde Spiel had continued to regard her position in her host country as a privileged one. The author, who was born in Vienna in 1911 (and died in 1990), had just completed her philosophy studies when she decided to turn her back on the Austrian corporate state. Her marriage to Peter de Mendelssohn in 1936 provided her with the opportunity to settle in England. Spiel, whose parents were converted Jews, was thus spared the precipitate escape forced on so many of her colleagues only two years later. Nevertheless, she too was unable to achieve the successful switch to another language without considerable effort, despite the support of her husband:

> mein Schulenglisch war ausreichend, um mich mit gebildeten Menschen zu unterhalten, ... aber wie ich nach London kam, hab ich gemerkt, daß ich nicht versteh, wie der Grünzeughändler redet oder die Greißler, oder sogar die Nachrichtensprecher hab ich nicht verstanden, weil das alles viel zu rasch war und viel zu sehr in einem lokalen Idiom vor sich gegangen ist. Also das hat Monate und dann später Jahre gedauert, bis ich mich getraut habe, Englisch auch zu schreiben. Das war ein sehr mühsamer Vorgang.[14]

> [My school English was good enough for me to converse with educated people, ... but when I came to London, I realised that I couldn't understand the greengrocer or the other shopkeepers, and I didn't even understand the radio announcers because they all spoke too fast, and much of what was said was in a local idiom. All that took months, and it was to be years before I dared to write in English. It was a very laborious process.]

Her novel *Flute and Drums*, published in English by Hutchinson in 1939, is evidence of her successful efforts, yet it still had to be written first in German before being translated into English with the help of de Mendelssohn and Eric Dancy. By now, Spiel felt even more relaxed and secure in English than in German ('müheloser und sicherer als im Deutschen').[15] Nevertheless, it was to be over twenty years before *The Darkened Room* appeared. This was because the shift to another language resulted in a change in genre: Spiel, the writer of prose fiction, became an essayist.[16] In spite of the block on her creative abilities as a novelist – her existential 'Lebensbruch' also coincided with a creative 'Schaffensbruch'[17] – she was to gain recognition as a cultural journalist, and she published in such reputable journals as the *New Statesman and Nation*. She considered her contributions to the feature page 'Books in General' to be the 'Akkolade einer in die Sprache eingewanderten Schriftstellerin' ('the accolade of a writer who had taken up residence in the foreign language').[18] This 'accolade' was endorsed with the award of British citizenship in 1941. It was in the literature of her new country that Spiel was to find an element which facilitated her identification with the English mentality: the painful homesickness of all those 'exiles from childhood' ('all jene[r] Exilierten der Kindheit')[19] which pervaded the work of many English writers:

> Solcher Exilierten gab es in England immer die Menge, und wie in keinem anderen Land haben sie das Schrifttum der letzten dreißig Jahre bestimmt. Die Kluft zwischen der Wirklichkeit der viktorianischen Nursery und der Wirklichkeit der erwachsenen Welt wird täglich weiter und unüber-brückbarer. ... Der traumatische Schock, den die Tiefenpsychologie der Geburt zugeschrieben hat, ereignet sich hierzulande erst im achten oder zehnten Jahr, wenn die Kinder aus ihrem Reich verstoßen werden und das erste feindliche Gebiet der Schule betreten. (*EA* 187–8)

> [In England, there had always been a host of such exiles and they have determined, as in no other country, the writing of the last thirty years. The chasm between the reality of the Victorian nursery and the reality of the adult world becomes wider and more unbridgeable by the day. ... The traumatic shock, which psychoanalysis ascribes to birth, is not experienced in this country until the age of eight or ten when the child is banished from the domestic realm and enters, for the first time, the enemy territory of school.]

This experience of exile and the search for the lost land of childhood had produced a literature which narrated the most brilliant of stories, and, in the same manner, Hilde Spiel tried to conceive of the forced change of language as a way of honing her craft as a writer. And as far as her essays are concerned, her schooling in the precision and inherent logic of the English language is indeed unmistakable. Spiel stated that her work in the foreign language was guided by two fundamental rules: 'erstens, den Wortschatz und die Syntax nicht zu überschreiten, die man in dem betreffenden Augenblick ohne Anstrengung beherrscht, und zweitens, den eigenen Gedankengang niemals aus dem einen in das andere Idiom zu übersetzen' ('first, to remain within the bounds of the vocabulary and syntax which one readily commands at any given moment, and second, never to translate one's own train of thought from the one idiom into the other').[20] What may appear here to be a modest principle which allows for a loss of nuance also proved itself to be an excellent discipline when writing in her native tongue. Neumann, too, was convinced that he had corrected his smooth German eloquence by exposure to the more rigorous medium of English, through which he gained a 'second linguistic virginity' ('eine zweite sprachliche Virginität').[21] In Hilde Spiel's case, she was able to combine complete mastery of English with a sovereign command of the German language. She main-tained that the 'spurious profundity' ('falsche Tiefe') of her German had been driven out by contact with the foreign language. The double linguistic necessity caused by exile was to develop, via a fruitful experiment in the synthesis of two languages and cultures, into a two-way linguistic perfection:

Jedes Gewebe von Worten, so wurde mir schließlich klar, ist ein andersgearteter Filter, durch den ein Destillat der Wirklichkeit zu gewinnen ist. Mehr als das kann es nicht sein. Aber wer die Realität nicht nur durch einen, sondern durch mehrere Filter sieht, der hat zuletzt die feinste und reinste Essenz gewonnen. (*vw* 552)

[I finally realised that every web of words is a different kind of filter through which a distillate of reality can be extracted. And that is all it can ever be. However, those who sieve reality through not one, but several filters extract the finest and purest of essences.]

Her gratitude is expressed in her choice of the words of St Stephen as the epigraph for her second volume of memoirs, entitled *Welche Welt ist meine Welt?*: 'Denn kraftlos und schwach ist das Königreich einer einzigen Sprache und Sitte' ('For the kingdom of a single language and culture is feeble and weak').[22] Evidence of the creative discipline which Hilde Spiel learned in England is provided by her journalism, which achieves both its greatest density and clarity in those essays devoted to the mastery, which she encountered in her adopted country, of the art of living, speaking and writing. In 1986, Hilde Spiel was awarded the Ernst Robert Curtius Prize, and even if one allows for the inevitable pathos of such an occasion, the official citation is by no means the only testimony to her success in combining two great historical traditions: 'die englische und die des deutschsprachigen Raumes'.[23] In her activities as editor[24] and journalist, she was to serve as an example to others of how to introduce the German reading public to English literature. Shakespeare[25] and Byron, Blake and Dickens, Shaw and Maugham, the 'Cambridge Apostles' and the exponents of the 'New Writing' featured in essays which combine a wealth of knowledge with the patience for a readership only familiar with such authors in anthologies and in translations.[26] Hilde Spiel proved herself to be a tireless intermediary in this often thankless area of literary activity. For example, she translated the poetry of W. H. Auden; prose works by Graham Greene, Elizabeth Bowen and Angus Wilson, and plays by James Saunders, Emlyn Williams and Tom Stoppard.[27] Her work as an intermediary, however, was to drop off markedly after 1945, when her publishing activity in England became increasingly restricted. Nevertheless, she could express her sense of being accepted ('wir sind akzeptiert ... obwohl wir gewußt haben, daß wir von da nicht herkommen'),[28] and for the time being she did not consider re-emigrating. Her initial and temporary return to Vienna, in February 1946, left her under no illusion as to the alacrity with which that city was jettisoning the legacy of the recent past. She felt no inclination to write in German ('Sprachwilligkeit zum Deutschen'),[29] and the subsequent record or 'diary' of this return was written in English and only appeared in German in 1968. The magnetic attraction of Vienna, however, had already begun to loosen Spiel's ties to her second homeland. It was only when certain quarters in England began to let it be known that the exiles were expected to leave that the pendulum swung in favour of her country of origin (*ww* 183–8). As a result, and notwithstanding Spiel's linguistic competence in English, it had once again proved to be a case of her having 'dropped in' on the foreign language, just visiting ('comme on visite des amis').[30] Nevertheless, it was to be 1963 before Hilde Spiel moved to Vienna for good. Hilde Spiel spent a final year in England (1983–4), living in a London town house – the kind of house she had always longed for (*ww* 279–81). For the rest of her life, it was only with considerable difficulty that she was able to bring into balance the different senses of belonging.

A Schizophrenic Age

The agony of a divided loyalty to her first and second homes had an initial effect on the 'psychology of exile':

> Schlimmer als körperliche Entbehrungen oder selbst Existenzsorgen waren, so meine ich, das gespaltene Bewußtsein, die schizophrene Geistes- und Gemütshaltung, unter denen, vor allem nachdem die Feindseligkeiten ausgebrochen waren, nahezu jeder der Emigranten litt. Was es nur hieß, den Krieg, dieses grauenhafte Übel, willkommen heißen zu müssen, weil sonst ein Schrecken ohne Ende in Aussicht stand. Dann, für die Niederlage, ja die Vernichtung jener beten zu müssen, denen man mit allen Fasern durch Herkunft, Kindheits-erlebnisse, Landschaft, Freundschaft und Verwandtschaft immer noch verbunden war.[31]

> [More severe than the physical privations, or even the existential fears were, in my opinion, the split consciousness, the schizophrenic mental and emotional states which afflicted almost every exile, particularly after the outbreak of hostilities. One can hardly imagine what it meant to have to welcome the war, this dreadful evil, because the only other prospect was a terror without end. And then, having to pray for the defeat, indeed the destruction, of those to whom one remained inextri-cably linked by virtue of background, childhood experiences, landscape, friendship and family.]

The émigré, this symbol of a 'schizophrenic age' ('Symbol unseres berühmten schizophrenen Zeitalters'),[32] is characterised by the stigma of a split personal-ity. Paradoxically, this form of emotional and mental affliction ('Gemüts- und Geisteskrankheit') was exacerbated even after the collapse of the National Socialist regime. The decision whether to stay or return once again subjected the respective loyalties to a stern test. Hilde Spiel's second husband, Hans Flesch-Brunningen, has also described how the return to Vienna mirrored the depersonalisation experienced in exile.[33]

Hilde Spiel felt that her whole existence had been shaped by a form of 'schizophrenia'.[34] *Anna & Anna*, which was conceived initially as a film script, before being produced in an abridged version as a play in the foyer of the Burgtheater, is the retrospective story of a 'Schizophrenie'.[35] The 'splitting of the personality' in question takes place in 1938: the girl Anna, who works in the administration of the State Theatres, stays on in Vienna after the Anschluss, as Anna 1 – and goes, as Anna 2, into exile in England. This plot combines autobiographical elements with historical documents. Posters, play-bills and newspaper cuttings, radio speeches and cinema newsreels all facili-tate the exact dating of individual sequences which take us from Schuschnigg's farewell speech (11 March 1938) and Churchill's inaugural speech as Prime Minister (10 May 1940), via the ceasefire with France (22 June 1940) and the bombing of Coventry (14 November 1940), to the Moscow Declaration (30 October 1943) and VE-Day (8 May 1945). The fellow exiles whom Anna meets are barely-concealed characters *à clef*, like the poet Theodor Kramer. Many short sequences provide an illustration of British refugee policy.[36] For example, Anna takes up a position as a housemaid because the immigration regulations initially prohibited employment of exiles except as domestics, nurses and agricultural workers.[37] The controversial internment of the 'enemy aliens' is also touched upon, as is the recruitment of Austrian émigrés to the 'Alien Companies' of the Auxiliary Military Pioneer Corps. The episodes set in the BBC's Bush House were undoubtedly inspired by the experience of Hans Flesch-Brunningen, who had worked for the World Service from 1940.

Anna's excursions into émigré circles provide a review of the politico-cultural activities of the Austrian organisations in exile, such as the 'Laterndl' cabaret or the Austrian Musicians' Group of the 'Free Austrian Movement'. *Anna & Anna* can thus be read as a brief history of British exile, while the various events taking place simultaneously in Vienna convey the precarious balance between opportunistic political acquiescence and resistance. The symmetrical structuring of the scenes between Vienna and London is compli-cated by contrapuntal developments in the plot. The shabby rented room, for example, in which the émigrés meet, contrasts markedly with the Viennese Salon where the upper classes and artists inadvertently display their oppor-tunism. Similarly, a performance of *Romeo and Juliet* at London's Old Vic Theatre is interrupted by an air raid, while in the scene which follows, Goebbels is shown praising the Vienna Burgtheater's production in German of *Romeo und Julia*. The original form of the screenplay routinely exploits the possibilities of simultaneous visual and acoustic fading techniques which Spiel had already analysed in her doctoral thesis.[38] In one scene, for example, Anna 1 watches a newsreel showing a bomb dropping on London; this very bomb then lands in the immediate vicinity of Anna 2's house. A further example is when Anna 2 becomes a BBC radio announcer in 1943, and Anna 1 listens to her reading a news bulletin. These 'cuts' mirror the division of the parts of the personality.

Anna & Anna, however, is more than just the formally accomplished presentation of 'inner' and 'outer' emigration and the congenial fictional realisation of a conflict of loyalties. It must be noted, however, that the 'schizophrenia' of its figure(s) does not refer to the political options offered, or to their possible room for manoeuvre.[39] The psychoanalytical term 'depersonalisation', therefore, would again be more appropriate in this context when describing the ensuing loss of the most important objects of identification (like homeland) and the destruction of the 'ego'. What is 'schizophrenic' is much more a question of the relationship to language; it is the functions of language which are divided. In her doctoral thesis, Hilde Spiel deploys the 'language theory' of her teacher, Karl Bühler, as a framework for the analysis of the semantic structures of film.[40] As a result, it would not be inappropriate to apply Bühler's dual conception of the 'denotative' and 'symbolic' fields of language ('Zeigfeld' and 'Symbolfeld') to *Anna & Anna*.[41] In the English-language environment, Anna 2's use of German loses its character of *parole*, of the speech act, because Anna has to use the foreign language in those situations requiring direct communication. She succeeds, however, in occupying linguistically the 'Zeigfeld': the direct deictic orientation, and the here and now, the cultural coordinates of the speaker's situation, are 'translatable' even when the 'Haus' where Anna has found lodgings is destroyed by a bomb: 'Don't worry. I'm still here' (*AA* 101). Conversely, Anna 1 experiences the destruction of the 'Symbolfeld' of language. If – following Bühler – the linguistic sign does indeed mirror reality in a manner which is 'relationstreu', then this correspondence is shattered by the linguistic lies perpetrated by the Nazis.[42] In National Socialist discourse, words and sentences were created or chosen deliberately to falsify their context. As a result, the 'Symbolfeld' which determines and delineates concepts becomes so distorted that every utterance about reality is perverted. It is to this extent that *Anna & Anna* is primarily concerned with language and speech.

Anna & Anna begins in a language and genre which no longer exists: the Yiddish couplet or music-hall song. The first scene is set in a basement theatre which is raided by a Nazi gang. The song of the Jewish chanteuse is the last act of an idiom which was part of the cultural diversity of the monarchy and which, quite literally, perishes beneath the jargon of the ss. The 'Schönbrunnerdeutsch' ('Emperor's German') of Anna's superior is also an old Austrian variant, but it proves itself subsequently to be capable of linguistic accommodation when confronted with the 'Reichsdeutsch' (nation-alistic German) of the new rulers. For the time being, Anna herself is speechless, as indicated by a series of stage directions. Indeed, the scene in which Anna is 'split' takes place in total silence ('völlig stumm', *AA* 43). Anna now embarks on a process of language acquisition which goes beyond Spiel's initial intention of characterising 'die zunehmende Sprachverwirrung und Sprachverwandlung einer Emigrantin durch immer deutlicher hervortretende Zuflucht zum Englischen' ('the increasing linguistic confusion and linguistic metamorphosis of an émigrée, as a result of her taking refuge in English to an ever more apparent extent') (*VW* 549). Anna makes rapid linguistic progress and comes into contact with a very differentiated sociolinguistic spectrum, which extends from the Cockney of the newspaper woman to the upper-class English of her employers. She learns how to find her way and express herself in this linguistic world. For example, she translates English idiomatic expressions into German and not vice versa: 'Clean-limbed – wie hätten wir das genannt?

Wohlgebaut?' (*AA* 101).[43] For Anna, the command of the foreign language also coincides with the fact that she can suddenly become the 'Sprecherin' (radio presenter) of her mother tongue. In the Austrian service of the BBC, she finds the 'code' with which she can combat the Nazi dictatorship and its totalitarian use of language.

Anna 1, in the meantime, is witness to the spread of the 'Language of the Third Reich' (*Lingua Tertii Imperii*). The cultural institutions with which she has contact – theatres and newspaper offices – are centres for the dissemination of the cultural and linguistic policies of the Nazis. The linguistic domination expresses itself in the elimination of foreign words, the naturalisation of Germanisms, and the advent of cynical euphemisms: Anna's Jewish grandmother, for example, is denoted as a 'Webfehler' ('slipped stitch') in her 'Ariernachweis' ('certificate of Aryan origin'). Anna's tentative expressions of protest are silenced; her opposition remains speechless. Although she supports a group of resistance fighters and organises the paper necessary for them to print and disseminate their various proclamations, her contribution is, quite literally, empty or 'blank'. The fact that Anna gives up her position in the theatre administration to become a (tight-lipped) nurse contrasts with the dual linguistic competence which Anna 2 ultimately possesses. Whilst Spiel has taken great pains to avoid her story of a split personality becoming a kind of 'Anna Jekyll and Mrs Hyde', and while the text does not side expressly with Anna 2, it is the latter's very eloquence which provides the endorsement of a language which can be neither corrupted nor silenced. It is not, however, the guarantor for a second homeland: Anna 2 returns to Vienna, the words 'You are coming back to Britain' are uttered too late, and Anna's last words are 'If only someone had said that before' (*AA* 172).

A Synthesis in the 'Spiritual Realm'

Anna 2 shares Hilde Spiel's experience of feeling at home in the language but not among its speakers, and the author has her fictional character object to a concept which Spiel herself had employed elsewhere: Hofmannsthal's notion of language as the 'spiritual realm of the nation' ('geistiger Raum der Nation'). When in *Anna & Anna* one character, Theodor, applies Hofmannsthal's phrase to the performance of Viennese plays and songs by an Austrian cabaret troupe in exile, the pragmatic Anna replies 'Wir schweben aber nicht im Raum über unserer Nation. Wir sind in England' ('We are not floating in a spiritual realm above our nation. We are in England') (*AA* 68). It must be remembered, however, that for Austrian exiles engaged in cultural pursuits, Hofmannsthal was a symbol of their lost homeland. An edition of the 'Kulturelle Schriftenreihe' of the 'Free Austrian Movement', for example, was dedicated to him in 1944 on the seventieth anniversary of his birth.[44] Hilde Spiel herself had also made a vain attempt to publish an article on Hofmannsthal in the *New Statesman*, and her efforts to interest the publishing house Methuen in an edition of the writer's selected poems were to suffer a similar fate.[45] Spiel regretted this failure all the more because she considered Hofmannsthal to be not only the author of an incomparable document on the crisis of language but also the product and champion of a supranational, multilingual cultural tradition.[46] Thus Anna's lapidary reply constitutes the rejection of a position which Spiel had initially found comforting and which had acted as a common bond between her and the English PEN Club, which she described as a 'home' that was immediately open to her ('sofort ein Zuhause)'.[47] She always paid tribute to the cosmopolitan generosity of the PEN Club, for example, in September 1941, when she was Austrian delegate to the London writers' congress with its theme of 'writers without languages':

> Unvergeßlich der Zusammenhalt, die Hoffnung dieser Menschen, dieser Tagung. Hier schwebte, im geistigen Raum, ein befriedetes und befreites Europa über unseren Köpfen.[48]

> [I shall never forget the solidarity, the hope of these people, of this congress. Here, floating in the spiritual realm above our heads, was a Europe which had been given peace and liberty.]

Spiel maintained that the 'geistige Raum' of the country of exile was international and cosmopolitan, and thus open to the exiles.[49] She referred to this space, however, not as a 'Haus' but as a 'Wolke' ('cloud'). When Spiel's 'innerer Standort' ('inner habitat') was shaken by her first return visit to Vienna, this metaphor began to take on a disquieting connotation of diffusion and uprooting: 'Ich muß befürchten, daß mein Schwerpunkt irgendwo in den Lüften über Europa liegt, in einer schwebenden Wolke über England, Österreich, Italien, Frankreich, abwechselnd angezogen und abgestoßen, ohne an diesem oder jenem Ort niederzugehen' ('I fear that my centre of gravity is floating somewhere in the air over Europe, in a cloud over England, Austria, Italy, France, attracted here and repelled there, never descending on any one particular place').[50]

Later, Spiel was to distance herself on many occasions from Hofmanns-thal's 'problematic essay' ('fragwürdig[em] Aufsatz').[51] In his speech of 1927, Hofmannsthal had made a plea for a synthetic German 'spiritual realm' which was evidently also to encompass Austria.[52] For the mature Spiel, Hofmannsthal's advocacy of a 'conservative revolution' was tantamount to 'self-obliteration' ('Selbstauslöschung'):[53] 'It is thus ... that Austria's most prototypical writer came to deny a separate identity and a separate Austrian literature, thereby negating his own *raison d'être*'.[54] Yet even the attempt to sever the link between Hofmannsthal's 'spiritual realm' and its fatal national-ism and to locate it in an imaginary republic of artists and scholars above national frontiers did not solve the concrete problem of where to live. The attempt to overcome in this 'space' the schizophrenia suffered by the émigrés was in vain. While offering an opportunity of surviving the period of exile, the retreat into the 'spiritual realm' could even be seen as pathological: 'eine krankhafte Abwehrreaktion' or 'realitätsfremde Selbstversenkung' on the part of the writer.[55] In 1981, Hilde Spiel even made a polemical attack on the allegedly unrealistic nature of contemporary Austrian literature, employing a quotation from Nietzsche as a warning of the effects of such nebulous indeterminacy ('Sonne bald, bald Wolke').[56] Here the precarious connotations which accompany the metaphor of the 'spiritual realm' are evident: an elitist separation of artist and public and a 'spiritual' attenuation are unavoidable.

Walter Benjamin chose similar imagery when describing the transfer, i.e. the translation, which would be the necessary prerequisite for the creation of such an international intellectual sphere: 'In ihr wächst das Original in einen gleichsam höheren und reineren Luftkreis der Sprache hinauf' ('In it, the original ascends, as it were, to a higher and purer stratosphere of language').[57] For Benjamin, this 'Luftkreis' is completely distinct from the pure function of language as a means of communication and is based on the 'translatability' of the original, not on the translation itself. The translation, however, with its educational aim of bringing together speakers from different cultural circles, is not alone in being a manifestation of language as a means of communication. The pragmatism required of the exile can sometimes reduce language criticism and language scepticism to the level of a luxury. This is because the language barrier as well as the shortage of outlets for expression require language to function primarily as a mediator of content and meaning; and it was this very function which the proponents of literary modernism deemed to have been rendered increasingly obsolete.

Exile scholarship has generally been loath to accept that a critical evaluation of its subject matter must take into account just how many of the works written in exile chose to put their trust in the affectivity of the content, in the educational and enlightening urgency of the 'story', instead of making the medium of language a central theme. This debate ought to be promoted rather than hindered by recognition of the fact that the literary avant-garde is occasionally more likely to be found 'on the other side', in the works of writers who offered no, or only token, resistance to fascism. In order to avoid from the outset awarding bonus points in the absurd competition between 'Gesinnung' (convictions) and 'Ästhetik' (the aesthetic) to those writers who display a lack of convictions, the crude factors of production and influence which were responsible for writers in exile having recourse to conventional aesthetic methods have to be considered thoroughly.[58] It must be recognised that the necessity to 'conserve' one's native tongue can result in 'conservative' literary techniques, as well as the tendency to depict a conservative view of the world which is accompanied occasionally by a preference for the historical novel.

Despite distancing herself from Hofmannsthal's essay of 1927, Hilde Spiel never ceased to regard him as perhaps the principal representative of an Austrian cultural tradition in which the antagonisms of multilingualism, in particular, appeared to be harmonised. In the domed reading room of the British Library – the exile's real 'spiritual realm' – she carried out research for a historical novel set in Vienna at the time of rapid economic expansion at the end of the nineteenth century. *The Fruits of Prosperity* was not accepted for publication, however, and appeared in German for the first time in 1981. As the story of a young Croat who rises to affluence in the imperial capital, the novel insists on a 'natural' homogenity, as it were, of the monarchy. When it rains in the novel, it does so in all the Habsburg crown lands simultaneously: 'ein meergeborener salziger Regen in Dalmatien, ein warmer und fruchtbarer Regen in Kärnten und Krain'.[59] Whenever characters in the book have a drink, they drink (and this is only a 'sample'!) cider from Upper Austria, Moravian beer, Gewürztraminer wine from the Southern Tyrol and Polish vodka (*FW* 139). And if food for a train journey is purchased, then it too develops into a celebration of Habsburg gastronomy: 'Zwieback in Graz, Marillen in Marburg, Pflaumenkuchen in Agram und istrische[r] Wein' (*FW* 284). Such agricultural 'fruits of prosperity' ('Früchte des Wohlstands') speak in a language understood by everyone.

This pre-industrial sense of belonging to Habsburg territory may well allow the rich diversity of the respective imperial provinces to emerge, but it ignores their conflicts.[60] While the story *Mirko und Franca*, set in the Trieste of the former empire, might still document the conflicts between the Slovenian and Italian populations, its private love-story offers the prospect of their harmonious resolution.[61] The Habsburg myth evoked here acts as a screen for the retrospective projection of a peaceful and multilingual coexistence. Occasionally, however, it becomes the 'haunted realm' ('Geisterreich') of an unattainable past. At the same time, a traditional narrative technique prevails which in no way achieves the brilliance of Hilde Spiel's essays.[62] Spiel also ignores, occasionally in a crass manner, the linguistic experiments in the works of other writers.[63] Both these aspects can be attributed to her adherence to the communicative capacity of literature. What appears aesthetically regressive is the result of an experience which make one's words disintegrate ('im Mund zerfallen') in a way far more terrible than any which Lord Chandos might have been able to imagine. And that the 'geistiger Raum' should prove itself to be so fragile demonstrates the extent to which the metaphor of the 'Haus der Sprache' has to be understood in a concrete material sense. This is the reason why Spiel's essay 'Das Haus des Dichters'[64] is, contrary to what one might have expected, not about language. Rather it provides reminiscences of the country house of Alexander Lernet-Holenia, in which the most simple of objects bear the history of their production and their purpose, a history which, for the exile, had disappeared forever. 'Mein Traum vom Haus', that dream of domestic security which was never to be realised, was to remain for Spiel the expression of an existential longing: 'der Begriff des Zuhauseseins in dieser Welt'.[65]

Spiel provided a further example of the 'Wohnrecht auf Zeit', or conditional right of residence, with its tangible solidity and latent insecurity, when she took documents on the life of Fanny von Arnstein (1758–1818) and turned them into a broad panorama of the age. This biography of the Berlin-born Jewess, whose marriage took her to Vienna where she kept a salon, is a case study in attempted integration and assimilation. The fact that Fanny is a woman who finds the forum for her 'public' appearances in the niche of the salon culture is of only secondary importance in the novel, although Hilde Spiel has also keenly observed how women have attempted to establish rights of residence in the cultural and political tradition. Examples are women writers like Virginia Woolf and Katherine Mansfield, as well as feminists ranging from Emmeline Pankhurst to Germaine Greer.[66] Fanny's 'emancipation', however, acts as a 'parable for the whole Biblical people'.[67] Fanny's family demonstrates both the contradictions of loyalties (between orthodoxy and assimilation, and between religious faith and enlightenment) and the outsider role which the Jewish population continued to play despite the Law of Religious Tolerance. The 'Haus' becomes the metaphor for 'Heimat', for a homeland which cannot be attained in the sense of 'real estate'. Fanny's husband, Nathan Adam Arnsteiner, became Austria's first Jewish baron in 1798, but he and his dependents were not allowed to become citizens: 'They were allowed to display their arms on their tents in attacks and battles, in jousts and tournaments, but they were still forbidden to own a house in the inner city' (*FA* 152). Consequently, Fanny's significance lies in drawing the attention of 'the great ones of this world to whom she opened her doors' to the question of 'whether or not there was room in the community of mankind for the children of the Old Testament':

> For this was what it amounted to – a piece of earth, a few untroubled breaths of air, a roof over one's head like everyone else in this transitory state that we call life. (*FA* 341–2)

Notes

1. Stella Rotenberg, *Scherben sind endlicher Hort: Ausgewählte Lyrik und Prosa*, ed. Primus-Heinz Kucher and Armin A. Wallas, *Antifaschistische Literatur und Exilliteratur – Studien und Texte*, vol. 6 (Vienna, 1991), p. 148.
2. Gabriele Kreis, *Frauen im Exil: Dichtung und Wirklichkeit* (Darmstadt, 1988).
3. Hilde Spiel, *Rückkehr nach Wien: Ein Tagebuch* (Munich, 1968), p. 23; cf. Hilde Spiel, *Die hellen und die finsteren Zeiten: Erinnerungen 1911–1946* (Munich, 1989), p. 194.
4. Cf. Gabriele Tergit, 'Die Exilsituation in England', in Manfred Durzak (ed.), *Die deutsche Exilliteratur 1933–1945* (Stuttgart, 1973), pp. 135–44 (p. 138).
5. *TLS*, 13 June 1942; quoted in Sylvia M. Patsch, *Österreichische Schriftsteller im Exil in Großbritannien: Ein Kapitel vergessene österreichische Literatur* (Vienna, 1985), p. 47.
6. Robert Neumann, *Ein leichtes Leben: Bericht über mich selbst und Zeitgenossen* (Munich, 1963), p. 157.
7. Cf. Waltraud Strickhausen, 'Schreiben in der Sprache des *Anderen*: Eine Vorstudie zu den Publikationsmöglichkeiten und der Wirkung englischsprachiger Exilwerke in Großbritannien', in Dieter Savin (ed.), *Die Resonanz des Exils: Gelungene und mißlungene Rezeption deutschsprachiger Exilautoren*, Amsterdamer Publikationen zur Sprache und Literatur, vol. 99 (Amsterdam, 1992), pp. 369–96 (p. 379).
8. Jean Améry, *Jenseits von Schuld und Sühne: Bewältigungsversuche eines Überwältigten* (Munich, 1988), p. 72.
9. Hilde Spiel, *The Darkened Room* (London, 1961), p. 86; German edn: *Lisas Zimmer: Roman* (Munich, 1965), p. 132.
10. Hilde Spiel, 'Das Haus der Sprache', in Ota Filip and Egon Larsen with the

assistance of Günter W. Lorenz (eds), *Die zerbrochene Feder: Schriftsteller im Exil* (Stuttgart, 1984), pp. 11–14 (p. 12).

11. 'Ich bin nur einer von den Epigonen, die in dem alten Haus der Sprache wohnen.' Karl Kraus, 'Bekenntnis', in his *Gedichte*, Schriften, vol. 9 (Frankfurt, 1989), p. 93.

12. Hilde Spiel, ['Vorstellung',] in *Jahrbuch der Deutschen Akademie für Sprache und Dichtung* (1972), pp. 93–4.

13. Cf. Marcel Reich-Ranicki, 'Wem sagen Sie das? Über einen Roman der vorzüglichen Essayistin Hilde Spiel', *Die Zeit*, 8 October 1965; as to the novel, cf. Dagmar C. G. Lorenz, 'Hilde Spiel: *Lisas Zimmer*: Frau, Jüdin, Verfolgte', *MAL*, 25 (1992), no. 2, pp. 79–95.

14. 'Interview mit Hilde Spiel ..., 22.2.1989', in Dokumentationsarchiv des österreichischen Widerstandes (ed.), *Österreicher im Exil: Großbritannien 1938–1945: Eine Dokumentation* (Vienna, 1992), pp. 406–7 (p. 406).

15. Hilde Spiel, 'Freuden und Leiden des Übersetzens', *Maske und Kothurn*, 23 (1977), 224–8 (p. 224).

16. Cf. Waltraud Strickhausen, 'Im Zwiespalt zwischen Literatur und Publizistik: Deutungsversuche zum Gattungswechsel im Werk der Exilautorin Hilde Spiel', *Publizistik im Exil und andere Themen: Exilforschung*, 7 (1989), 166–83.

17. Hilde Spiel, 'Der Erzähler Peter de Mendelssohn', in Peter de Mendelssohn, *Die Kathedrale: Ein Sommernachtsmahr* (Hamburg, 1983), pp. 237–64 (p. 239).

18. Spiel, *Die hellen und die finsteren Zeiten*, p. 219.

19. Hilde Spiel, *Englische Ansichten: Berichte aus Kultur, Geschichte und Politik* (Stuttgart, 1985), p. 236 (henceforth cited in the text as *EA* and page number).

20. Hilde Spiel, 'Das vertauschte Werkzeug: Schriftsteller in zwei Sprachen', *Literatur und Kritik*, 8 (1973), 549–52 (p. 551) (cited as *VW*).

21. Neumann, *Ein leichtes Leben*, p. 157.

22. Hilde Spiel, *Welche Welt ist meine Welt? Erinnerungen 1946–1989* (Munich, 1990), p. 6 (cited as *WW*).

23. *Ernst-Robert-Curtius-Preis für Essayistik: Dokumente und Ansprachen* [Hilde Spiel] (Bonn, 1986), p. 37.

24. Cf. *England erzählt: Achtzehn Erzählungen* (Frankfurt, 1960) (selected and intro-duced by Hilde Spiel). The volume contains, among others, stories by E. M. Forster, James Joyce, Katherine Mansfield, Virginia Woolf, Graham Greene, Evelyn Waugh, Dylan Thomas and Doris Lessing.

25. Cf. her edition of William Shakespeare, *König Richard III: Vollständiger Text des Dramas in der Übersetzung von August Wilhelm von Schlegel: Dokumentation* (Frankfurt, 1964), which includes a long essay entitled 'Shakespeares König Richard III'. In her essay, Spiel does justice to the historical Richard and attributes Shakespeare's own portrayal of the king to the distorted historical accounts of the day which he had used as his sources.

26. Cf. for example the collections of essays: *Der Park und die Wildnis: Zur Situation der neueren englischen Literatur* (Munich, 1953); *Kleine Schritte: Berichte und Geschichten* (Munich, 1976).

27. Cf. the bibliographies in Peter Pabisch, 'Hilde Spiel – Femme des Lettres (Mit Werkübersicht)', *MAL*, 12 (1979), no. 3/4, pp. 393–421 and Waltraud Strick-hausen, 'Das Thema Exil im Werk Hilde Spiels', unpublished ms (Vienna, 1987), pp. xi–xiii.

28. Interview mit Hilde Spiel ..., 22.2.1989', in *Österreicher im Exil*, p. 627.

29. Peter Pabisch, 'Hilde Spiels Rückkehr nach Wien – eine besondere Thematik der Exilliteratur', in Donald G. Daviau and Ludwig M. Fischer (eds), *Exil: Wirkung und Wertung: Ausgewählte Beiträge zum fünften Symposium über deutsche und österreichische Exilliteratur* (Columbia, 1985), pp. 173–83 (p. 180).

30. Améry, *Jenseits von Schuld und Sühne*, p. 72.
31. Hilde Spiel, 'Psychologie des Exils', in Dokumentationsarchiv des österreichischen Widerstandes and Dokumentationsstelle für neuere österreichische Literatur (eds), *Österreicher im Exil 1934–1945* … (Vienna, 1977), pp. xxii–xxxvii (p. xxxiii).
32. Hans Flesch-Brunningen, *Perlen und schwarze Tränen: Roman* (Munich, 1980), p. 108. The novel, entitled *Spirits of Night*, had been written in English and was not published. The first German-language edition, published by Wolfgang Krüger, appeared in 1946.
33. Hans Flesch-Brunningen, *Die verführte Zeit: Lebenserinnerungen* (Vienna, 1988) (ed. with an afterword by Manfred Mixner), p. 139.
34. Spiel, ['Vorstellung'] p. 93.
35. Hilde Spiel, *Anna & Anna* (Vienna, 1989), p. 13 (cited as *AA*).
36. See particularly Helene Maimann, *Politik im Wartesaal. Österreichische Exilpolitik in Großbritannien 1938–1945*, Veröffentlichungen der Kommission für Neuere Geschichte Österreichs, vol. 62 (Vienna, 1975), pp. 11–21.
37. Cf. Hans-Albert Walter, *Deutsche Exilliteratur 1933–1950*, vol. 2, *Europäisches Appeasement und überseeische Asylpraxis* (Stuttgart, 1984), pp. 122–3.
38. Hilde Spiel 'Versuch einer Darstellungstheorie des Films', unpublished doctoral thesis (Vienna, 1935), pp. 74–7.
39. For a political assessment of the text, cf. the critical commentary by Hans Heinz Hahnl, 'Durchwursteln oder emigrieren', *Arbeiter-Zeitung*, 15 April 1988, and the more moderate discussion by Maria Klanska, '*Anna und Anna* von Hilde Spiel und *Nordlicht* von Helmut Schwarz – zwei Stimmen zur Bewältigung der Nazizeit in Österreich', *Mnemosyne*, 13 (1992), pp. 11–26.
40. Subsequently, Spiel was to criticise the theoretical foundation of her thesis; cf. Margit Steiner, Margit Suppan and Theo Venus, '*In Österreich wurde ich eigentlich vernachlässigt. Ein Gespräch mit der österreichischen Publizistin Hilde Spiel*', *Medien & Zeit*, 2 (1987) no. 1, pp. 8–16 (p. 9).
41. Cf. Karl Bühler, *Sprachtheorie: Die Darstellungsfunktion der Sprache* [1934] (Stuttgart, 1982) (foreword by Friedrich Kainz).
42. Cf. Harald Weinrich, *Linguistik der Lüge* (Heidelberg, 1966), pp. 35–7, 57–8.
43. In an essay on 'Lady Diana Cooper', Spiel offered early assistance in this regard when she translated 'clean-limbed' with 'edel gewachsen': *Welt im Widerschein: Essays* (Munich, 1960), pp. 47–59 (p. 55).
44. Cf. Herbert Steiner, 'Die kulturelle Tätigkeit des Free Austrian Movement in Großbritannien', in Johann Holzner, Sigurd Paul Scheichl and Wolfgang Wiesmüller (eds), *Eine schwierige Heimkehr: Österreichische Literatur im Exil 1938–1945*, Innsbrucker Beiträge zur Kulturwissenschaft, Germanistische Reihe, vol. 40 (Innsbruck, 1991), pp. 153–67 (p. 160).
45. Hilde Spiel, 'Bekenntnis zu Hofmannsthal', in her *In meinem Garten schlendernd: Essays* (Munich, 1981), pp. 22–4 (p. 23).
46. Her many essays on Hofmannsthal include '*Die Erben laß verschwenden*: Eine Umfrage über Hofmannsthal', in her *Das Haus des Dichters: Essays, Interpretationen, Rezensionen* (Munich, 1992) (selected and edited by Hans A. Neunzig), pp. 334–8; on her relationship to Hofmannsthal, see Ingo Hermann (ed.), *Hilde Spiel: Die Grande Dame: Gespräch mit Anne Linsel in der Reihe 'Zeugen des Jahrhunderts'* (Göttingen, 1992), pp. 53–4, 80, 86–7.
47. 'Exil und Rückkehr. Hilde Spiel im Gespräch', in Neue Gesellschaft für Bildende Kunst (ed.), *Kunst im Exil in Großbritannien 1933–1945* (Berlin, 1986), pp. 289–95 (p. 289).
48. Hilde Spiel, 'Keine Klage über England', *Ver Sacrum* (1972), pp. 21–5 (p. 25).
49. E.g. Spiel, 'Das Haus der Sprache', p. 13.
50. Spiel, *Rückkehr nach Wien*, p. 152.

51. E.g. Spiel, 'Bekenntnis zu Hofmannsthal', p. 23.

52. Hugo von Hofmannsthal, 'Das Schrifttum als geistiger Raum der Nation', in his *Reden und Aufsätze III (1925–1929): Aufzeichnungen*, Gesammelte Werke (Frankfurt, 1980), pp. 24–41 (p. 41).

53. 'Die österreichische Literatur nach 1945. Eine Einführung', in Hilde Spiel (ed.), *Kindlers Literaturgeschichte der Gegenwart: Autoren – Werke – Themen – Tendenzen seit 1945: Die zeitgenössische Literatur Österreichs* (Zurich, 1976), pp. 13–127 (p. 16).

54. Hilde Spiel, *Vienna's Golden Autumn 1866–1938* (London, 1987), pp. 226–7; German edn: *Glanz und Untergang: Wien 1866–1938*, tr. Hanna Neves (Vienna, 1987), p. 216.

55. Spiel, 'Psychologie des Exils', p. xxxii.

56. Hilde Spiel, 'Kafka, Flaubert und das elfenbeinerne Dachkämmerchen', in Harald Seuter (ed.), *Die Feder ein Schwert? Literatur und Politik in Österreich* (Graz, 1981), pp. 170–5 (p. 171). The actual title of Nietzsche's poem, quoted from the 'Vorspiel' to *Die fröhliche Wissenschaft*, is 'Der Weise spricht'.

57. Walter Benjamin, 'Die Aufgabe des Übersetzers', in his *Gesammelte Schriften*, Werkausgabe, vol. 10 (Frankfurt, 1980), pp. 9–21 (p. 14).

58. Cf. Wulf Köpke, 'Die Wirkung des Exils auf Sprache und Stil: Ein Vorschlag zur Forschung', *Gedanken an Deutschland im Exil und andere Themen: Exilforschung*, 3 (1985), 225–37 (p. 235).

59. Hilde Spiel, *Die Früchte des Wohlstands: Roman* (Munich, 1981), p. 27 (cited as *FW*).

60. For very different views, see Waltraud Strickhausen, 'Hilde Spiels historischer Roman *Die Früchte des Wohlstands*', *Exil*, 10 (1990), no. 1, pp. 27–42, and Kurt Klinger, 'Bekenntnis zu Hilde Spiel' [1981], in his *Theater und Tabus: Essays – Berichte – Reden* (Eisenstadt, 1984), pp. 205–14 (p. 208).

61. Hilde Spiel, *Mirko und Franca: Erzählung* (Munich, 1980).

62. Cf. Marcel Reich-Ranicki, *Reden auf Hilde Spiel* (Munich, 1991), esp. pp. 81–6.

63. For example, in a comment in the programme 'Kultur aktuell', broadcast by Austrian Television (ORF) on 15 May 1972.

64. [1958], in her *Das Haus des Dichters*, pp. 27–36.

65. In her *In meinem Garten schlendernd*, pp. 34–6 (p. 36).

66. Cf. e.g. 'Virginia Woolf. Bildnis einer genialen Frau' and 'Katherine Mansfield: Ein Leben und eine Legende', in her *Der Park und die Wildnis*, pp. 13–35, 36–65; 'Virginia Woolfs innere Vision', in her *Welt im Widerschein*, pp. 126–36; 'Emmeline Pankhurst (1858–1928)', in Kurt Fassmann with the assistance of Max Bill et al. (eds), *Die Großen der Weltgeschichte*, vol. IX (Zurich, 1970), pp. 365–79; 'Selbstkastrierung einer Feministin' (*EA* pp. 39–46).

67. Hilde Spiel, *Fanny von Arnstein: A Daughter of the Enlightenment 1758–1818*, tr. Christine Shuttleworth (New York, 1991), p. 341 (cited as *FA*); German edn: *Fanny von Arnstein oder Die Emanzipation: Ein Frauenleben an der Zeitenwende 1758–1818* (Frankfurt, 1962), p. 236.

Austrian Zionism in Exile

The Work of Josef Fraenkel

Evelyn Adunka

Josef Fraenkel, who lived in London from 1939 until his death in 1988, was a Jewish refugee from Vienna whose career exemplifies the paradoxes of Austrian Zionism. He was born in 1903 in Ustrzykidolne in Galicia, a shtetl of 4,000 inhabitants, 2,000 of them Jews. His father, Moses Fraenkel, was mayor of this little town for twenty-five years and had been a follower of the Zionist movement since 1898. Moses Fraenkel was also the first person to establish an oil refinery in the region.[1] The gifted young Josef Fraenkel went to grammar school first in Vienna and later in Bielitz, where his religious teacher was Michael Berkowitz, the Hebrew translator of Herzl's *Der Judenstaat* (*The Jewish State*). It was Berkowitz who inspired him not only to devote himself to Zionism but also to develop an interest in historical research.[2] As a young man, Fraenkel participated in the inaugural meeting of the Agudath Hanoar Haivri (Hebrew Youth Organisation). But in 1925 he joined the recently established Revisionist Movement led by Vladimir Jabotinsky. Taking issue with the more moderate policies of Chaim Weizmann, the Revisionists demanded the establishment of a Jewish state on both sides of the Jordan and a more militant stance towards both the British and the Arabs in Palestine.

Fraenkel studied law at the University of Vienna, although he never graduated, and became a member of the Zionist student duelling fraternity Ivria, taking a leading role in Zionist student politics. At the same time, he began to publish articles on Herzl and Zionist history in the Austrian Jewish press. During the 1930s, Fraenkel became one of the closest followers and collaborators of the prominent Austrian politician Robert Stricker, an adherent of Radical Zionism and one of the founders of the 'Judenstaatspartei', the Jewish State Party, formed after the split in the Revisionist movement in 1933 caused by Meir Grossmann.[3] In August 1932, the Union of the Zionist Revisionists and the Revisionist Students Club, of which Fraenkel was then the chairman, organised the World Conference of Revisionist Students in Vienna. At this conference, which took place in the Leopoldstadt, a predominantly Jewish district of Vienna, Fraenkel gave a lecture on the Hebrew University, opened only seven years earlier in 1925.[4]

During the 1930s, Fraenkel also began to attend the International Zionist

Congresses as a delegate. In 1936, he participated in the foundation session of the World Jewish Congress (WJC) in Geneva, together with Robert Stricker, who was one of the members of the Administrative Committee. There he became the secretary of the Austrian section of the WJC and chairman of the Boycott Committee against Germany (which 'served as European clearing house for the Joint Boycott Council in New York').[5] Looking back on this episode thirty years later in an article entitled 'Congress Memories 1936–1966', Fraenkel records his impressions of those momentous days in Geneva:

> I had the privilege of attending that Congress and I can still hear ringing in my ears the prophetic speeches by Stephen S. Wise and Nahum Goldmann. Why should the world worry about the Jews if the Jews themselves did not worry? asked Wise. And Goldmann again called on the Jews to unite and organise themselves – otherwise 'time will sweep over us without mercy'. Wise and Goldmann, and with them the best among our people, redoubled their efforts in an attempt to save Jewry. But the Second World War was soon to break out. Had the World Jewish Congress been in existence before 1933, it may well be that our tragedy would never have reached such gigantic proportions and we would not have lost six million people.[6]

In his memorial book on Robert Stricker, published in 1950 in London, Fraenkel also describes in detail the last days of the Ivria and the circle around Stricker, indeed the end of the old Viennese Jewish community in the days following the Anschluss:

> Ivria used to meet at its recognised table in the Cafe Astoria in Währingerstrasse. The leading Zionists in Vienna had been meeting there for years. I passed it several times without having the courage to enter, but at last I went in. There were several Nazis there in uniform. But the blue-white Jewish National Fund Box, the Ivria Banner with the Magen David, and the attendance book were still on the table. I opened the book and found a few entries made by I. H. Koerner, the founder of the Hakoah – we used to call him 'Klofac' – and by Dr Edward Pachtmann, known to us as 'Navi'.

He also discovered a message addressed to himself:

> 'Rebbe, report immediately to Klofac and Navi. The Chief Rebbe needs you urgently.' Rebbe was my Ivria name, and Robert Stricker was the 'Chief Rebbe'. I rushed at once to 10 Kohlmarkt, met Koerner and Pachtmann there, and we went to the Seitenstettengasse, where Stricker had his office as Vice-President of the Vienna Jewish Community ... Stricker took me aside and whispered to me. Dr Koerner said: 'Speak up, Robert, so that we can all hear you. Your whispering irritates us.' Stricker looked at Koerner, lifted up the carpet, pointed to some wires there and said, again whispering: 'There were two Nazis here today. They said they came to repair the telephone. Just think how worried

they are about us. They want us to do a lot of telephoning, so they have put in their instruments to listen in and hear what we say.' Stricker wanted me to go at once to Czechoslovakia, to transmit certain messages to Dr Kafka, President of the Prague Jewish Community, and to Dr Wurmbrand, of the Jewish Telegraphic Agency. Before I left Vienna, I saw Stricker again at his home. He gave me instructions, and said repeatedly: 'The Jews must keep on protesting, they must shout, set everything in motion, or they will slaughter us like sheep'. His wife Paula suddenly went on her knees and wept: 'Robert, please go with him. There is still time, you can still do it.' But Stricker answered: 'I can't. I owe it to my constituents. I must stay with my constituents.'[7]

Fraenkel stayed for several years in Prague, where he became co-editor of the journal *Der Judenstaat*, published by Oskar K. Rabinowicz, and corre-spondent of the Jewish Telegraphic Agency. In this function, Fraenkel was the last journalist to report the persecutions of the Jews in Czechoslovakia. In August 1939, he went to Geneva as delegate of the Jewish State Party to the 21st Zionist Congress and from there was able to reach the safety of London. After he lost a part of his family in the Shoah, he never again returned to Germany or Austria, even for a visit.[8] An edition of the newsletter of Ivria, circulated during 1940 in Palestine, reported that in London Fraenkel was able to earn a modest income as representative of the Jewish Telegraph Agency and as member of an organisation for the support of Polish refugees. Later that same year, however, Fraenkel was interned by the British as an enemy alien in the camp at Huyton. He responded to this traumatic experience with characteristic energy, founding (as he later recalls) 'a Zionist organisation with 1,000 members', which organised a meeting almost every day. Martin Freud, the eldest son of the founder of psychoanalysis, who was also interned at Huyton, was one of the lecturers who – according to Fraenkel – spoke at one of these meetings 'in the presence of thousands of professors, doctors and scientists' about his father Sigmund Freud.[9]

After the war, Fraenkel became the Research Officer of the Information Department of the British Section of the World Jewish Congress in London, until it was dissolved in 1973, when the Board of Deputies of British Jews itself affiliated with the WJC. In this function, he founded a press survey called 'Weekly Review of the Jewish Press', which he edited until his retirement, when it ceased to exist (in the age of television it had lost its former importance). With the help of the Cultural Department of the WJC, which was headed by Aaron Steinberg, and of his friend Joseph Leftwich, the well-known translator of Yiddish literature, Fraenkel organised Yiddish lectures and meetings at the Ben Uri Gallery in London, which were regularly attended by forty to fifty people.[10] In England, Fraenkel also became active in numerous Zionist groups, as chairman of the Jewish State Party in Great Britain and of the Nahum Sokolow Society, as co-founder of the 'Unity Group', as Honorary Secretary of the Jacob Ehrlich Society and the Conti-nental Zionists, as well as in the Theodor Herzl Society, the Jewish Record

Office and the Zionist Federation.[11] In 1952, on the occasion of the opening of the Binyanei Ha'umah, the big Jerusalem Congress Centre, Fraenkel proposed to name the rooms of the Centre after the twenty-three Zionist Congresses and to document them and their delegates there – 'in order to inspire their grandchildren for new efforts for the Jewish people'.[12] In 1970, Fraenkel tried in vain to initiate a club for past and present Zionist Congress delegates and a 'non-partisan society aimed at recording the unacknowledged achievements of British Zionism'.[13]

The early history of Zionism is also recalled in Fraenkel's contribution to the memorial volume for Simon Dubnow, edited by Aaron Steinberg in 1963. In his autobiographical introduction, he emphasises the special importance of Dubnow for his own generation in Vienna:

> Simon Dubnow was the outstanding historian of my generation. He, and Heinrich Graetz, were our teachers and provided us with the signposts to Jewish history. Though we had all heard of Dubnow and knew who he was, the first volume of his *Weltgeschichte des Jüdischen Volkes* (World History of the Jewish People) came as a revelation and took us by storm; we welcomed it with enthusiasm. It is difficult to explain exactly why this was the case; possibly, because the words 'World History' in the title filled us with pride ... We had been waiting for someone like Dubnow for a long time and his work appeared just at the appropriate moment ... We were looking for a link with the era of modern Zionism. Hence the excitement with which we welcomed every volume published by Dubnow; each new volume increased our veneration for him, though we did not, by any means, invariably agree with his conclusions.[14]

At the conference of the World Jewish Congress in Stockholm in 1959, Fraenkel convened a meeting of seventy Jewish journalists under the chairmanship of Meir Grossmann. This led to the founding of the World Union of Jewish Journalists, which held its first conference in 1960 in Jerusalem and whose honorary secretary Fraenkel then became. In an article about the programme of the World Union, he called for the establishment of a 'House of the Jewish Press' in Israel, which should collect all Jewish periodicals and newspapers since the first had appeared in 1678 in Amsterdam. He also envisaged a Research Institute for the History of Jewish Journalism, an Emergency Fund for its members, and a periodical to be called 'The Jewish Journalist'. The idea of a 'House of the Jewish Press' was never realised, but many of the activities proposed by Fraenkel are now carried out by the Jewish National Library of the Hebrew University and other academic centres in Israel, although there are still many Jewish journals which cannot be found in Jerusalem and are even untraceable in their native country.[15]

As early as 1953, Fraenkel published his booklet *The Jewish Press of the World*, the seventh edition of which came out in 1972 listing no less than 954 Jewish journals published in seventy-seven countries. It recorded the name of the editor, the editorial board, the date of foundation, the address and the circulation of the journals. As a preface, Fraenkel wrote a short history of the Jewish press, in which he also reviews the brochure about the Jewish press published in Vienna in 1882 by Isidor Singer under the title *Presse und Judentum* (Press and Jewry). He also describes the blooming of the (predominantly Yiddish) Jewish press in Central Europe before the Shoah, adding a section on Jewish papers published during the Nazi regime and later even in the camps for Displaced Persons. Fraenkel identifies a twofold duty for the Jewish journalist after the war, emphasising that the fate of the Jewish press is inextricably linked with the situation of the Jews:

> Today, one of the chief functions of a Jewish press is undoubtedly the preservation and strengthening of the Jewish spirit and of Jewish morale. But there is also the formation of Jewish public opinion. In the very few countries where the publication of a Jewish press is barred, limited or made deliberately difficult, the right of Jews to live a Jewish life is also in jeopardy: a country with a Jewish community, deprived of the basic right to communicate among themselves by means of the printed word, i.e., bereft of their own press, is thereby also cut off – or almost so – from the Jewish people beyond that community's border ... Finally, no Jewish editor ought ever to forget that it is one of his duties to acquaint the non-Jewish world with the Jewish situation of the day and to explain and justify – again, not merely propound – Jewish grievances and demands ... The Jewish press must always remember that it can only fulfil its main function – that of a link uniting the Jewish people all over the world – if it remains fair, free and fearless![16]

As an aid for the Jewish journalist, Fraenkel also compiled the booklet *Every Day in Jewish History*, which lists almost 2,000 dates according to the days of the civil year and the Hebrew calendar. With this publication, Fraenkel wanted to remind the Jewish world 'not to forget the great personalities of Jewish History, the poets and writers of Jewish literature in Hebrew, Yiddish and in other languages, the builders and leaders of the Zionist Organisation, of the State of Israel, of the World Jewish Congress and other organisations, the outstanding achievements of the Nobel Prize Winners'. Fraenkel wanted especially to 'help editors and journalists of the Jewish Press to remember the anniversaries of our immortals and to recall their works and life and to draw the attention of their readers to past events, both good and bad'. But Fraenkel also thought that this publication should serve even greater educational purposes, helping 'schools and cultural societies to arrange meetings on historic dates, lectures and symposiums; to encourage the study of Jewish History and Literature and the reading of Jewish books'.[17]

Besides his work for the World Jewish Congress, Fraenkel collected material for the Central Zionist Archives (CZA) in Jerusalem, about which he also published an interesting article. Alex Bein, the director of the archives, wrote an article on the occasion of Fraenkel's seventieth birthday saying how grateful he was for his friendship and support, adding that an inventory of the thousands of documents, which Fraenkel discovered and gave to the CZA, would consist of several volumes. He also wrote that he knew few people who had so devotedly served Zionism and everything concerning the Jews. Bein correctly observed that in Zionist circles of London Fraenkel had become an institution, to whom anyone who wanted to know something about Zionist history could refer, and never in vain.[18] Indeed, many of Fraenkel's articles were devoted to the life and work of Herzl. He also published short biographies of Herzl both in German and in English, and in 1950 he became involved in the controversy about the true identity of the anonymous editor of the original German edition of Herzl's diaries. In one of his articles, he also urged the transfer of Herzl's remains to Israel, several years before this was actually achieved in 1949, appealing in 1946 to the Zionist Action Committee to appoint a special committee for that purpose.[19] Another landmark in the commemoration of Austrian Zionism was the transfer to Israel of the remains of Zwi Perez Chajes, the famous Zionist Chief Rabbi of Vienna from 1918 until 1927, who inaugurated a spiritual and religious renaissance of the Jews of Vienna. To mark this occasion, Fraenkel published an appreciation of Chajes in German, in which he remembered that he was once one of the representatives of the Jewish students who were appointed as guard of honour for the Chief Rabbi in Vienna.[20]

In his numerous articles for the Jewish press and other publications, written in Yiddish as well as English and German, Fraenkel continued to defend his own distinctive vision of Zionism, often challenging the official line. For example, in 1949 he wrote an extremely critical review of the autobiography of Chaim Weizmann, *Trial and Error*, which lists a number of factual errors in the book and censures Weizmann for his self-centredness.[21] But he was also resolute in his defence of the State of Israel. In two English reviews on Arnold Toynbee, he vehemently attacked the famous historian for his deep-seated anti-Zionist and anti-Semitic tendency:

> Toynbee is consumed by his Jewish psychosis. He seems to have donned the mantle of a professional agitator against Jews, Judaism, Zionism and the State of Israel. He is not alone in wielding his pen in order to spread hatred against the Jews. Unfortunately, we have always had   and still have – thousands of such writers. The Jews have managed to survive them all and will, no doubt, continue to do so in the future.[22]

In 1967, Fraenkel published his best-known book, *The Jews of Austria: Essays on their Life, History and Destruction*, which soon became a classic. The book had a very interesting genesis which is not generally known. In 1959, Fraenkel initiated a project for a 'Chajes Institute of Jews in and from Austria'. According to a memo by Fraenkel, the Geneva conference of the World Council of Jews from Austria proposed and decided to create this institute. Its task should have been to collect and publish material in order to record the great tragedy of the Jews of Austria in the period 1938–45. Apparently the Chajes Institute was promised support from the Vienna Jewish Community, and the institute was to be located in Vienna with branches in London, New York and Tel Aviv. In Geneva it was proposed to appoint a president, a director, and a board for publications and for organisational and financial matters. Fraenkel was delegated to draft the constitution of the new institute with the help of Fritz Lothar Brassloff, a lawyer who came originally from Austria and now worked for the World Jewish Congress.[23] The Claims Conference was also asked to support the Chajes Institute financially. But the Leo Baeck Institute for the History of the Jews of Germany (LBI), which evidently was the model for the planned Chajes Institute, strongly opposed Fraenkel's initiative, feeling that it might provide unwelcome competition. S. Adler-Rudel from the LBI in Jerusalem wrote a letter to the head of the LBI in New York, Leo Kreutzberger, explaining that he had met Fraenkel in London and suggested – as a compromise – the creation of a special department of the LBI for Austria, with or without the name of Chajes. But Fraenkel rejected this idea because he apparently wanted to become director of a Chajes Institute under any circumstances, even without material support. Adler-Rudel even noted in his letter that he was not convinced that his own idea could be realised, because the attempt to combine the distinctive traditions of Chajes and Baeck in a single institute would probably be opposed by the followers of the two great Rabbis. According to Adler-Rudel, Fraenkel in principle had some claim to be considered a historian of the Zionist movement, with special regard to Theodor Herzl, but in practice was merely a minor official of the World Jewish Congress, struggling to consolidate his social position and his material existence. Fraenkel had mentioned to Adler-Rudel a list which he had compiled of forty to fifty Austrian Jewish researchers who were prepared to cooperate with the Chajes Institute, although he had actually sent him a copy of the list (apart from mentioning that he was counting on the cooperation of Salo W. Baron, a leading Jewish historian in the United States). But on the other hand, Fraenkel had explained that he only wanted to edit five or six books, which left Adler-Rudel with the impression that Fraenkel had mainly his own books in mind. This unpublished correspondence gives us a glimpse of the professional and personal rivalries which inevitably formed one element in the activities of German and Austrian Jewish exiles. Kreutzberger's reply to Adler-Rudel expressed his satisfaction that the projected Chajes Institute was far from realisation, since he too feared an unnecessary overlapping of fields of work.[24]

This story had an equally instructive epilogue ten years later, when Hugo Gold, another very meritorious (but non-academic) historian of Austrian Jewry who lived in Tel Aviv, announced in 1969 his own plans for the foundation of a Chajes Institute, linked with a new publication series on Austrian Jewry. The announcement of this series, a circular letter and a form designed for applications for membership, constitute the only evidence of the activities of this second proposed Chajes Institute that has survived.[25] For the LBI reacted even more unfavourably towards Gold's project than towards that of Fraenkel ten years earlier. Hans Tramer, one of the leading figures at the Leo Baeck Institute in Jerusalem, wrote that he wanted to have nothing to do with Gold, refusing to become a member or to collaborate with Gold in any way.[26] Nevertheless, brief announcements appeared in the *Jewish Chronicle*, both in 1959 and during the 1960s, reporting the establishment of the Chajes Institute in Vienna, London, Tel Aviv and New York as if it had really happened. Without mentioning Gold's name, the paper wrote in 1968 that 'former students and friends of the late Chief Rabbi of Vienna, Dr Z. P. Chajes, who would be interested to participate in the formation of a Z. P. Chajes Institute, should get in touch with the Preparatory Committee' in Tel Aviv.[27]

Fraenkel's efforts nevertheless did have some practical results. The first was a special issue of the German Bulletin of the Leo Baeck Institute devoted to the history of Austrian Jewry, edited by Hans Tramer. Even more significant, however, was the collection of articles edited by Fraenkel himself, published in London in 1967 under the title *The Jews of Austria*. Given the difficult circumstances described above, it is all the more remarkable that he succeeded in compiling such a substantial work of collaborative cultural history. In 1962, the following note appeared in the *Jewish Chronicle*: 'A History of the Jews in Austria is to be published by the World Council of Jews from Austria next year. More than 20 historians and scholars have promised their cooperation with the editor, Josef Fraenkel of London.' The paper also mentioned Fritz L. Brassloff and Charles Kapralik, two originally Viennese lawyers in London, as members of the editorial board.[28]

Almost all the thirty-five contributors to *The Jews of Austria* belonged to the generation which had participated in the flourishing Austrian Jewish culture before 1938. A brief overview of its contents will give a sense of the wealth of different subjects which the book covers. The essays in the first part describe the extraordinarily original and creative contributions of Austrian Jews in the fields of art, music, jurisprudence, medicine, literature, journalism and sport (by Walter Pillich, Peter Gradenwitz, Franz Kobler, Moshe Atlas, Harry Zohn, Richard Grunberger and Erich Juhn). A second part includes personal memoirs by S. Birnbaum, Martin Freud, Sol Liptzin, Joseph Leftwich, Max Brod, Martha Hofmann and Ernst Waldinger. The historical part combines essays by such well known authors as Wolfgang von Weisl, Arieh Tartakower and N. Tur-Sinai and contributions on the history of the Jews in the Austrian provinces and of the Hasidic and Sephardic community in Vienna by Rabbi J Heshel and Rabbi Manfred Papo. The final section is devoted to the destruction of the Austrian Jewish community. In one of the few German contributions, Gustav Jellinek summarises the sad history of the Austrian financial restitution, followed by a useful bibliography on the subject, compiled by Ilse R. Wolf of the Wiener Library.

Although the book gives prominence to precious reminiscences, and to authoritative first-hand accounts of important subjects which might otherwise have passed unrecorded, the final result is not entirely satisfactory. Certain functionaries of the Viennese Jewish Community, who were still alive in the 1960s, were evidently not invited to contribute. The reader thus gets the impression not of a systematic and balanced history of the Jews of Austria, but of a collection of fragmentary essays and memoirs about certain specific aspects of that phenomenon. Conscious of the limitations of his project, Fraenkel stresses in his introduction that one of the aims of the book is to inspire further investigations: 'May this book find readers; and may it inspire future research into history, in order to record the great deeds of nearly fifty generations and to preserve the memory of Austria's Jewish martyrs'.[29]

On the occasion of the publication of the book, the World Jewish Congress in London organised a reception at which Norman Bentwich, Peter Pulzer and Fritz Lothar Brassloff spoke.[30] But the reception of the book in the international press was rather mixed. A review by Janko Musulin in the *Frankfurter Allgemeine Zeitung* noted that a:

> unified and detailed history of the Austrian Jews ... would be a task for one of the most important and informative books that could ever be written about Austria. The book *The Jews of Austria*, published by Valentine Mitchell in London, is not such a work, but it provides a survey of available material, acquaints us with the problems and sources, and covers both political and intellectual history – and anybody who is interested in this topic should consult it.[31]

Despite this emphasis in a leading German newspaper on the fundamental importance of the subject, Fraenkel's book was never translated into German, nor was any serious attempt made by German or Austrian historians to improve upon his work. Not only were the Jews themselves expelled from German-speaking Europe, but for several decades after the defeat of Nazism the task of reconstructing the great mosaic of German-Jewish life was systematically neglected at German and Austrian universities. Not until the 1980s did Jewish Studies re-emerge in Germany and Austria as a central field of historical inquiry. It is exiles like Josef Fraenkel who deserve the greatest credit for their pioneering works of commemoration. The paradox of his career is that, despite his lifelong commitment to Zionism, Fraenkel's most enduring achievement is a book which records not simply the activities of religious communities and Zionist organisations, but above all the achievements of assimilated German-speaking Jews. The experience of exile led him to look back on the culture of the Jews of Austria not simply with nostalgia, but with a defiant pride in their achievements.[32]

Notes

1. I gratefully acknowledge an interview with Fraenkel's daughter, Ruth Deech, which took place in Oxford in 1992 and which was a valuable source of information for this chapter. See also *Zionist Year Book* (London, 1963/64), pp. 326–7.
2. *Neue Welt*, July 1963 (article to mark Fraenkel's sixtieth birthday).
3. Ibid.
4. Harald Seewann, *Zirkel und Zionsstern: Bilder und Dokumente aus der versunkenen Welt des jüdisch-nationalen Korporationswesens*, vol. 1 (Graz, 1990), p. 182.
5. *Unity in Dispersion. A History of the World Jewish Congress* (New York, Institute of Jewish Affairs, 1948), pp. 78–9.
6. Fraenkel, 'Congress Memories 1936–1966', *World Jewry*, 7/8 (1966).
7. *Robert Stricker*, ed. Josef Fraenkel (London, 1950), pp. 11–12.

8. *Neue Welt*, July 1963; see also *Biographisches Handbuch der deutschsprachigen Emigration*, vol. 1 (Munich, 1978), pp. 184–5.

9. Fraenkel, 'Sigmund Freud und die "Kadimah"', *Das Jüdische Echo*, 5 (1957), no. 5/6.

10. I gratefully acknowledge information provided by interviews with Elizabeth Eppler and Stephen Roth, Fraenkel's colleagues at the World Jewish Congress (which took place in Jerusalem and London in 1992), and with S. J. Goldsmith, Fraenkel's friend and colleague (also in London in 1992).

11. Fraenkel, 'Bemerkungen eines jüdischen Journalisten', *Neue Welt*, May 1963.

12. *Jewish Chronicle*, 25 September 1970 and 5 February 1971.

13. Fraenkel, 'Ein Symbol für die Judenheit', *Neue Welt*, September 1952.

14. Fraenkel, 'Simon Dubnow and the History of Political Zionism', in *Simon Dubnow. The Man and his Work*, ed. Aaron Steinberg (Paris, 1963).

15. *Zionist Year Book*. 1963/64: Fraenkel, 'Weltverband jüdischer Journalisten', *Neue Welt*, November 1959; 'Programm des Weltverbandes Jüdischer Journalisten', *Neue Welt*, December 1960.

16. Fraenkel, *The Jewish Press of the World*, 7th edn (London, 1972), pp. 10–11.

17. Fraenkel, *Every Day in Jewish History* (London, n.d.), p. 1.

18. Alex Bein, 'Josef Fraenkel zum 70. Geburtstag', *Allgemeine Wochenzeitung der Juden in Deutschland*, undated press cutting from the archive of Desider Stern, Literaturhaus, Vienna; Fraenkel, 'Das Zionistische Zentralarchiv in Jerusalem', *Neue Welt*, December 1965.

19. Jewish Chronicle, 8 March 1946; *Neue Welt und Judenstaat*, April–October 1950.

20. Fraenkel, 'Oberrabbiner Hirsch Perez Chajes kehrt heim', *Jüdische Rundschau Maccabi* (1952), no. 35/36.

21. Fraenkel, 'Trial and Error', *Neue Welt und Judenstaat*, August 1949.

22. Fraenkel, 'Travesty of History', *World Jewry* (1969), no. 11/12; 'A Love Affair with Zionism', *World Jewry* (1967), no. 11/12.

23. File of letters concerning the Chajes Institute, no. 480, Leo Baeck Institute, Jerusalem; transcript of Fraenkel, 'Chajes Institute of Jews in and from Austria', London, 27 October 1959.

24. Letter from S. Adler-Rudel to Leo Kreutzberger, 21 June 1960 (copies to S. Moses, H. Gerling and H. Tramer).

25. Membership form in the above-mentioned file; archive of Desider Stern about Hugo Gold.

26. Tramer file, not dated, File 480, Leo Baeck Institute, Jerusalem. The publication series of the 'Zwi-Perez-Chajes-Institute' included Hugo Gold, *Zwi Perez Chajes*; Harry Zohn, *Österreichische Juden in der Literatur*; and Wolfgang von Weisl, *Die Juden in der Armee Österreich-Ungarns*.

27. *Jewish Chronicle*, 20 November 1959; 5 July 1968.

28. *Jewish Chronicle*, 14 September 1962.

29. *The Jews of Austria*, ed. Josef Fraenkel (London, 1967), p. xiv.

30. F. L. Brassloff, *Die Gemeinde*, 31 January 1968.

31. *Frankfurter Allgemeine Zeitung*, 8 August 1969.

32. The most significant of his other publications are: *Palästina lacht* (Vienna, 1936), *Sigmund Werner: Ein Mitarbeiter Herzls* (Prague, 1939), *Theodor Herzl: A Biography* (London, 1946) and *Dubnow, Herzl and Ahad Ha'am* (London, 1963).

Joseph Otto Flatter

The Politicisation of a Portrait-Painter

Dorothea McEwan

Often, artists may anticipate events which have not yet broken through to public consciousness. Intuitively, they give definition to developments which seem to the contemporary onlooker too unreal, too crass or too shocking to express. The experience of exile brought about the politicisation of the work of many writers and artists who had previously avoided such commitments. The most celebrated example is Kokoschka, who during the 1930s painted a number of allegories dealing with the dangers of fascism and later became a leading member of exile organisations, including the Freie Deutsche Kultur-bund in London. An even more striking instance is provided by the career of Otto Flatter, which has remained relatively little known. Flatter, who had trained as a portraitist, foresaw the implications of political events long before the majority of his contemporaries. And once he had left his native Austria, he felt compelled to warn the British people of the impending dangers.

Born of Jewish parents in Vienna in 1894, he had just completed his school career and begun studies at the Academy of Fine Arts in Vienna when the First World War began and he was conscripted into the Imperial and Royal Army. In the course of an army career lasting over three-and-a-half years, he spent two years at the front in South Tyrol as a junior officer in the 4th Viennese Hoch- and Deutschmeister Infantry Regiment. He was awarded medals for bravery, which he said were won by sheer endurance in his case. From his autobiographical writings, we know how terrifying an experience war had become for him, how tedious and indeed how futile. In his unpublished autobiography, he movingly describes a night watch in South Tyrol:

> The hour before the daybreak is the loneliest, the hardest to bear for the entrenched prisoner ignorant of the cause of punishment and of the sentence passed on him. There is usually an hour of silence before the night recedes. Both sides, tired from the night watch, are quietly waiting for their relief. The sky is changing its tints, first to a misty purple, then to a band of silver slowly rising on the horizon. The searchlights make their last, feeble sweep over the valley as if to try to wipe it clean of the obscenity of war before the new day. Now the peaks

104

of the mountains, one after the other, carry the message of light ... And then the sun reveals himself, reveals the prison and its huge place of execution.[1]

The description is that of a painter who keenly feels the importance of light and misery of its absence.

When peace returned, he resumed his studies at the Academy. After the disintegration of the Austro-Hungarian Empire, difficult financial circumstances forced him to leave before he could complete the curriculum and to make a living travelling extensively throughout the area of the former Empire as an itinerant portrait-painter. His self-portrait of 1932 (Figure 1) shows a vigorous man, confidently painted in broad brush-strokes. Over the years, he exhibited at the Künstlerhaus and the Sezession, then the leading traditional and modern exhibition venues of Vienna respectively. The year 1934 found him teaching in Brno. Together with his second wife Hilde Love, who was a concert pianist and composer and who was touring the British Isles, he travelled to England to study English and Scottish portraitists in preparation for a lecture course in Brno. Very soon he decided to go back only to deliver his lectures and then to pack and leave for good.

Inclined by his liberal ideas to a critical view of the society of his time, Flatter had seen through the dangers of Nazism from an early stage. He returned briefly to Vienna in 1936 to dispose of his studio. Glimpsing a portrait of Hitler in the flat of his seemingly harmless next-door neighbours, he realised that they had secretly become National Socialists. Flatter harangued the wife with untypical vehemence and prophesied that Hitler would bring ruin to himself and them. At the time, he was embarrassed by his conduct and by no means certain of the future he foretold with such confidence, but he felt he must do something to challenge what he saw:

> As National Socialism was an illegal creed in Austria at that time, Frau M. may have feared that I could denounce her husband to the police (not that I had any intention of doing so, or that I expected the corrupt police to act in any way). Frau M's face reddened, her hands trembled, she had to sit down. It was perhaps petty of me to take revenge on the little woman sitting cowed before me. Oratory was never my strong side. On this occasion, however, I talked as if Europe was at my feet and listening to me. Hitler means war, I said, and Hitler's war means world war; look at the world map and see how small Germany is; she will stand alone, who, except Austria, will want to be her ally? her towns will crumble into dust, millions will die, your Fuehrer will drag you down, will burden you with unforgivable guilt, and if you do not die in the holocaust, you will curse the man you so much admire now, until the bitter end of your life. 'Tell your husband he is a damned fool', were the last words I said to Frau M. This my performance as a prophet, which at that time I regarded as melodramatic overacting, has but proved only too true.[2]

By 1938, greatly concerned at the course of events in Europe and convinced of the need to alert people to Hitler's evil designs, he set aside portraiture, the work he had engaged in for the past twenty years, to create a series of drawings which would publicise the ignorance, brutality and cynicism of *Mein Kampf* in Britain. The more than sixty drawings and cartoons which illustrate this theme were viewed initially by some of the British press as too extreme, indeed as an incitement to war. 'Some, hypnotised by enemy propaganda, thought I was endangering my life. A visitor to one of my exhibitions was heard to remark that he could not condemn the German people for their patriotic fervour, but would condemn me, the artist, for my barbarity'.[3] Once war had broken out, the series was eagerly adopted under the title *Mein Kampf Illustrated* for a travelling exhibition. His artistic activity had taken an abrupt change of direction with this discovery of a political mission in Britain. Despite the evidence in the earlier paintings and drawings of his thorough academic training, we are unprepared for the self-assurance and quality of his work in this new genre. The genre (as Ernst Gombrich perceptively observes) derives its effect from the use of metaphor 'to comment on the topical reports of the day. It relies on a public that enjoys the wit of the comparison which may not explain but sum up a situation.'[4]

There is no evidence of a lengthy period of preparation or apprenticeship. Quite suddenly there is a substantial body of new work of remarkable quality and fluency. It is not innovative or particularly individual in terms of style. He links the familiar with the unfamiliar, offering an explanation for events which makes them appear part of the old story, 'as if there was really never anything new under the sun. ... Hence nothing is more characteristic of pictorial satire than its conservatism, the tendency to draw on the same old stock of motifs and stereotypes.'[5] And so the cartoon, like the caricature, serves to reassure, to explain by making connections, by making use of the most mundane and unoriginal. Each picture has a clear and memorable composition apt for the subject, relying on a simplicity of expression which puts each idea across tellingly. Flatter, commenting on events, showed himself to be an artist with a political mission.

This series was the foundation of his wartime career as a cartoonist. But before he could embark on it, he had first to submit to a common experience of many an exile in Britain, internment on the Isle of Man, even though he had been judged a 'harmless' alien – as he put it – by a tribunal some months previously. For almost three months, he turned his hand to cooking, giving some drawing lessons for variety, until his anti-Nazi credentials were recognised.

> I had only been back a few hours in my home, when I was called to the telephone. It was the police, the police again. Could they have released me from detention by mistake? Was I to be sent back again? I was told to stay at home and wait for a telephone call from the Ministry of Information. 'They have been searching for you, they did not know you had been His Majesty's guest on the Isle of Man' said the voice at the other end.[6]

He was told to present himself at the Ministry, and once there he was instructed by an official to 'submit ideas for leaflets whose purpose it was to intimidate the German soldier preparing for the invasion of England. He impressed on me that this meant highly secret work, that I was not to talk about or show my sketches to anyone, not even to my wife, that I would have to keep the drawings overnight in a sealed portfolio at my bedside.'[7] In the excitement, Flatter had taken the wrong hat from the stand and had to return it. He realised that 'in an incredibly short space of time I had risen from the status of a distrusted alien to that of an officially sanctioned conspirator in secret work. (I later learnt that Lord Vansittart, the then chief adviser at the Foreign Office, who knew of me and my work, had acted as my sponsor.)'[8] In his unpublished autobiography, which he started in the 1970s as a septuagenarian, he added as a touching postscript that although an official asked him to give a vow of secrecy, he revealed his commitment to his wife: 'she knew; how can you in the precincts of your home keep a secret activity concealed from your wife! The official must have been a bachelor.'[9]

Thus Flatter was launched on his very own war effort. While the mordant caricatures and fiercely sardonic drawings of the *Mein Kampf Illustrated* series were aimed at the British minds and hearts, the broadsheets and cartoons on which he was now embarking were aimed at 'Wehrzersetzung', at sapping the morale of the German troops. Leaflet drops over enemy territory had been part of modern warfare ever since the First World War. Alfred Harmsworth, later Lord Northcliffe, was convinced that 'the bombardment of the enemy mind is almost as important as his bombardment by guns'.[10] Neither Churchill ('This is a war of deeds, not words!') nor Air Marshal Harris, the head of Bomber Command, which had to drop the leaflets on Germany, was particularly interested in propaganda leaflets. But in order to enlighten the people on the other side, the leaflet drops of broadsheets, pamphlets, newspapers in miniature and official declarations formed a classic method of spreading information. Balloons and aeroplanes were used to get in touch with these people. In Europe alone, 95 million leaflets were dropped by the British government from balloons and 1.4 billion from aircraft.[11] In order to avoid endangering the air crews, everything was strictly regulated and streamlined, and the procedure of leaflet-dropping became quite a science, incorporating rules on the size of the leaflets and the quantity to be dropped at any one time. Of crucial importance were the date, time of day and most importantly the weather, so as to maximise the effect over a large area. Like everything else in wartime, this freight, the product of an artist, was subject to the rules of logistics. Leaflets were dropped throughout the war, but their effectiveness is hard to measure. Was the civilian population really swayed by little bits of paper crammed full of information, jokes, biting criticism, visionary solutions? Did these little bits of paper really sap the fighting morale of the soldiers? Did the leaflets influence the people, emotionally, intellectually, to concede that violence, bloody warfare and racial hatred lead nowhere? How could propaganda which vilified the 'enemy' create an atmosphere in the enemy population which accepted the other side's points of view? These are complicated

Figure 1 *Self Portrait*, 1932

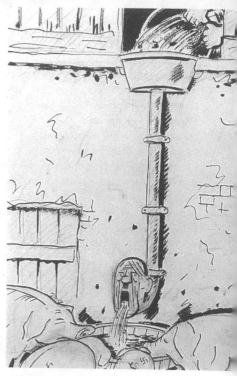

Figure 2 *The Mouthpiece*

Figure 3 *Much rehearsed, but never performed*, 1940

questions which will never be satisfactorily resolved. The opinions which were expressed in the political caricatures could be smiled at or cursed at, but we simply do not know what effect they had. The war was won on the battlefield. But the war on the field of propaganda was nevertheless pursued with great vigour. David Low from Australia, who worked for the *Evening Standard*, Cyril Kenneth Bird, who designed posters, Walter Trier from Czechoslovakia, book illustrator and cartoonist, and Otto Flatter himself were the leading figures in this propaganda offensive.

The starting point for a representation of the enemy is the leader himself, who personifies the system and its ideology. The craft of the cartoonist is to translate ideas into pictures, to make visible what is talked about. In 'The Mouthpiece' (Figure 2), the swill from Hitler's mouth pours into a trough round which pigs with swastikas on their behinds bustle to lap it all up. The inference is immediately clear. It is the political artist's mission to make people realise what is behind Nazi ideology: the gutter, appealing to people's basest drives.

Another publication, *Struwwelhitler*, published in 1941, had the same mission.[12] It used the well-known format of a children's book first published in 1845, Heinrich Hoffmann's *Struwwelpeter*, which in ten short chapters, with verse and pictures, inculcated correct behaviour into children. It showed cruel children, fidgety children, children who did not eat up, who played with dangerous things, in short, who needed a heavy patriarchal hand to knock them into shape. During the war, two brilliant English linguists, Robert and Philip Spence, used it to ridicule the main Nazi leaders. The first chapter, 'The Story of Cruel Adolf', introduces the reader to the wickedness of this character who slaughtered 'little neutral birds' (neutral countries), who 'tore each pact', who 'screamed until his voice was cracked', who did not feed his four-legged friend Fritz, but on the contrary whipped the 'Greedy scamp! / To the Dachau concentration camp'. But Fritz bit him so badly that the doctor (the United States) had to come, who could not save him from dying, whereupon Fritz 'on Ribby's [Ribbentrop's] fizz his thirst he slakes / and eats all Adolf's creamy cakes'. Those who fight back will win, so the satire of *Struwwelhitler* suggests, and all the bullying, the taunting and the cruelty will come to nothing. Hence, a cartoon like 'The Mouthpiece' or a satire like 'The Story of Cruel Adolf' point to the same frame of mind, the unsavoury thoughts and the unacceptable behaviour of the Nazi leader. The public is left with a double message: the Führer is wicked, but at the same time rather absurd.

One of the first results of this bullying is captured in the brilliantly-drawn 'Rape of Czechoslovakia' (C 014). Here, in place of the 'little neutral birds', Flatter effectively exploits the biblical allusion of wolf devouring sheep, the wolf coming from the West, in his fangs Czechoslovakia, a peaceful lamb, shedding its blood. But whereas the rape of Czechoslovakia is portrayed as a tragedy, Hitler's preparations for the invasion of Great Britain are rendered comic in 'Much rehearsed, but never performed' (Figure 3). Flatter commented later in life that he had intended to kill himself, should the Nazi army overrun the British Isles; but he treated the threat in a way which made it appear absurd theatre. He chose a very famous passage in Wagner's *Lohengrin*, where the hero departs on a fabled swan. But Hitler, his sword and arm raised high, is about to step into a wooden contraption drawn not by an elegant swan, but by a rather homely duck.

Flatter often used Wagner operas as a foil for political points. If this drawing was designed for a leaflet drop over Germany, it would effectively have conveyed the message that the invasion was a fantasy. Flatter had to submit three to five sketches per week commenting on the twists and turns of the war, the developments abroad and at home. Unknown to him, two would be selected to be printed by the million and to be dropped over enemy territory. The drawings were then finished and printed, but not signed. Although the research by Klaus Kirchner does not list Flatter among the artists working for the Ministry of Information, documentary proof of Flatter's work exists in the Public Record Office.[13] The artistic work was financially remunerated, but it was a very haphazard income, Flatter never knowing how many of his sketches would be adopted.

Another fantasy concerns the fulfilment of Nazi prophecies, the cartoon 'Hitler working on Volume Two of "My Struggle": Let's think of a happy ending to Volume Two' (C 136). The Nazi bigwigs behind Hitler look troubled. From the title illustration of Volume Two a stern-looking Hitler stares at us, but behind the desk Hitler is agitated, clenched fist and hunched shoulders denoting acute writer's block, while his entourage has little to contribute. They look downcast; there is no fury or venom left, just sheer brainlessness. The fantasy of the fulfilment of Nazi prophecies becomes the prophecy of a doomed ideology. This cartoon superbly illustrates the hollow fantasies of the Nazi regime, the wild accusations and acts of aggression, the hard dictatorial hand and the cruel language of arms. Cut down to size, the fantasies are revealed as groundless. Therein lies the task of the prophet, not to be taken in by rhetoric and appearances, but to see behind the masks.

What sounds like a superb promise, like the tender care of a devoted gardener, 'I will turn Austria into the most beautiful garden' (C 208), turns in Flatter's hand into a ghoulish nightmare. Again the tension between what is said, and how it will turn out is expertly handled. Hitler, the gardener complete with watering-can and apron, and Himmler, holding an urn, meet at a special type of garden, a cemetery. Austrians lavish a great deal of care on the graves of their loved ones, so, in fact, cemeteries are places of natural beauty with a profusion of flowers and wildlife. But here nothing is growing. Hitler, water as he might, will not get a single flower to bloom. Crosses inform us of stark facts, suicides and treasons. There are no names, only reasons for death. Austria, the beautiful garden of the quotation from a Hitler speech in 1938, is a graveyard, full of people driven to death by suicide or slaughter.

The cartoon of 1941, 'Austria and Hitler crucified on the swastika' (Figure 4), is again a prophetic appeal and a gruesome warning. Austria has her head bowed low in shame or anguish, while Hitler is yelling in pain. A man holding firebrands puts the fettered pair to the torch. The impact of this drawing is stark, a violent and brutal scene of pain and suffering. One is reminded of the long tradition of demonstrating pain in pictorial form, the gruesome torture scenes of Christian saints or, most famous of all, the Laocoon group, depicting the sufferings of the Trojan priest Laocoon, who warned his countrymen not to accept the wooden horse into Troy. The gods, fearing their plans of destroying Troy may be thwarted, 'send two gigantic snakes from the sea which catch the priest and his two unfortunate sons in their coils and suffocate them. It is one of the stories of senseless cruelty perpetrated by the Olympians against poor mortals.'[14] The dramatic struggle, the pain and agony, create movement in this famous sculpture. In Flatter's cartoon there is also a sense of struggle, perhaps even of cinematic movement. To move the onlooker to feelings of compassion for Austria with a scene which of necessity looks static, but conveys motion, is a considerable achievement. A short poem in Flatter's hand on the back of the cartoon, addressed to the Austrian people, drives home the message:

> Willst Du gehaßt von aller Welt verderben,
> An diesem Schandmal schuldbelastet sterben?
> Steh auf und peitsch hinaus die braune Bande,
> Sei wieder Herr in Deinem Vaterlande!

> [Do you want to perish hated by all,
> Do you want to die on this heinous symbol laden with guilt?
> Get up and whip them out, the brown-shirt thugs,
> To be again the master in your fatherland.]

The artist comes into his own as a visionary with the following cartoon, dated 1939, 'Your victories will be like this onion, Herr Hitler' (Figure 5). Hitler is not quite sure what to make of this clairvoyant with her curious crystal ball, for an onion, as everyone knows, is made up of layers: as soon as one has been peeled off, another layer is there to be taken off, for there is no centre. Hitler's victories will be peeled off and there will be nothing left. When Flatter drew this cartoon in 1939, it was by no means clear that this would be the case; the artist, however, was sure that policies built on the contempt of people would prove as insubstantial as the innermost part of an onion.

The homely setting, the lovingly-drawn details like the footstool of the old woman or the cat curling round Hitler's feet, serve to add reality to an otherwise unreal scene. The cartoonist has to convince with a few lines. He does not delineate every feature, but highlights what is most prominent, exaggerating what is significant so as to make his characters easily recognisable. He can leave out lines and shadows where appropriate, he is free to hint at things with few brushstrokes or smudges. 'We have learned how far the limits of our understanding of images can be extended beyond the indication of natural appearances.'[15] Thus some details which do not seem significant at first sight take on importance in juxtaposition with the centre-stage narrative. While the message of doom is expressed in the 'Onion' cartoon calmly and convincingly, the cartoon 'German Carnival' (Figure 6) expresses the same message with a mixture of ridicule and horror. Carnival is a time of processions

Figure 4 *Austria and Hitler crucified on the swastica*, 1941

Figure 5 *'Your victories will be like this onion, Herr Hitler'*, 1939

Figure 6 *German Carnival*, 1941

and dances, of festivities and exuberance, giving way to Lent, the period of mourning before the passion of Christ. While the caption suggests joyful celebrations, the pictorial message shows us the opposite: Hitler, as Prince Carnival, is sitting aloft on a dais with his crown and coat of ermine, but he does not enjoy his ride on the shoulders of four hooded bearers (pall bearers?). He grimly clutches his throne, while Goebbels crouches like a goblin beneath it. The procession is led by an inanely grinning skeleton dressed up as a harlequin, while soldiers following the dais drag with them an emaciated woman – not exactly a festive occasion. The cartoonist, who has the licence to shock, has also the right to mock.

The very titles of cartoons, both those executed as warning to the British and those designed as propaganda for the Germans, reveal this dual method, setting up an ironic counterpoint to the visual image: 'He [Hitler] loves children' (C 005), 'Thanksgiving Service – Only the Devil Comes to Pray' (C 007), 'The Führer and the Riders of the Apocalypse' (C 017), 'Göring Implores the Witches for Help' (C 019), 'John Bull and the Bully of Europe' (C 102), 'Frog Mussolini' (C 126), 'Don't forget, Comrade Stalin, that I [Hitler] want to shave you afterwards too' (C 131), 'Now I am going to tell you something about the German Lebensraum, Herr Sumner Welles' (C 135), 'Last Appeal: "Believe me, I won't talk any more of Living Space, if you only give me some Breathing Space!"' (C 201) 'The German Samson' (C 207), 'I Was a Giant Until I Met Giants' (C 214), 'A Lesson in Broomstick Flying' (C 220), 'The Führer's Comfort to Millions of German Mothers' (C 225), 'Don Quixote's Final Assault' (C 240), 'Lohengrin Ersatz' (C 250), 'German Culture is at Stake' (C 260), 'Poet Goebbels' Complaint' (C 261), 'De Gaulle as Swan of Peace' (C 267). The breadth of developments commented on, the wealth of allusions employed and the range of feelings expressed are truly astounding. Flatter evidently worked hard, for the oeuvre catalogue lists some 400 cartoons for the wartime period alone. Some are not fully finished designs, some are recycled ideas, but all of them are vividly drawn, fuelled by a paradoxically creative form of hatred:

> Though I had read much of the enemy's literature and had listened regularly to his propaganda, the subjects I drew had seldom a direct connection with what I read or heard. The ideas for the cartoons, so it seemed to me, were sparked off my my pencil while it moved over the drawing paper. The moving force was hatred, it took concrete shape before my eyes. And my hatred of those responsible for the wanton cruelty done to so many innocent victims was boundless. I went about in the shape of my adversaries, I crept into their skin, I 'drew, hanged and quartered' them.[16]

'The Axis Powers' (Figure 7) is an effective caricature of a concrete political situation. Hitler, his brow furrowed with apprehension, awkwardly carries the structure, hinted at by a frieze. A proud eagle with swastika in the middle, the fascist axe on one side and the rising sun of Japan on the other side, symbolise the three totalitarian systems. The structure has no substance,

Hitler carries it all on his own, for Mussolini, the figure that used to support the entablature under the fascist axe, is flat on the ground like a doll, while Hideki Tojo, the Japanese Prime Minister between 1941 and 1944 and later chief of staff, holds up his arms pretending to carry the pediment. The message inscribed on the structure is a message without substance. It is a superb example of yoking together different metaphors to produce a striking new result. The artist's insight and his view of events are personal; but translated into visual images they become instruments with which to teach, to warn, to coax the onlooker into taking sides.

The visionary element is particularly prominent in those of Flatter's cartoons which anticipate the downfall of the Hitler regime. In *Struwwelhitler*, the 'Story of Fidgety Adolf' presents the reader with this kind of prophecy through pictorial images which politicise the children's story. Adolf is a restless, hyperactive child, who is dining with Uncle Sam and Aunt Britannia. But his antics make the grown-ups cross, and when he eventually rocks the chair so wildly that he falls and pulls everything to the ground – 'Down upon the ground they fall, / glasses, plates, knives, forks and all', Adolf is in disgrace. The verdict of Aunt and Uncle is a masterpiece of understatement: 'He must go to bed without'. Flatter's own variant on this transposition of a familiar fable into a political allegory is demonstrated in 'Teutonic Loyalty: Do you feel safe now, darling' (C 205). It plays on the well-known poem *Erlkönig* by Goethe, which narrates an epic ride across a very sinister countryside. The rider, who holds a sick child in his arms, has to reach his destination before the child's health collapses. The rider just makes it, but the child dies. In Flatter's treatment, the rider is Hitler, the horse has lost his hind legs and buttocks, its blinkers are decorated with swastikas. Hitler holds the reins with one hand, in the other hand he holds a small fat Mussolini, who threatens to slip from the firm grip of his arm. Together they rush headlong into perdition. The caption 'Teutonic loyalty', the much-vaunted German esprit de corps among comrades in arms, takes on the opposite meaning: from a relationship of trust arises a relationship which spells disaster for both parties.

Flatter's economical technique, using no recognisable landscape or any other markers, makes this cartoon highly effective and instantly understandable. The opposite method, surprisingly, achieves a similar result. In 'The Nazi Head Quarters: "Who will stab me in the back?"' (C 203, drawn well before the attempted coup of 20 July 1944), we are confronted with Hitler, rumpled and fearful, pointing to the positions on the army staff map in front of him. Things are not going well for him, but he is even more afraid of all those standing behind him and towering over him. They fill every inch of background, the tiny Goebbels looking nervous, fat Goering, Himmler looking inscrutable, von Papen looking alarmed, and rows of others who stand and watch and wait for the moment to put in the knife. Who will be the one who delivers the fateful stab in the back? Here, the mastery of the portrait-painter comes into its own. Flatter highlights the members of the Nazi leadership with a few lines, catching their physique and features, the poise and peculiarity of their anatomy. Those are not types, but individuals. Hitler is pre-occupied not with the disastrous situation on the battlefields, but with considerations for his own survival.

In contrast to these recognisable individuals, Flatter had used types in his series *Mein Kampf Illustrated* to ridicule the inflated language of Hitler's notorious tract. The visual comments on Hitlerian quotes are very effective as they again juxtapose the captions with visual images which give the quotation a particular slant not intended by the author. The line about Austria in chapter 5: 'and then from the dim past will emerge the immortal vision of those solid ranks of steel helmets ...' caused Flatter to lash out against his countrymen.[17] The cartoon, entitled 'The Austrian last line of defence' (Figure 8), shows two characters sporting featureless military uniforms. One has a huge unkempt beard, the other has a neck unnaturally extended by a lifetime of yodelling. The lower part of the face hints at a sour disposition, with the mouth turned down. To top it all, they wear not steel helmets but upturned chamber pots, complete with handles and swastikas. The characters do not give the impression of solid ranks of fighters. The Austrians, definitely not a martial race, cannot possibly realise an 'immortal vision' with soldiers like these.

Flatter's work explored such a wide range of motifs and emotions that by the end of the war his work was in great demand. 'I could not draw quickly enough to provide the Belgian refugee government, the Ministry of Information, the Free French paper and later on *Die Zeitung*, a German London paper, with leaflets and illustration.'[18] Needless to say, he was driven above all by an urge to unmask the Nazi atrocities against humankind: 'I felt for the first time in my life the satisfaction of being engaged in a work that was urgently wanted'.[19] And even as an old man, he wrote: 'I still look at my wartime activity with pride,'[20] adding that he 'could not believe that such a man – Hitler – could triumph in the end'.

When Hitler was finally defeated and the Nazi leadership put on trial at Nuremberg, Flatter was commissioned to sketch the proceedings for two weeks. He attended as official war artist and sketched fast and furiously, producing memorable images of those 'In the dock at Nuremberg' (Figure 9). The trial gave him the opportunity to draw from life the actors on the Nazi stage whom, for so many years, he had drawn from his imagination. But he responded with mixed emotions: 'I had neither hatred nor pity for them. They looked like marionettes forsaken by their master.'[21] In an article entitled 'Captive Nazi Lions Have Become Dachshunds' in the *News of the World* (11 August 1946), he wrote:

> I was somewhat disappointed when I entered the courtroom at Nuremberg for the first time. The distance from the press gallery to the dock was greater than I had expected, and I had to use binoculars – a cumbersome aid. I had expected to see 21 unrepentant Nazi fanatics ready to die heroically for their creed, their deeds, their Führer. I had prepared myself to draw the faces of tyrants, bullies, and sadists; my pencil was to be the sword to slay them. What I saw was a band of timid, dejected men, the plea for mercy inscribed on their faces. I had to brace myself

Figure 7 *The Axis Powers*, 1942

Figure 8 *The Austrian last line of defence*, 1944

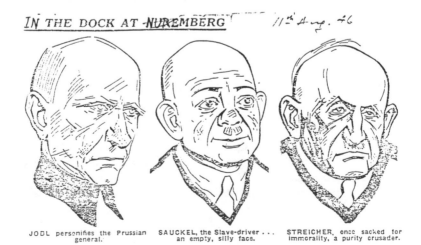

Figure 9 *In the dock at Nuremberg*, 1946

lest I should feel pity for them, and had to remember how these men once claimed to be supermen, entitled to exterminate like vermin people they pretended to regard as inferior. Now, scared of their fate, they were ready to denounce everything they stood for. Hitler, like all fools who talk a lot, sometimes talked sense; he pronounced his judgment on these men when he said in 'Mein Kampf': 'Of course, grovellers and lickspittles never want to die for their master'. ... In captivity the former lions had turned into dachshunds, and they outdid each other in trying to convince each other that they just followed the whistle of their master.

The fruit of his work is contained in hundreds of sketches, as well as the watercolour 'The Nuremberg Trial. The Accused in the Dock' (D 401), which confirms Flatter's credentials as a portraitist. Each head is highly individual. Goering, the ex-field marshal, staring gloomily in front of him; Hess, his neighbour, burying his nose in a book so as to demonstrate that he does not have to pay attention to what is going on; Ribbentrop, 'the conceited champagne-merchant, who, by Hitler's permission, wore gorgeous beribboned and bemedalled uniforms', displaying a 'hypocritical face as a clown's white mask. I am certain that this assistant-producer of the Nazi stage will not die a hero'. The 'hangman' Frank's face was to Flatter 'a satanic one'; the face of the 'slave-driver' Sauckel, 'so remarkable for its emptiness', was difficult to draw. Streicher, 'the former schoolmaster, who became gauleiter of Nuremberg, was once sacked for his immoral conduct', but posed as the crusader for the 'cleanliness and purification of the German blood'.

> Hitler's obedient servant in military matters, Keitel, sat in the dock as motionless as a grey marble bust ... Papen, Schacht, and Fritzsche tried hard to distinguish themselves from the other accused, regarding themselves as belonging to a much higher social or intellectual caste. Another aristocrat is Baldur von Schirach, the Youth Leader and Gauleiter of Vienna ... The man who was once regarded by the Nazis as the paragon of Aryan beauty certainly looks better now, when personal suffering and fear have marked his face. He was once a fat and more distinctly feminine fellow.

Such are Flatter's perceptive comments on the accused in the *News of the World*. By contrast, the GIs surrounding the accused are stylised to the point of looking uniformly angelic. Was Flatter also hinting at another court?

After the war, the *Evening Standard* offered Flatter a post as cartoonist, but he feared that as a specialist in hate he was ill-equipped to comment humorously on a wide range of current news, including such matters as cricket! A political cartoonist without exhaustive knowledge of cricket faced insurmountable problems, as he put it in his old age, and so he declined. But even in peacetime he retained a sceptical attitude towards political events. It is no surprise that, later in life (he remained active as an artist until his death in 1988) he was as clear in his criticism of the Common Market as earlier in his criticism of the steamrolling Nazi ideology. He turned to gouache painting, commenting on political events with reference to their impact on ordinary people, as if on a stage. For him, the Common Market was in tune with dictators' visions of unified territories, starting with Napoleon's fraternité through Hitler's Thousand-Year Reich to the European gospel of 'integration'. His political instinct made him suspicious of pathos-mongers who are more interested in abstract questions than in the living relationships between people. He had seen too much suffering to espouse causes of extreme emotional sacrifice for the greater good.

Flatter's art focuses on the sufferings and the everyday experiences of ordinary people, not the great schemes and grand solutions. Where he uses pathos, as in the 'Invasion' cartoon, it is used as a tool to ridicule big words and empty gestures. He is at his best when he portrays a concrete situation, even if the specific instance is an imaginary event, like the forced ride in *Erlkönig*. His sketches and designs, drawings and cartoons did not use tricks to master difficult formal problems; they used human scenes to demonstrate, to teach and to warn, putting them into a manageable perspective. When he adapted visual terms for expressing violent action, he did so in the pursuit of truth and justice. The moral stance which finds expression in his works was the social conscience of an ordinary man, which enabled him to see through the empty rhetoric of political leaders. This theme has by no means lost its relevance with the passage of time. When his works were shown in Vienna in 1981, the walls outside the Künstlerhaus were daubed with swastikas by Austrian neo-Nazis. His comment aptly summarises his artistic creed: 'The operatic Viennese probably expected me to express in my work my undying love for my fatherland, for the "city of my dreams". But what I gave them was a sermon, and they did not like that very much.'[22] But then, who is ever a prophet in his own country?

Notes

Numbers given in brackets after the titles of cartoons by Otto Flatter refer to the oeuvre catalogue numbers in the estate, except for Figure 3 which is in the collection of the Imperial War Museum, London.

1. Otto Flatter, *A Painter's Monologue*, unpublished autobiography (not dated), p. 16, in the possession of the author of this chapter. Subsequent quotations from this source are identified as Flatter, followed by the page reference.
2. Flatter, pp. 52–3.
3. Flatter, p. 57.
4. Ernst H. Gombrich, 'Magic, Myth and Metaphor: Reflections on Pictorial Satire', *L'Art et les Révolutions*. Conférences plénières. Congrès International d'Histoire de l'Art (Strasbourg, 1990), p. 44.
5. Gombrich, op. cit., pp. 43, 47.
6. Flatter, p. 55.
7. Flatter, p. 56.
8. Ibid.
9. Flatter pp. 56–7.
10. *Propaganda, the Art of Persuasion. World War II*, ed. V. Margolin and A. Rhodes (London, 1975), p. 107.

11. Cf. Klaus Kirchner, 'Flugblattpropaganda: Das nichtgewaltsame Kriegsmittel', in *Flugblattpropaganda im Zweiten Weltkrieg* (exhibition catalogue), ed. Hartwig Gebhardt and Adolf Wild (Bremen, 1980), p. 22.
12. Robert and Philip Spence, *Struwwelhitler*, ed. and introduced by Karl Riha (Cologne, 1984).
13. Pressmark in the Public Record Office, Kew, London, FO 898, 498.
14. Ernst H. Gombrich, *The Story of Art* (Oxford, 1989), p. 74.
15. Ernst H. Gombrich, *Art and Illusion: A Study in the Psychology of Pictorial Representation* (Oxford, 1988), p. 196.
16. Flatter, p. 57.
17. Adolf Hitler, *Mein Kampf*, tr. Ralph Manheim with an introduction by D. C. Watt (London, 1969), p. 152 (Flatter quotes from an earlier translation).
18. Flatter, p. 57.
19. Ibid.
20. Ibid.
21. Flatter, p. 59.
22. Flatter, p. 103.

Felix Pollak

An Austro-American Poet

Gregory Mason

Felix Pollak (1909–87) abandoned his university studies in 1938 and fled his native Vienna for America. There he quickly mastered English, pursued a successful career as a rare books librarian, and made his mark as an American poet. In 1974, glaucoma forced him retire from his librarian's post, but he continued to write both in German and in English. Blindness gave Pollak's experience of exile a special poignancy and became the major theme of his later poetry. He remained largely unknown outside of poetry circles in America, until a successful reading tour in Germany and Austria in the last months of his life introduced him to a new generation of his compatriots. Substantial belated recognition followed with the posthumous dual-language publication of his poetry and his aphorisms.[1]

Felix Pollak was born on 11 November 1909, the older of two sons, to middle-class Jewish parents in Vienna. A sensitive youth and aspiring writer, Pollak claims that his mother 'violated' his 'vulnerable budding-poet soul' since she 'liked to brag in the most superficial fashion about me to her friends and acquaintances'. Describing himself as 'the typical misunderstood child and youngster', Pollak admitted that there was 'some romanticism connected with that role that appealed to me'.[2] At seventeen, he won a young writers' competition, and his winning story, followed by one or two others, appeared in the Vienna *Neue Freie Presse*. These stories, such as 'Finale' and 'Rufe, die man nicht hört' (Cries that no-one hears), pictured isolated protagonists close to insanity or suicide. Reinhold Grimm sees in Pollak's early writings an 'inborn and inherited feeling of separation and loneliness, of outsiderness and exclusion, even of ... "existential exile"'.[3] Before he was forced to become an actual exile, Pollak was already an exile in temperament.

While Pollak's mother had embarrassed him as a youth, his father pressured him as a young man to pursue a course of university study that would lead to a 'breadwinning' occupation. 'After many a stormy domestic scene', Pollak enrolled to study both jurisprudence at the University of Vienna and theatre at the Theatre Seminar of Max Reinhardt. Throughout his life and work, Pollak's predominantly cautious choices in the public world fought against extravagant yearnings in his inner life; the needs of the survivor conflicted with the dreams of the artist. As a highlight of his theatrical apprenticeship, Pollak directed a production of *Midsummer Night's Dream* under Reinhardt's tutelage at the Salzburg Festival in 1933. Under a full moon, in front of Klessheim Castle, the open-air performances were a great success (*A* 11).

Two days after Hitler's annexation of Austria in March 1938, Pollak had his passport confiscated. It took him three months of standing in queues to get it back. Pollak recalls that his 'friends were arrested and began to disappear in increasing numbers' (*A* 12). With an affidavit for immigration to the United States, but with no visa to enter a European country, Pollak hazarded an escape in September 1938. He sent telegrams to all the French contacts he could muster, and hoped that a French citizen would materialise to vouch for him at Paris airport. If turned back by the French authorities, he would certainly have been sent to a concentration camp. Fortunately, one couple did show up, and Pollak was free. Aided by the Jewish Refugee Committee, he made his way first to London and then to New York, arriving on 7 December 1938 on board the *Queen Mary*.

In an essay written a few weeks after his arrival, Pollak captured the pain of the reluctant new immigrant:

> Ja, es sticht in See, aber es sticht auch ins Herz. Plötzlich spürst du es, plötzlich bricht das Gefuhl aus, das dich schon die ganze Zeit über dumpf erregt und beunruhigt hat, das Gefühl: dieses Schiff fährt nach Hause, nach Europa ... dorthin, wohin du gehörst – und du stehst am Ufer, in der Fremde, siehst es wegfahren und kannst nicht mit! Und etwas würgt dich in der Kehle, doch mit 'Heimweh' ist das nicht zu erklären, Heimlosigkeitsweh, das ist's schon eher.

> [Yes, the boat is striking out to sea, but something is striking your heart as well. Suddenly you sense it; suddenly the feeling that has been agitating and unsettling you deep down all this time, breaks out. This ship is sailing back home, to Europe ... over there where you belong – and you are standing here on the shore, in a foreign country, watching it sail away – and you can't go with it! It's like a choking feeling, and 'homesickness' doesn't quite describe it. 'Homelessness-sickness' would be a better word.][4]

Sick at heart, the Romantic in exile wanders the streets, languidly absorbing the scene. His thoughts wander back to Austria. Tyres squeal. An angry motorist screams at the daydreamer. Jolted back to present reality, the young immigrant resolves: 'Du bist jetzt in New York, mein Lieber, und du mußt das Licht sehen lernen, rot, grün, oder übertragen, sonst kommst du unter die Räder' ('You're in New York now, my friend, and you'd better watch out for the lights – red, green or yellow – or else you're done for').[5] Pollak, the survivor, resolves to go to the agency the next morning and take the first job offered to him.

Pollak recalled again how he felt at this critical moment in a letter congratulating Hermann Hesse on his seventieth birthday in 1947:

121

Ich entsinne mich, daß ich Ihnen im Herbst 1938, als ich meine oester-
reichische Heimat verlassen mußte, vom Schiff aus einen symbolischen
Abschiedsgruß sandte – Ihnen als dem lebenden Repräsentanten all
dessen, was ich unwiederbringlich hinter mir ließ. Europa, meine
Jugend, eine versinkende Welt. Es war mir immer seither ein Trost, daß
ich einige der lieben und vertrauten blauen Bände, Ihr Bild, und einen
Brief, den Sie mir anläßlich Ihres 60. Geburtstags zur Antwort nach
Wien gesandt hatten, aus den Trümmern nach Amerika retten konnte.

[I remember, when I had to leave my Austrian homeland in autumn
1938, that I sent a symbolic parting greeting to you as the living
representative of everything that I was leaving inexorably behind me.
Europe, my youth, a foundering world. It has always been a comfort to
me since then, that I was able to rescue from the ruins and bring to
America a few of those familiar and beloved volumes with the blue
bindings, your picture and a letter that you sent in reply to the sixtieth
birthday greeting I had sent you.][6]

The jobs that Pollak landed in New York, doughnut-baker and door-to-door
salesman, were not exactly suited to his talents. When the Jewish Refugee
Committee recommended that he move to Buffalo in upstate New York where
he might more easily find employment, Pollak readily consented. Things moved
slowly there too until, with a stroke of chutzpah, Pollak presented himself to
the Head Librarian of the Buffalo Public Library. After the elderly adminis-
trator had subjected the young immigrant to a mumbling, two-hour disquisi-
tion on the American Civil War, he promptly offered Pollak a job as a clerk,
without inquiring about his qualifications. Pollak was on his way. He took a
library degree at the University of Buffalo and was launched in a new career.
    In 1943, Pollak was drafted into the United States Army. He gladly joined,
since he believed in the cause, and his induction expedited his application for
American citizenship. Assigned to the American South, he acted as an
interrogator of German and Austrian prisoners of war. Pollak admitted to
'very ambivalent feelings toward the German and the Austrian people'.[7] He
continued to feel outrage at the way in which Hitler had 'moved into Austria
greeted jubilantly by the majority of the population [while] Jews like me had
to scramble out of their native city and country, to save their naked lives' (*A*
12). The recalcitrant attitude of the prisoners amazed him. 'They threatened
us that we should be careful because Hitler's secret weapon would come and
then we'd be in the compounds and they would be on the outside. Then,
when the war was won, they all lined up and said they were really anti-Nazis
all along. Which was shameful, and of course not true' (Davis, pp. 29–30). He
was angered at the idea of the supposed ignorance of large parts of the
population and the convenient amnesia of former Nazis. 'The average
German citizen will tell you that he was never involved, didn't know from
nutt'n and besides saved a Jew.' This was 'standard procedure by the
deloused and de-nazified and very transparent'.[8] He indicted this hypocritical
and cowardly behaviour in the poem 'Niemalsland':

Wir haben es niemals gewußt.
Wir sind es niemals gewesen.
Das hat es niemals gegeben.

Das ist uns niemals gelungen.
Das haben wir niemals versucht.
Das wurde uns niemals bewiesen ...

Ja, im Niemalsland lebt sich's behaglich.
Man erinnert sich niemals an nichts.
Uns selber hat's niemals gegeben.

Trotzdem sind wir niemals ganz glücklich.
Wir können halt niemals vergessen.
All das, was hier niemals geschah.

(Vom Nutzen, p. 73)

[Neverland. We never knew anything about it. We never had any part in it. It was something that never happened. It was something we never achieved. It was something we never even tried. It was never proved against us. Yes, in Neverland, we live a comfortable life. We never remember this 'nothing'. It never happened to us. Still we're never entirely happy. We still just can never forget, everything here that never took place.]

After the war, Pollak took a Masters degree in Library Science at the University of Michigan, and in 1949 he was appointed Rare Books Librarian at Northwestern University in Evanston, Illinois, a suburb of Chicago. There, he met Sara Allen, whom he married in 1950. Sara played a crucial role as a source of stability and support for Pollak in all the years that followed. American citizenship, an excellent job and a good marriage established Pollak in his new homeland, and helped him find his way as an American poet.

Exiles in other fields have an easier time than writers do in picking up and continuing their careers. Whereas scientists, musicians and visual artists work in a 'universal' language, the verbal artist depends on his native tongue. In the last few days before his flight, Pollak took long walks in the Vienna Stadtpark with a friend (who later vanished in his attempted flight to Palestine). On these walks, the two lamented the imminent end of their fledgling writing careers, since neither could imagine giving up his mother tongue. Pollak had taken a classical course of study at the Gymnasium, and was poorly versed in English when he arrived in America. A quick learner, however, he had 'an ear for speech melodies and rhythms and a fascination for colloquialisms (I remember I was endlessly puzzled and intrigued by expressions like "he got my goat")'. He was very proud of the first article which he published in English in 1942, and he felt that 'it established a connection and continuity with myself, a bridge to the past which I felt was irreparably broken' (*A* 21).

Once he had mastered the new language sufficiently, he joined a small reading circle of poets in Evanston and began writing poetry in English. His first published volume, *The Castle and the Flaw* (1963), takes its title from this poem:

> The disk spins on the phonograph
> thick silky strands of music, wall to wall.
> But when I enter from the outer hall,
> I hear but needle-scraping, silk turned chaff.
>
> Perhaps it's only in the jail of metaphor
> that I can enter unoblique
> *das Ding an sich?* The flaw which I deplore
> may be the castle which I seek.
>
> The needle drains the music from the disk,
> seeding the grooves with silence as they sing,
> unravelling the weave of the black mask,
> weaving the web of its unravelling,
>
> till the flawed song is covered by the shroud
> of flawlessness: the songless void.[9]

Here is technical mastery of a very high order, with subtle thematic development in the imagery. The sound imagery of the phonograph record takes on almost concrete dimensions in the second line, 'thick, silky strands of music, wall to wall', but the anticipated harvest becomes 'silk turned chaff' as the poet approaches closely enough to hear the 'needle-scraping'. While metaphor is not the thing itself but another thing named in place of it, the poet then wonders: 'Perhaps it's only in the jail of metaphor / that I can enter unoblique / *das Ding an sich?*' The poem becomes a meditation on poetry, which Pollak elsewhere calls 'the art of conveying in words what words cannot convey'.[10]

The third stanza further extends concrete imagery by playing on the ambiguity of the phonograph 'needle', now like a pine-cone needle, 'seeding the grooves with silence as they sing'. The work of art, itself an imperfect recreation of its subject matter, achieves its own perfection in the act of its own making/ unmaking, 'weaving the web of its unravelling / till the flawed song is covered by the shroud / of flawlessness: the songless void'. This is a virtuoso accomplishment within the rigorous formal scheme of the Shakespearean sonnet. Its imagery and thematic richness recall Wallace Stevens's 'The Idea of Order at Key West'. Pollak was a poet's poet, with a subtle and playful feel for language. In 'Aesthetics', he turns both his classical training and his status as a newcomer to the English language to advantage. He sees terms from the medical dictionary with fresh eyes and he makes them sound musical and heroic:

> There are such beautiful
> exotic
> words in the dictionary,
> euphonic songs that taste good
> in the mouth – salmonella,

```
glaucoma, catatonia, ataxis,
words like the names of
legendary heroines or goddesses
– Acne, Hysterectomy,
Emphysema, Peritonitis, or thunderous
appellations reminiscent of old
warriors and lovers – Tetanus,
Staphylococcus, Stupor,
Cyanide, Carbuncle...
```
(Vom Nutzen, p. 128)

Pollak saw the poet as a verbal artist of the highest order. 'Poetry demands an effort: you should learn the language of poetry as you would a foreign language or musical notation standard.' Philosophically, however, he cast the poet in more Romantic lights. 'Only the man tortured by dissonance appears able to sing the glories of harmony.' Furthermore, he claims that 'If by chance no foreign agent finds its way into the artist's soul to disturb and bedevil it, his first creative act will unfailingly be the artificial fabrication of such an invader: he will fashion the needed thorn in his flesh, to have the frustration he must have for the purpose of overcoming it in his work' (Judson, pp. 12–13).

At the same time, Pollak never lost his sense of humour. 'Felix's Romanticism', as Lisel Mueller recalled, was 'always leavened by his wit' (Davis, p. 31). The ironical and the self-deprecating were essential to Pollak. 'The poet', he aphorised, 'is a man who matures earlier than others, and who stays immature longer' (Judson, p. 12). He valued humour highly and esteemed it as 'almost equivalent to intelligence' (Powell, p. 14). Pollak the poet forged unexpected congruences between words and breathed new life into dead metaphors. Pollak the humorist saw the joy of sudden dissonance in phrases, ideas and situations that native speakers of English commonly overlook. In 'How I Got Myself Trapped', loath to accept the shackles of a bourgeois existence, he pokes fun at his own timidity:

```
It was easy.
I took one right step
after another.
```
(Vom Nutzen, p. 144)

In 'Musings of Late', he even has fun thinking of how his habit of showing up late might affect him in 'later life':

```
I was born late, I think,
and came late – wouldn't you know? to my wedding
after marrying late. Preferring to be in time to being
on time, I do hope I'll be late also for my funeral.
So they can call me the late late
```
Felix Pollak
(Vom Nutzen, p. 150)

Pollak published his poems steadily in little magazines nationwide, and in 1957 he received a congratulatory note from William Carlos Williams, who found 'so much to praise' in Pollak's verses.[11] He had become an accomplished poet in the American vein of terse, concrete imagery, but at the same time he remained a European. Walter Grünzweig has commented on the cultural synthesis implied in the title of the dual-language edition of Pollak's selected poems, *Vom Nutzen des Zweifels* (*The Uses of Doubt*).[12] This points both to the sceptical, European dimension, and to the pragmatic American aspect of Pollak's writing, while *Benefits of Doubt,* the American edition of Pollak's selected works, evokes a spirit of affirmation no doubt influenced by his American experience.[13] Hans Magnus Enzensberger praised Pollak's poetry both for its Viennese sensitivity to the nuances of language, and for its American forthrightness: 'Die alte Schule höre ich aus all Ihren Arbeiten heraus, auch wenn es noch so amerikanisch darin zugeht ... gänzlich amerikanisch ohne Ehrfurchtsgesten' (*Collection*, 22 March 1982) (I hear the old school in everything you write, even when it's still so American ... completely American, without any bowing and scraping).

While Pollak was finding time, 'at the tired edges of my days',[14] to produce this considerable body of poetry, he also had an impressive career as a librarian. In 1959 he was appointed Curator of Rare Books at the University of Wisconsin in Madison. In his new position, he made an important contribution to American letters by building up the Marvin Sukov collection into the largest collection of little magazines in the world. Pollak's tastes and temperament were well matched to this speciality. In his Vienna days, he had greatly admired Karl Kraus and his little magazine *Die Fackel.* Now in his adopted setting, he could foster the Krausian spirit not just as curator of the little magazines, but as their advocate.

During the 1960s, Madison, Wisconsin became a hotbed of protest against the Vietnam War, and a centre of the counter-culture. With an office on the second floor of Memorial Library, he sat, in the parlance of those days, 'in the heart of the beast'. He stoutly defended the little magazines' elitism and saw them as heralds of the avant-garde and of minority culture, asserting that 'true art has always been a conspiracy, an underground movement operating out of caves (sometimes disguised as attics), forever imposing the *status nascendi* of various media on the *status quo* of society'. He insisted that 'the expression "subversive art" is a tautology'.[15] He saw the size of little magazines as the touchstone of their integrity, their badge of rank: 'Littleness guarantees the littles their independence and unbeholdenness without which they would cease to be what they are'.[16] For Felix Pollak the exile, the little magazine, *in* but not *of* the cultural mainstream, provided just the right forum to voice his convictions.

During this time, Pollak wrote 'Speaking the Hero'. Widely quoted, translated and pirated, this poem gained him considerable fame:[17]

I did not want to go.
They inducted me.

I did not want to die.

They called me yellow ...

They said I gave my life.
I had struggled to keep it.

They said I set an example.
I had tried to run ...

I wanted to live.
They called me a coward.

I died a coward.
They call me a hero.

(Vom Nutzen, p. 58)

This poem's public theme stands in sharp contrast to the predominantly private themes in Pollak's previous work. Its dualistic structure and strident, satirical tones diverge distinctly from his earlier, subtler accents.

Pollak had become a public American intellectual, with his essays in little magazines and the mainstream press, and through his poetry readings, especially a recitation of 'Speaking the Hero' to an audience of 14,000 in 1969. Two further volumes of verse, *Say When* (1969) and *Ginkgo* (1973), each went into several printings and consolidated Pollak's stature as a poet.[18] No longer principally an exile or an émigré, he had become a voice in the American cultural scene in his own right.

Nevertheless, Pollak continued to feel like a 'FRIENDLY ALIEN', words which had been stamped on his papers when he first arrived in America. In his extensive correspondence, especially with novelist Anaïs Nin, Pollak described his despair at what he saw as the 'lonely desperation and orderly dreariness' of certain American cities. He saw the American publishing world as ruthless and philistine, and university campuses as intellectually barren. In Nin's novel *Winter of Artifice*, Pollak caught the aura of 'an indefinable, intangible European air' that he pined for, 'the smell of the streets of Paris, the strong, unique exhilarating odor of the Metro' (*Collection*, 30 July 1954).

During the late 1950s, Pollak's discontent festered, with a vague Romantic 'hunger / for being elsewhere / from where' ('What It Always Comes Down To', *Vom Nutzen*, p. 126). He tried unsuccessfully to change employment, applying for travel fellowships and for a post at the United Nations in New York. When he first learned of his appointment to the University of Wisconsin in Madison, with its reputation for cultural and intellectual vitality, Pollak felt 'as if a burden had been lifted from me'. But the deracinated exile already anticipated disillusionment. He knew that at his next stop 'there was another burden already waiting', and concluded that 'sometimes the interim period between two burdens is best, the period of floating' (*Collection*, 16 April 1959). Favouring a 'period of floating', with its latent sense of possibility, over situated fulfilment, with its inevitable workaday disappointments, Pollak again showed his fundamentally Romantic temperament.

Where is the homeland of a man who is reluctant to take up the burdens which come with putting down roots? Pollak answered this question in part, in thanking Hermann Hesse in 1949 for a letter he had just received from him: 'Es war heimweh-erweckend und zugleich -stillend, denn die Heimat, die einzig übriggebliebene, und wahrscheinlich auch wahre, die je bestanden hat, war in diesem Briefumschlag' (*Collection*, 17 December 1949) (It awoke a feeling of homesickness in me and calmed it at the same time, because my homeland, the only one left to me, and probably the only true one that there ever was, was in this envelope). Perhaps Pollak's true homeland lay in a sense of community with kindred spirits in the inner world of letters: Karl Kraus, Rainer Maria Rilke, Hermann Hesse, Alfred Polgar. Pollak was particularly fond of Polgar's aphorism 'Die Fremde ist nicht zur Heimat geworden. Aber die Heimat zur Fremde' (The foreign country has not become my home, but my homeland a foreign country). This captures Pollak's own ambiguous feelings towards his native Austria.

Pollak's attitude towards Vienna went to the emotional heart of the matter. It was much easier to condemn his venal fellow countrymen than to dismiss the city in which he had had so many vital, formative experiences and relationships. His attitude to the city of his birth remained extremely emotional, feeling by turns like a mistreated lover or a stepson: 'Vienna to me is like one of those women one can never quite get away from, no matter whether they treat one well or badly'. He came to call Vienna his 'stepmother town'.[19]

After the war, Pollak did in fact return to Vienna in 1952 and 1953 to complete his Doctor of Jurisprudence degree. This was a quixotic venture, since the qualification had no practical value in America, but Pollak saw it as 'a symbol and a kind of triumph, untranslatable into dollars and cents' (*A* 20). He was claiming back part of his past that had been denied to him and officially flouting the declaration which he had had to sign when he left in 1938, that he would never again set foot on Austrian soil. He was impressed to see that the citizens of Vienna had decided rebuild the opera before they rebuilt public housing. 'That is a symbol to me and to the world. Art is not a luxury. It goes to the core' (Powell, p. 15). More strongly, Vienna stirred in him the sense of visiting a former battle site, as 'Vienna 1967' makes clear:

> Though my
> roots are
> cut off
> here, they
> hurt like
> an old
> scar when
> it rains.

> (*Vom Nutzen*, p. 114)

When he visited Vienna in 1979, he heard his 'New York' essay broadcast over the radio, and recalled:

It was a strange feeling to sit in a room overlooking the roofs of a city that had kicked me out half a life ago, and to hear my words being sent now into the very living rooms of the people who had uprooted me and threatened my life itself. But it was too late to feel any sense of triumph, just a kind of wonder and awe. (*A* 14)

In an article entitled 'The Polarity of Jewish Traits', Pollak had argued that, while Jews seemed to occupy extreme ends of various ideological spectrums, they had a fundamental trait in common, 'the striving for salvation in this world, for self-preservation'.[20] This theme of survival preoccupied Pollak, and it occurs repeatedly in his poetry. In an early draft of the poem 'Circus', he wrote: 'Success is measured by survival, / the head retrieved from the lion's mouth' (*Collection*, March 1975). His poem 'Refugee' drama-tises the human cost of survival and its alternatives:

He was born in Vienna
he died in Auschwitz
he is living in New York...

(*Vom Nutzen*, p. 54)

The refugee has not perished, but part of him has died with the terrible suffering and displacement of his people: 'In seiner Seele ging etwas vor, eine große Zäsur, ein großes Trauma'.[21] (Something happened in his soul, a great caesura, a great trauma). In 'Concerning Survival', the poet muses uneasily on his own quasi-immortality as 'the lone survivor'.[22] Survival has begun to seem more of a burden than a blessing. The space traveller in 'Astronaut', himself an exile from earth, concludes: 'I do not wish to re-enter' (*Vom Nutzen*, p. 62).

In 1963, Felix Pollak first experienced symptoms of the disease which was to claim his eyesight. By 1974, he was forced to take early retirement, having become legally blind. Blindness had made a near-mockery of his tenacious will to survive:

And so the terror without end
becomes routine. Survival
is purchased at the price
of incapacity.[23]

As Pollak's blindness worsened, a more stringent voice entered his poetry. His mood darkened in *Subject to Change* (1978), and in *Tunnel Visions* (1984) Pollak devoted a whole volume to the theme of his blindness.[24] Moving to a freer, unrhyming verse form, he transmuted painful testimonial into moving verse.

In 'Visit to the Institute for the Blind', the poet documents his baffled rage and helplessness:

Swimming against the coarse grain
of sun-streaked air, I am intercepted
by the crisscross of fins, the sparkle
of black diamond scales and the greetings

of strangers of long standing, who slip
their arms under mine, steering me like a
shipwreck. 'Watch out' they cry, 'there's
a step!' and heave me off my feet so that I
stumble and slip, leaving my arm behind.
When they finally leave me and dissolve
into fibres of mist, my thankyous damn
their eyes.

(*Vom Nutzen*, p. 178)

Pollak tried 'not to indulge in self-pity, hard as it is not to break out in an occasional howl, but to convey a degree of universality to my personal affliction'. He wanted his readers to realise that 'our handicaps are, after all, only metaphors for the general existential situation of human beings, for the human condition itself'.[25] Blindness becomes both metaphor and enactment of the progressive isolation that comes to all with old age – loss of personal strength, loss of the people of one's prime, including one's former self, loss even of the memory of it all:

I remember what they see, the people
who know me, but they're strangers
to my country of shadows. I am walking
the tightropes of memory, afraid of
false steps, bruised by forgotten
winds. The long shadow of my past
is creeping up on me behind my back,
pointing ahead now into echoing
hallways of fear. I walk on,
with a sureness I do not feel.

('I Walk', *Vom Nutzen*, p. 186)

In his later Vienna poems, Pollak's major themes of exile, survival and blindness combine with great poignancy. Initially, his images of the past have only blurred with the passing of time, as he shows in 'Vienna: The Street':

A different barber. Eyes my clothes
And greets me in bad English. The manicurist
(face of a tired nurse) must
be his wife. My best friend bit his nails.

Yes, cut my golden locks. He laughs
obliging. (*Amerikaner* like to joke.)
The rocking horse is gone. The clock
reads backward in a mirror full of blindspots.

(*Vom Nutzen*, p. 118)

Mistaken by a local for an American on the street where he had attended elementary school, the poet is being told that he no longer belongs there,

130

whether he feels that way or not. The rocking horse of childhood has surely vanished, and a sinister new note is sounded in the closing line. From his seat in the barber's chair, he catches sight of the clock reflected in the mirror. The clock 'reads backward' which suggests that the poet is on a futile journey back through time. Worse still, the mirror is 'full of blindspots', spots caused not only by the poet's slipping memory but also by the encroaching symptoms of glaucoma.

More and more, as in a nightmare, the poet sees passers-by on the streets of Vienna only as gruesome smudges. Like someone walking in a hellish landscape among the dead, he feels guilty to be a survivor:

> Ghosts, misty shapes of blood, charge me with living:
> to walk alive amidst the dead is guilt: am I worth having
> what they lost?
>
> (*Vom Nutzen*, p. 116)

In 'The Finger', Vienna lives on for him now only in dreams. fading images that can no longer be refortified by experience:

> I may pass through once more next month.
> But it will not be Vienna. It will be
> London's fog. I will not see that finger,
> nor that statue. If I am lucky,
> I'll go to my hotel one night
> and have a dream.
>
> (*Vom Nutzen*, p. 174)

In 1985, Felix Pollak wrote to Egon Schwarz, reporting on what he thought would be his last visit to Vienna. He attributed his profound ambivalence, an attitude of 'love-hate nostalgia', to 'der Gleichzeitigkeit und dem Nebeneinander von der Utopie Wien und der Wirklichkeit Wien' (the simultaneity and proximity of Vienna the utopia, and Vienna the reality). The blindness which now hindered him from fully experiencing his old home town acutely aggravated his sense of dissonance: 'In Madison, I'm dreaming of Vienna, and in Vienna I'm still dreaming of Wien' (*Collection*, 11 August 1985). 'Vienna' is the Americanised version of his home town, now lost to him across the divides of exile and blindness, while 'Wien' remains the city of his youth, which he can no longer revisit.

Events turned out differently. Pollak gained belated literary recognition in Germany and Austria, and returned once more to give a reading tour in 1987. In a radio interview in Siegen, he found fresh images to describe his sense of continuing exile. This time, he experienced his return 'home' as 'ein merkwürdiges Zusammenfallen von Realität und Unrealität, Vorwelt und Nachwelt, nicht mehr irgendwo zu Hause' (a curious implosion of reality and unreality, of the life before and the life after, being nowhere any more at home).[26]

Felix Pollak fought to the end against his failing faculties. He collaborated with Reinhold Grimm in translating his own poetry into and out of German, became involved in local radio broadcasting, and gave readings of poems which he had memorised. He was hospitalised while proof-reading the collected edition of his poetry in English, *Benefits of Doubt,* and died a few days later. Forced to flee Hitler or face dire consequences, Pollak adapted to a new set of circumstances with imagination and creativity. His achievement as an accomplished poet in two languages was rare. He also experienced by turns the relief of deliverance from and the pull of nostalgia for his native Vienna. Through his return to his native city as an acclaimed writer, he entered into dialogue with a new generation of his compatriots and achieved a sense of reconciliation. Throughout his long and eventful life, Felix Pollak made exile into his muse, as in the poem 'Beim Schreiben meiner Autobiographie' ('While Writing My Autobiography'):

> Wer schläft heute nacht in meinem Kinderzimmer?
> Ich bin ein alter Mann.
> Wie lang die Zeit, die mir so kurz verrann!
> Einst ist für immer ...
>
> Nur jetzt ist wirklich: dieses ist mein Zimmer.
> Was einst Zuhause war, ist nicht zuhaus.
> Etwas geht ein und aus.
> Nichts ist für immer.

(Vom Nutzen, p. 139)

[Who is sleeping in my childhood bedroom tonight? I am an old man. What a long time, that has slipped away from me so soon! Once is for ever ... Only now is real: now this is my room. What was once home, is home no longer. Something just comes and goes. Nothing is for ever.]

Notes

Poems from Pollak's collection *Vom Nutzen des Zweifels* (Frankfurt am Main, 1989) are cited in the text as *Vom Nutzen* (followed by page number).

1. *Lebenszeichen: Aphorismen und Marginalien,* ed. Reinhold Grimm and Sara Pollak (Vienna, 1992).
2. 'Felix Pollak: An Autobiographical Sketch', *Northeast,* 5.5 (Winter 1991–2), pp. 11–24 (p. 22). Subsequent references are cited in the text as '*A*' (followed by page number).
3. Reinhold Grimm, '"My Stepmother Town": Felix Pollak and Vienna', in Jeffrey B. Berlin (ed.), *Turn-of-the-Century Vienna and its Legacy: Essays in Honor of Donald Daviau* (Boulder, CO, 1993), pp. 507–28 (p. 518).
4. Felix Pollax, 'New York: ein Schiff, ein Emigrant' (New York. A steamship. An Emigrant), *Akzente,* 3 (June, 1979), pp. 314–20 (p. 315).
5. Ibid., p. 320.
6. Felix Pollak Collection, University of Wisconsin – Madison Memorial Library, Department of Rare Books and Special Collections, Madison, Wisconsin, USA. Subsequent references are cited in the text as *Collection,* sometimes followed by date.
7. Davis, 'Against the Dying of the Light', *Isthmus* (9 November 1984), pp. 29–30 (p. 29); subsequently cited in the text as 'Davis'.

8. Sanford Smoller, 'Felix Pollak's Last Journey: A Remembrance', in *Pembroke Magazine*, 22 (1990), 10–14.
9. 'The Castle and the Flaw' in *The Castle and the Flaw* (New Rochelle, NY, 1963), p. 22.
10. Felix Pollak, 'Of Wording & Poeting: An Aphoristic Mosaic', in John Judson (ed.), *Voyages to the Inland Sea, II* (La Crosse, WI, 1972), pp. 11–25 (p. 12); cited as Judson.
11. See Reinhold Grimm, '"So Much to Praise": On Felix Pollak and His Poetry', *Wisconsin Academy Review*, 37.2 (Spring 1991), pp. 6–8 (p. 8).
12. Walter Grünzweig, 'Der Exilautor und sein Publikum: Über den Lyriker Felix Pollak', *Das Jüdische Echo*, 1.29 (October 1990), pp. 164–8 (pp. 166–8).
13. Felix Pollak, *Benefits of Doubt: Selected Poems*, (Peoria, IL, 1988).
14. Pat Powell, 'Interview with Felix Pollak', *Wisconsin Academy Review*, 29.3 (June 1983), pp. 12–15 (p. 12); cited as Powell.
15. Felix Pollak, 'Excerpts from Various Essays on Little Magazines', in *Prose and Cons* (La Crosse, WI, 1983), pp. 10–24 (p. 11).
16. 'Excerpts', p. 23.
17. See Davis, p. 30.
18. *Say When* (La Crosse, WI, 1969); *Ginkgo* (New Rochelle, NY, 1973).
19. See *A*, p. 19, and Smoller, p. 13.
20. *Recall*, 11.4 (1962), pp. 30–5 (p. 32).
21. Gerhart Lampe, 'Die Fremde ist nicht Heimat geworden. Aber die Heimat Fremde. Felix Pollak: ein Wiener Exilschriftsteller', Radio broadcast (Siegen, October, 1988).
22. *Minnow* (January, 1977), p. 20.
23. 'Eyewitness Report', *Pembroke Magazine*, 13 (1981), pp. 132–4.
24. *Subject to Change* (La Crosse, WI, 1978); *Tunnel Visions* (Peoria, IL, 1984).
25. 'In Memoriam: Felix Pollak', *Wisconsin Academy Review*, 34 (March 1988), pp. 24–5 (p. 25).
26. Lampe, Radio Broadcast.

A Passion for People

Elias Canetti's Autobiography and its Implications for Exile Studies

Harriet Murphy

In his short piece from 1979 on 'Methodological Problems in German Exile Literature Studies', Joseph Peter Strelka suggested that the main and 'entirely proper' way out of the dilemmas confronting scholars of literature known as exile literature was to treat *exile* literature as exile *literature*.[1] This route, Strelka maintains, leads us away from sociological and political divergences, from methodological chaos, pedestrian journalism and population statistics, to a country of the mind, an 'inner country', worthy of investigation because of its timeless beauty, grandeur and significance. This concept of timeless artistic significance may appear old-fashioned, but it does draw attention to the one-sidedness of positivistic approaches to exile studies.

Elias Canetti's three-volume autobiography, which covers the years from 1905 to 1937, ends at a critical moment, just before Canetti's decision to flee Vienna at the time of Hitler's annexation of Austria, a flight which subsequently led to the choice of London and Zurich as his new, long-term homes. Interestingly, considering the popularity of autobiography among those living in exile, Canetti's three volumes were not written in close temporal proximity to the events which they actually chronicle. *Die gerettete Zunge* appeared in 1977, although it chronicles life between 1905 and 1921. *Die Fackel im Ohr* appeared in 1980; it chronicles life between 1921 and 1931. Finally, *Das Augenspiel* appeared in 1985, although it chronicles life between 1931 and 1937. Richard Critchfield notes that Ernst Toller, Stefan Zweig, Klaus Mann, Heinrich Mann, Alfred Döblin, Gustav Regler and Ludwig Marcuse all, by contrast, produced their autobiographies or memoirs almost immediately after the initial decision to live in exile.[2] While this issue of the timing of publication may partly explain Canetti's absence from so many of the major collections of essays or studies of exile literature,[3] it may also explain why Canetti's autobiography has not been taken seriously as a historical text. My contention in this chapter will be that Canetti's near-exclusion from exile studies is suggestive of two interconnected points, which may help to qualify Strelka's contention that critics should elevate artistry above thematics.[4]

While the near exclusion of Canetti's work from exile studies is the responsibility of scholars and critics, it also suggests that Canetti's writing may be resistant to the critic's desire that narratives should also be impersonal metanarratives, offering conceptual paradigms of human experience. For Canetti's narrative has little to say about the virtue of giving priority to the collective, whether in terms of racial, linguistic, religious or cultural groupings. It is thus implicitly critical of the very methodological criteria which critics use to justify their choice of subject matter on the basis of national or ethnic premises. Authors are taken seriously because they can provide documentary or testimonial evidence of what it might mean to survive as a Jew or as a German-speaking intellectual in exile from some kind of original homeland as a consequence of the ideology of National Socialism. Exile studies further identifies home in impersonal and spatial terms, and as synonymous with language, race, religion or culture.

If one isolates points relating to language in Canetti's autobiography, however, it is clear that language is always presented as if it were an aspect of Canetti's personal biography. Although the autobiography is written exclusively in German, it is hardly a sustained attempt to promote the German language as such. Its references to the fact that German was specifically chosen as Canetti's literary language, and one chosen from a number of possible languages, do not indicate that Canetti felt particularly moved by the ideological debate about how 'proper' it would be to use a language so apparently devalued by the National Socialists. The polyglot members of Canetti's family in Rustschuk are not primarily presented as if they were linguists (the fact that Canetti's grandfather spoke seventeen languages becomes a relatively incidental detail). Rather they are shrouded in charisma, remembered as they are through the eyes of an impressionable child who is entranced by the aura that surrounds the adult world. A fair amount of narrative space is dedicated to the gruelling experience of acquiring German in Lausanne, yet only in terms of Canetti's extraordinary awareness of the extent of his mother's passion for high standards. That Canetti has chosen to write exclusively in a language, German, which was not his first language, *can* be read as an almighty tribute to his mother and to the punishing experience of learning from her. By the same token, the fact that German was a private language between his parents is recorded in terms of Canetti's appreciation of its role in the development of their love. There is a plain and simple appreciation of the theatrical aspects of language, particularly of 'Wienerisch'. Above all, there is an appreciation of the way in which words can be used economically and with power, a point which will become clear in my discussion of Canetti's relationship with Fritz Wotruba.

Canetti's narrative shows by example that the desire to appropriate narratives for metanarratives is reductive. His fascination with highly personal details suggests that such an attitude is destructive of the inalienable uniqueness of each human experience, and each human subject. Indeed, his attention to the inalienable truth of detail undermines the abstract, totalising drive of metanarrative. There is thus little in Canetti's autobiography on what it 'means' to have to leave, or to choose to leave, a linguistic, cultural, religious or national home, not least because Canetti rejects definitions of home which equate home with geographical *space*.[5] His concept of *resistance is* not directed towards sociopolitical issues, as in the case of authors like Ernst Toller and Klaus Mann, for whom existence is primarily a matter of taking on sociopolitical causes.[6] Canetti's aesthetics and politics of resistance are of a different kind, and have little in common with the idea of resistance normally encountered in exile studies, where it is usually equated with resistance to political or racial persecution.

Canetti's narrative works with a very challenging assumption, namely that the individual should make a priority of those personal details of his life which are *emotionally* meaningful to him, as a way of *preserving* the full integrity of the self and protecting it from violation by sociopolitical ideology of any kind. This is a substantially different point of departure from the view that the priority should be with *defending* the self against impersonal forces in the world beyond the individual's imagination. By being brutally clear about the wealth and depth of each individual human experience, Canetti also becomes capable of defying and celebrating as life-giving, in terms of dynamic human relationships, something that other exiled authors tend to assume only exists in the sociopolitical realm, namely power. Canetti chooses to meet and negotiate the challenge of power as it is embodied in individual personalities. Finally, in denying that identity should be constituted by impersonal factors and repudiating membership of those communities founded on very general notions of purity or exclusivity, whether of language, culture, religion or nation, he reveals how we can open up possibilities for ourselves related to an ideal freedom, which celebrates personal identity. Such possibilities preserve the uniqueness of each human subject. As such, they cannot seriously promote discrimination.

The silent subtext of the autobiography is thus very aware of the fact that all thinking which makes an issue of the determinants of human behaviour and experience in terms of race, sex, class, colour or creed is vulnerable to exploitation by the very evils which it wishes to combat. The subtext is shot through with the knowledge that the repeated use of common denominators stifles the scope for uniqueness and originality: repeatedly to make an issue of the impersonal may imply a failure of the imagination as an instrument of creativity, above all of happiness.

Despite the attempts made by critics, like Sander Gilman, to isolate aspects of the Jewish 'issue' in Canetti's autobiography, and to appropriate his insights for metanarratives, the bulk of narrative space in Canetti's autobiography is actually dedicated to human relationships and what sustains them.[7] The narrator is fascinated by those highly personal communities of self-selecting; elect sister souls, so boldly promoted by his hero, Stendhal.[8] Canetti, like Stendhal, does not believe, emotionally, in the state or experience of exile. He firmly believes in the possibility of freedom and happiness at all times, in spite of the endless constraints that may be imposed on individuals in the course of their lives. Canetti, throughout his narrative, promotes 'the happy few', those individuals who love one another because they share a delight, both personal and social, in self-creation. Such people choose one another because they enjoy cooperating with those who make a priority of the humanist goal of subordinating social culture to the goal of personal culture, especially with those who believe that identity is best constituted by the uniquely personal experience. The only justification for this strategy for living lies in the way in which it yields practical fruits in terms of personal happiness and pleasure: personal culture tends to nourish, complement and perpetuate natural bonds, such as those of love. Finally, a survey of Canetti's favourite people indicates, rather unusually in terms of the history of love in Western literature, that his 'passion for people' is really love, which may also be construed as a synonym for friendship.[9]

While it is obvious that very little in the autobiography lends itself to documentary interpretation, partly because of Canetti's easy cosmopolitanism, one could nevertheless reply that this can be accounted for by the kind of socioeconomic privileges which Canetti inherited at birth. He may simply have reacted positively to his new surrounding after 1938, when he first settled in 'exile' in London, because of these privileges. This ability to create a sense of home is corroborated, amusingly, by John Willett, who writes that Canetti, when he lived in London, was able to transform an ordinary English café in Hampstead into a Viennese-style literary coffeehouse.[11] And the same idea must have been in Steven Beller's mind when he coined the witty phrase: 'If you like: is not London NW6 one of the last bastions of the Habsburg Monarchy?'[12] While this would be an easy way of dismissing the achievement of the autobiography, the passages which I have chosen should reveal that the rhetorical drive of the narrative questions such a response.

Canetti's refusal of the categories which are common in exile studies and susceptible to exploitation is expressed by implying that the details of his life are unique to him as a named individual in the first instance, and then unique as such in the second instance. This curious ability to see *both* the general in the particular *and* the particular in the general is reflected in the very way in which the narrative assumes that the reader is a creator himself, and a believer in the power of creativity. The details of Canetti's life are narrated in ways which appeal to the imagination of his readers in terms of inventiveness and resilience and in terms of the reader's ability to appreciate the art of self-preservation as a necessary life-skill.[13]

If the autobiography asks, primarily, to be read in terms of the relationships which it depicts between two individuals, it does so in ways which turn all aspects of relations between individuals into powerful rituals, fuelled by the power which lies at the heart of the personalities which Canetti celebrates in his life-story. In the classic account of the death of his father, the representation of his mother's reaction enacts the violence of shock and, in doing so, asserts the importance of passion as a way of life:

> Er ging wie immer zum Frühstück hinunter. Es dauerte nicht lang und wir hörten gellende Rufe. Die Gouvernante stürzte die Treppe hinunter, ich ihr nach. Von der offenen Tür des Speisezimmers sah ich den Vater am Boden liegen. Er lag seiner ganzen Länge nach, zwischen Tisch und

Kamin, ganz nah am Kamin, sein Gesicht war weiß, er hatte Schaum um den Mund, die Mutter kniete neben ihm und schrie: 'Jacques, sprich zu mir, sprich zu mir, Jacques, Jacques, sprich zu mir!'[14]

[He went down to breakfast as usual. Before long we heard loud yells. The governess dashed down the stairs, I followed at her heels. By the open door to the dining-room, I saw my father lying on the floor. He was stretched out full length, between the table and the fireplace, very close to the fireplace, his face was white, he had foam on his mouth, Mother knelt at his side, crying: 'Jacques, speak to me, speak to me, Jacques, Jacques, speak to me!'][15]

The breathtaking, ruthless authority and determination of Canetti's mother as a teacher are likewise remembered in ways which both ritualise the experience itself and make her power as a creator and passion as a human being self-evident:

Ich weiß nicht, wieviel Sätze sie mir das erste Mal zumutete, sagen wir bescheiden: einige; ich fürchte, es waren viele. Sie entließ mich, sagte: 'Wiederhole dir das für dich. Du darfst keinen Satz vergessen. Nicht einen einzigen. Morgen machen wir weiter.' Sie behielt das Buch, und ich war ratlos mir selber überlassen. (p. 83)

[I don't know how many sentences she expected to drill me in the first time; let us conservatively say a few; I fear it was many. She let me go, saying: 'Repeat it all to yourself. You must not forget a single sentence. Not a single one. Tomorrow, we shall continue.' She kept the book and I was left to myself, perplexed.]

That this encounter between mother and son, so punishing in itself, resulted in the exclamation 'Ich habe einen Idioten zum Sohn!' (My son's a complete idiot) is not an invitation to self-pity or pathos. It is simply proof of the extent to which Canetti abhors any of the emotions which are debilitating in terms of self-preservation. Hence the frequency of laconic understatement in the course of the narrative. At the conclusion to the above episode, for instance, the sentence 'Den Terror, in dem ich lebte, hielt sie für pädagogisch' (She felt that the state of terror in which I lived was all part of the teaching process) states the obvious – only a wantonly fantastic reading of the scene could conclude otherwise. At the same time it refuses, utterly, to indulge in the business of recrimination, thus expressing a vote of confidence for dignity in the face of power. Here, Canetti's mother's power is really a synonym for an ability to do things with passion, *as if you thought they were worth while*; and the power of her son is enshrined in his dignified acceptance of his mother's power and passion, and in his refusal to minimise the extent of either. There is no explicit commentary and no analysis of the implications of her behaviour in terms of theory. It is simply given, as power is given.

There are also countless examples of the way in which Canetti's intersubjective encounters are productive of a sense of life. Whereas Sander Gilman dredges the text for themes pertinent to the cause of promoting the categories dear to exile studies – in the case of his survey in *Jewish Self-Hatred*, the apparent hostility of the Western Jew to the Eastern Jew – the autobiography actually excels at the artistry involved in creating and sustaining human relationships.[16] It does so, not primarily in the sense that it is admiring of the relationships which formed the substance of Canetti's actual life, but in terms of the way in which the text relates to its readers. The text presupposes the kind of reader who relishes intersubjective encounters of all kinds.

Dominating the story of his life is Canetti's relationship with his mother, a relationship which has inevitably attracted attention on account of its strength and intensity, and on account of the way in which it inverts the normative conventions usually thought to inform mother-son relationships.[17] Waltraud Wiethölter sees in the relationship evidence of Elias Canetti's omnipotence fantasy, of a rivalry between mother and son and of an Oedipus complex.[18] Friederike Eigler sees in the autobiography, more generally, evidence of Canetti's psychological need to define himself in opposition to other selves, as a way of protecting his own ego and his unquestioning sense of his own superiority. While it goes without saying that theory has a wonderful ability to deny individuality in favour of blank anonymous ideas about the workings of the human mind, it would be appropriate to remember the number of times that Canetti pays tribute to his mother's power as a creative influence, in terms of small, local details. His mother's amazing fear of mice makes her particularly human, when it is set alongside her terrifying strength of character. Her withering hatred of anything resembling secular success or material ambition, and her overriding passion for all pursuits of the mind and intellect, for anything which could be seen, heard and discussed, for all human beings who have any kind of character, above all her idealism – these qualities are all felt very powerfully. Indeed, Canetti's autobiography is so capable of distilling her spirit that one feels personally implicated in her almighty challenge to her son, as she lies on her death-bed, punishing him with her eyes for having hurt her by having married the woman he loved, Veza, and kept it a secret:

> Es war wieder ihr Gesicht mit den unersättlichen Nüstern. Die Augen, viel größer, blickten auf mich und sie sagte nicht: Ich will dich nicht sehen! Was tust du hier! Ich habe dich nicht gerufen! Im Duft, den sie erkannte, hatte ich mich eingeschlichen. Sie fragte nicht, sie ergab sich ganz dem Duft und mir war, als weite sich ihre Stirn und als müßten ihre unverkennbaren Worte kommen. Ich wartete auf harte Worte und fürchtete sie. Ich hörte ihren bitteren Vorwurf, als hätte sie ihn wieder ausgesprochen: Ihr habt geheiratet. Du hast mir nichts gesagt. Du hast mich belogen.[19]

> [Once again she had that look about her, her nostrils insatiable. Her eyes, which were larger, looked at me. She did not say: I don't want to see you again! What are you doing here! I didn't call you! I crept in with the air which she recognised. She did not ask me anything, she

acknowledged my air, I thought that her forehead indicated she was about to give me the benefit of more of her utterly unmistakable words. I waited for hard words and was afraid of them. I heard her bitter reproach, as if it had been expressed out loud again: You married, the pair of you. You didn't tell me anything about it. You lied to me.]

That elusive quality which Henry James called the sense of 'felt life' characterises the autobiography, in the sense that the enactment of experience flatters the reader's own ability to live life intensely. Yet the autobiography does not make a virtue out of Canetti's own uniqueness by implying that he is exceptional or superior, as so many autobiographies do: it assumes that we are all equal in our capacity to live life to the full. The extent of the intensity of experience in the autobiography is such that one soon forgets that Canetti is *re*membering or *re*collecting the past. On balance, far more creative and imaginative energy is committed to the dramatic enactment of scenes already experienced, *as if* they were still real, not just to the Canetti who is remembering as he writes and writing as he remembers, but to the reader as (s)he reads. In this sense they have been salvaged, altogether, from the possibility of loss and destruction.

We can turn now to the relationship with another loved one, Veza. First and foremost, given that Canetti married Veza and that *Die Fackel im Ohr* is dedicated to her, the story of the relationship is fiercely protective of itself, a feature of the narrative which has caused Bernd Witte to comment that the portrait of Veza is 'strikingly abstract and impersonal' ('seltsam abstrakt und unpersönlich').[20] Veza is known to us as a lover of books, and as an independent spirit, not as Elias Canetti's lover. Again, a feature of this close relationship is the sense in which it is possible to cooperate with another person's powerfully individual, unique and idiosyncratic differences. One can argue that Canetti tends to equate love with intellectual intimacy and friendship above all, not sentiment as such: while he admired Gogol and Stendhal, Veza liked Flaubert and Tolstoy and the two positively relished intellectual combat: 'Es gab Kämpfe, doch nie einen Sieger'[21] (There were battles, but never a victor). Veza's delight at Elias's ignorance of Büchner's *Woyzeck* underlines the sense in which a relationship is positively enriched by differences of opinion and differences in experience. It also leads on to another important point about the way in which experience is treated in the autobiography.

My example here is taken from the passage in *Das Augenspiel* where Canetti relates how he ran to visit Veza and wake her up one night, after he had read *Woyzeck* for the first time. Veza appears to be full of contempt, and Canetti expects her to indicate that she does not think much of Büchner's work. He is proved wrong:

> 'Und davon hältst du nichts?' Ich sagte es drohend und böse, sie merkte plötzlich, worum es ging.
> 'Wer? Ich? Ich halte davon nichts? Ich halte es für das größte Drama der deutschen Literatur.'

Ich traute meinen Ohren nicht und sagte irgend etwas: 'Es ist doch
ein Fragment!'
'Fragment! Fragment! Nennst du das ein Fragment? Was darin fehlt,
ist noch besser, als was in den besten anderen Dramen da ist. Man
möchte sich mehr solche Fragmente wünschen.'
'Du hast mir nie ein Wort darüber gesagt. Kennst du Büchner schon
lange?'
'Länger als dich. Ich habe ihn schon früher gelesen. Zur gleichen
Zeit als ich auf Hebbels Tagebücher und auf Lichtenberg stieß.'
'Aber du hast über ihn geschwiegen! So oft hast du mir Stellen aus
Hebbel und aus Lichtenberg gezeigt. Über den Wozzeck hast du
geschwiegen. Warum nur? Warum?'[22]

['And you don't think anything of it?' I said this in a threatening and
malicious kind of way, and she immediately picked this up and knew
what I was about.
'Who? Me? I don't think much of it? I think it's the greatest play in
German literature.'
I couldn't believe my ears and said something like: 'But it's a
fragment, you know!'
'Fragment! Fragment! You call that a fragment? What's lacking there
is much better than what you normally find in the best plays. I wish
there were more fragments like that one.'
'You never said a word to me. Have you known about Büchner for a
long time?'
'Longer than you. I read him some time ago. At the same time I came
across Hebbel's diaries and Lichtenberg.'
'But you kept quiet about him! And you kept showing me bits of
Hebbel and Lichtenberg. You kept quiet about Wozzeck. Why, why?']

Canetti makes frequent use of what Henry James described as the 'scenic
method' – the exploitation of dialogue in prose to make experience seem as
vital as it is in non-literary life. It is the use of dialogue which makes it
possible for the reader to experience what Canetti describes with absolutely no
loss of intensity. Not only has the very spirit of life been successfully distilled
from the historical moment to which the details of his life are linked: it has
been preserved intact. It is in this way that Canetti's autobiography is in a
class of its own: it destroys the division of time into mutually exclusive units
– the past, the present, the future – a division absolutely crucial to those
writers who believe in Exile and its corollary Loss. And it does so to
demonstrate that linear time can be transcended in favour of something like
the perpetual present of the imagination, a perpetual present which has very
little to do with memory as a place where memories are stored, and everything
to do with the way in which the imagination is endlessly capable of creating/
recreating the past *as if it were still present.*[23] The timelessness of Canetti's
autobiography, to which Strelka obliquely refers in his insistence on the
importance of the kind of literature which has the status of art, has, therefore,

nothing to do with linear time at all. The timelessness is Canetti's attitude to life, and that attitude to life implies an unusual degree of pride, as indeed love. The two combine in favour of the idea that preservation is crucial to survival on qualitative terms: you can preserve what you love and keep its sense of life and meaning intact by an act of the imagination, and without having to sell out to the devils lurking in the shadows. Canetti's imagination is alive enough not to be vulnerable to apocalyptic thinking, and it never degenerates into melancholia.

In *Das Augenspiel*, Canetti discusses at length his relationship with the sculptor Fritz Wotruba. I have implied that the narrative of Canetti's relationships with his mother and with Veza are tributes to them as people, and the narrative space dedicated to Fritz Wotruba, his 'twin brother', is no exception.[24] Here, one can marvel at Canetti's ability to approve of another person's being. Wotruba's creation of the sculpture 'Der schwarze Stehende' itself becomes the centrepiece of their relationship. Canetti marvels at the discriminating *man* in him, the creator who does not reserve his creativity for sculpture, who knows that there is an art to life:

> Seine Worte waren von der Kraft geladen, mit der er sie zurückhielt. Er war nicht schweigsam und äußerte sich zu vielem. Aber er wußte, was er sagte, ein müßiges Geplätscher habe ich von ihm nie gehört. Auch wenn es nicht um seine eigentlichsten Anliegen ging, hatten seine Sätze immer Richtung ... Wotrubas Sprache hatte mit Nestroy vielleicht nur das eine gemein: die Herbheit, eben das Gegenteil dessen, was sonst als Wiener Süße überall in der Welt beliebt und verrufen ist. (pp. 109–10)

> [His words were loaded with the power with which he kept them under control. He was not the silent type and had something to say about a lot of things. But he always knew what he was talking about, a mere dabbling with words was something you would never have expected of him. Even if the issue had nothing to do with his own concerns, his sentences always knew where they were going. That was the only thing Wotruba's language had in common with Nestroy: austerity, that very quality not generally associated with the Viennese language, which tends to be admired or despised for its sweetness.]

This analysis of the most important relationships in Canetti's life has indicated that his life-story is all about personal culture, about the rituals of life with one's loved ones. It has become clear that the *way* in which Canetti narrates his life-story is symbolic of his conviction that his readers are capable of living life intensely: he stages his scenes in ways which appeal to our artistic skills as creators, capable of negotiating power when it is at work in personalities around us and of using such dynamic intersubjective encounters to create and perpetuate bonds of love. This achievement may also be read ideologically, as a vote of confidence in our ability to sustain a sense of the uniqueness of ourselves and our experiences, if we want to survive and resist discrimination.

In so many of the accounts of exile literature, as in so many of the primary texts on which they focus, the silent view taken, if rarely expressed, is an opposed one, namely that the possibility of sustaining the self under pressure does not exist. The focus on loss, on rootlessness, on non-assimilation, on the failure of sociopolitical commitment and the problem of 'being' a German in a post-1 945 world, conspires to suggest, especially in autobiographical narratives, that those writers who were more directly affected by 1939–45 than Canetti effectively lost their faith in the purpose of life and in humanity as a whole. While this is obviously understandable, it seems that exile studies may be doing violence to the dignity of those testimonial accounts of loss, in its rigorous determination to exploit such accounts for other purposes. The first generation of writers to chronicle the experience of loss has now given way to a generation of critics, whose preoccupation with the spoils of the destructive past is suspect. Exile critics tend to privilege the works of writers who identify themselves racially or nationally as exiles. Because of the prominence given to race and nationality as 'methodological' criteria for selection, this has the effect of perpetuating the very ideology which such writers found abhorrent when it took the form of National Socialism. Yet the implications of this ideology remain hidden because such critics tend to celebrate their subjects as victims, making them into martyrs to the cause of truth. The recent dramatic increase in the number of publications which have been produced under the rubric of exile studies may indeed reflect a belated awareness of German guilt about the Second World War.

Adorno and Horkheimer attempted in their *Dialektik der Aufklärung* to attribute the rise of National Socialism to the spirit of the Enlightenment, identified as the evil which fostered the dogmatic mind-set which produced the ideology of fascism, and hence also its human victims. Yet the very paradigm which they develop in the course of their survey is one which instates the model of innocent victim and guilty aggressor: reason is identified as guilty of the evils associated with National Socialism, just as reason gave birth to innocent human victims. This binary thinking has been used repeatedly since 1945 by intellectuals on the political left, especially in Germany. Heinrich Böll and Günter Grass created the framework for 'critiques' of German society based on a relentlessly naive and imaginatively paralysing model of innocent victim and guilty aggressor. Exile studies form part of this large and diffuse phenomenon, which tends to *encourage* people to think in binary terms that render combative action or thinking redundant. Some of the most prestigious German newspapers implicitly endorse this binary model. *Die Zeit* thought it pertinent to republish Adorno's essay 'Erziehung nach Auschwitz' in the wake of the racist attacks in Rostock. In doing so, it further endorsed the links which intellectuals on the left like to see between Auschwitz and the present, yet in terms which do not allow for *negotiating* ways out of chaos and disorder. And in an article published in 1994 in the same newspaper, Ulrich Greiner, commenting on the popularity of Spielberg's *Schindler's List*, bemoaned the way in which 'Germans' still have to learn 'about' 'Auschwitz' from Hollywood. In so doing, he endorsed the polarised model on which the film was based, according to which all Jews are victims deserving of our sympathy and almost all Germans are perverse and worthy of our condemnation. The recent reminder by Rafael Seligmann in *Der Spiegel* that the continued identification of the Jews with Auschwitz would constitute the formal triumph of Hitler's thinking, and his emphasis on the tendency among those who reflect on Auschwitz to be intellectually numbed by the details of the Holocaust, only goes part of the way towards disentangling these deep confusions.[25]

Canetti's continued vote of confidence in creativity, his celebration of artistry and his insistence on the inviolable uniqueness of personal detail, can be read as a reminder, therefore, of the vulnerability to abuse of so many of the largely thematic criteria invoked by exile studies. There is a danger not simply of sustaining a perverse romance of Exile and Loss, but also of sustaining a perverse romance of covert racism and covert nationalism based on the model of aggressor and victim. Canetti admires power when it becomes a synonym for passion, and in his willingness to negotiate power in the spirit of passion he not only celebrates those who treat life seriously as a challenge, but also reminds us that power and passion produce the kind of systematic commitment which is creative of life. He reminds us that power and passion are destructive of the debilitating drive of that melancholy which induces the paralysis which has led to the continued, widespread acceptance of the binary model as a way of 'negotiating' the world. Ernst Toller ends his autobiography with a series of rhetorical questions which reinstate German nationalism, and the possibility of a messianic comeback by Germany. Klaus Mann ends his autobiography with a series of rhetorical reflections on the 'meaning' of German national identity. In Canetti's autobiography, we have a sustained use of rhetorical *devices,* all of which bespeak the conviction that to identify oneself as a unique individual, without recourse to race, religion, creed, nationhood or colour, is to secure both the possibility of non-discrimination and the advantages of compelling personal encounters with other human beings.

Notes

1. Joseph Strelka, 'Material Collectors, Political Rhetoricians, and Amateurs: Current Methodological Problems in German Exile Literature Studies', in *Protest – Form – Tradition: Essays on German Exile Literature*, ed. Joseph P. Strelka, Robert F. Bell and Eugene Dobson (Alabama, 1979), pp. 1–14 (p. 11).
2. Richard Critchfield, 'Autobiographie als Geschichtsdeutung', in *Deutschsprachige Exilliteratur: Studien zu ihrer Bestimmung im Kontext der Epoche 1930 bis 1960*, ed. Wulf Koepke and Michael Winkler (Bonn, 1984), pp. 228–41 (p. 228).
3. See Reinhold Grimm and Jost Hermand (eds), *Exil und Innere Emigration: Third Wisconsin Workshop* (Frankfurt, 1972); Peter Uwe Hohendahl and Egon Schwarz (eds), *Exil und Innere Emigration II: Internationale Tagung in St Louis* (Frankfurt, 1973); Ingeborg Drewitz, *Die zerstörte Kontinuität: Exilliteratur und Literatur des Widerstandes* (Vienna, 1981); John M. Spalek and Robert F. Bell (eds), *Exile: The Writer's Experience* (Chapel Hill, 1982); Joseph Strelka (ed.), *Exilliteratur: Grundprobleme der Theorie: Aspekte der Geschichte und Kritik* (Bern, 1983); and Andreas Dybowski, *Endstation, Wartesaal oder Schatzkammer für die Zukunft: Die deutsche Exilliteratur und ihre Wirkung und Bewertung in der westdeutschen*

Nachkriegsrepublik (Frankfurt, 1989) for examples of the way in which Canetti has been formally excluded from consideration. In a volume edited by Manfred Durzak, *Die deutsche Exilliteratur 1933–1945* (Stuttgart, 1973), a short article by Viktor Suchy entitled 'Exil in Permanenz. Elias Canetti und der unbedingte Primat des Lebens', pp. 282–90, only celebrates the autobiography in terms of something as vague as its sense of life.

4. For a recent attempt to look at the autobiography in terms of its artistry and internal tensions, see David Darby, 'A Literary Life: The Textuality of Elias Canetti's Autobiography', *Modern Austrian Literature*, 25 (1992), 37–49.

5. For a reading of Canetti's own relationship to the German language, see Yaier Cohen, 'Elias Canetti: Exile and the German Language', *German Life and Letters*, 42 (1988), 32–45. See also Hans Fabian, 'Die Sprache bei Elias Canetti: Exil als Asyl', in *Das Exilerlebnis: Verhandlungen des Vierten Symposium über deutsche und österreichische Exilliteratur*, ed. Donald Daviau and Ludwig Fischer (Columbia, 1982), pp. 497–504.

6. For a review of the various branches within exile studies, consult Wulf Koepke and Michael Winkler (eds), *Exilliteratur 1933–1945* (Darmstadt, 1989), in particular Werner Mittenzwei, 'Ästhetik des Widerstands' (pp. 141–65), who argues for the creation of the aesthetic category of resistance writing to honour those who used writing as a means of fighting against fascism.

7. See Sander Gilman, *Jewish Self-Hatred. Anti-Semitism and the Hidden Language of the Jews* (Baltimore, 1986) for evidence of Canetti's distancing himself from the 'Ostjude' in *Die Fackel im Ohr*. By classifying Canetti as a polyglot, Westernising, assimilated Jew and referring exclusively to the chapter involving Eva Reichmann and Backenroth (the Ostjude), Gilman tends to perpetuate binary thinking, ignoring the possibility that Canetti's non-response to Backenroth might just be an unusual case of his passivity.

8. See Ingeborg Brandt, '"Stendhal war meine Bibel": Gespräch mit Elias Canetti, dem Autor der *Blendung*', *Welt am Sonntag*, 8 November 1963. Also see Christine Meyer, 'La vie de Henry Brulard comme modèle pour l'autobiographie de Canetti', *Austriaca*, 33 (1991), 89–107.

9. Elias Canetti, *Das Augenspiel*, reprinted (Munich, 1988), p. 136.

10. See Gerhard Hirschfeld (ed.), *Exil in Großbritannien. Zur Emigration aus dem nationalsozialistischen Deutschland* (Stuttgart, 1983).

11. See John Willett, 'Die Künste der Emigration', in *Exil in Großbritannien*, pp. 183–204 (p. 186).

12. Steven Beller, 'The Jewish Intellectual and Vienna in the 1930s', in *Austria in the Thirties: Culture and Politics*, ed. Kenneth Segar and John Warren (Riverside, 1991), pp. 309–27 (p. 323).

13. See Harriet Murphy's study of Canetti's *Die Blendung* (forthcoming with the State University of New York Press).

14. Elias Canetti, *Die gerettete Zunge*, reprinted (Munich, 1977), p. 68.

15. All translations are by Harriet Murphy.

16. See note 7 above.

17. The most important full-length or detailed studies of the autobiography look at Canetti ahistorically and psychologically. See Barbara Saunders, *Contemporary German Autobiography: Literary Approaches to the Problem of Identity* (London, 1985); Madeleine Salzmann, *Die Kommunikationsstruktur der Autobiographie mit kommunikationsorientierten Analysen der Autobiographien von Max Frisch, Helga M. Novak und Elias Canetti* (Bern, 1988); and Friederike Eigler, *Das autobiographische Werk von Elias Canetti: Verwandlung, Identität, Machtausübung* (Tübingen, 1988).

18. Waltraud Wiethölter, 'Sprechen-Lesen-Schreiben: Zur Funktion von Sprache und Schrift in Canettis Autobiographie', *DVjs*, 64 (1990), 149–71.

19. Elias Canetti, *Das Augenspiel*, p. 300.
20. Bernd Witte, 'Der Erzähler as Tod-Feind: Zu Canettis Autobiographie', *Text und Kritik*, 28 (1982), 65–72 (p. 72).
21. Elias Canetti, *Die Fackel im Ohr*, p. 207.
22. Elias Canetti, *Das Augenspiel*, p. 17.
23. Wolfgang Paulsen, *Das Ich im Spiegel der Sprache: Autobiographisches Schreiben in der deutschen Literatur des 20. Jahrhunderts* (Tübingen, 1991), misses the point when he merely marvels at the capacity of Canetti's memory, in his cursory glance at the autobiography (pp. 162–5). Alfred Doppler also marvels at the epic breadth of the autobiography in terms of its ability to realise a whole period and to remember so many details: Alfred Doppler, 'Gestalten und Figuren als Elemente der Zeit- und Lebensgeschichte: Canettis autobiographische Bücher', in idem, *Geschichte im Spiegel der Literatur: Aufsätze zur österreichischen Literatur des 19. und 20. Jahrhunderts* (Innsbruck, 1990), pp. 197–204 (p. 204).
24. See Harriet Murphy, 'Fritz Wotruba: The neglected master of stone', *The European*, 12 October 1990.
25. Rafael Seligmann, 'Republik der Betroffenen' *Der Spiegel*, 14/1994, pp. 92–3 (p. 93).

Part Two
Review Articles

The Exodus from Austria

J. M. Ritchie

Wolfgang Muchitsch (ed.), *Österreicher im Exil. Großbritannien 1938–1945. Eine Dokumentation* (Vienna: Österreichischer Bundesverlag, 1992), 652 pp., 290 Sch.

Wolfgang Muchitsch, *Mit Spaten, Waffen und Worten: Die Einbindung österreichischer Flüchtlinge in die britischen Kriegsanstrengungen 1939–1945* (Vienna: Europa Verlag, 1992), xii + 266 pp., 348 Sch.

Peter Weibel and Friedrich Stadler (eds), *Vertreibung der Vernunft. The Cultural Exodus from Austria* (Vienna: Löcker Verlag, 1993), 394 + 172 pp.

Jörg Schöning (ed.), *London Calling: Deutsche im britischen Film der dreißiger Jahre* (Munich: edition text und kritik, 1993), 172 pp.

Christian Cargnelli and Michael Omasta (eds), *Aufbruch ins Ungewisse. Österreichische Filmschaffende in der Emigration vor 1945*, 2 vols (Vienna: Edition Wespennest, 1993), 484 pp. 340 Sch./DM 50.

Wolfgang Benz (ed.), *Das Exil der kleinen Leute. Alltagserfahrungen österreichischer Juden in der Emigration* (Munich: Beck, 1991), 344 pp., DM 48.00.

Adi Wimmer, *Die Heimat wurde ihnen fremd, die Fremde nicht zur Heimat* (Vienna: Verlag für Gesellschaftskritik, 1993), 236 pp., 248 Sch.

Whereas until recently the Austrians could have been accused of being very slow to come to terms with their National Socialist past, especially as far as the enforced emigration and systematic annihilation of Austrian citizens are concerned, there is no doubt that serious efforts are now being made to catch up. The volumes under review provide tangible evidence of this. Since 1975, the Dokumentationsarchiv des österreichischen Widerstandes (DÖW for short) has been collecting information on Austrians in Exile 1934–45, building on the support of the Bundesministerium für Wissenschaft und Forschung. For various pragmatic reasons, this massive project was broken up on a regional basis, and volumes have appeared on Austrians in France, in Spain (the

149

Spanish Civil War) and in Belgium. Further volumes are to follow on the USA, Latin America, Switzerland, the Soviet Union and Czechoslovakia. As far as Great Britain is concerned, the project has been extremely fortunate to find a quite outstanding editor in Wolfgang Muchitsch, who first showed his mettle with his diploma dissertation for the University of Graz in 1986: *Der Anschluß. Die Darstellung und Beurteilung des Anschlusses Österreichs an Deutschland in der englischen Geschichtswissenschaft.* This gave him the necessary firm foundation in British source-work, for his later book *Mit Spaten, Waffen und Worten* is quite immaculate, not only in the presentation in highly readable form of very complicated material, but also in the evident mastery of the subject. The same mastery and clarity of presentation are the features of his edition of documents devoted to Austrians in exile in Great Britain 1939–45, a volume which by its very subject matter is bulkier than any of the preceding volumes in the series.

In this documentation volume, Wolfgang Muchitsch is responsible for all the introductory material to the different sections, and for the selection and processing of the material itself, all of which must have presented an extremely arduous task. The volume itself is introduced by Herbert Steiner, who can speak not only as an academic authority on the subject of exile in Great Britain, but also as one who was there. In May 1988, fifty years after the National Socialist occupation of Austria, some 400 former members of Young Austria in Great Britain came together, though sadly the numbers were affected by sickness and death. Erich Fried was one who had to cry off on grounds of ill-health – he died not long afterwards. Great Britain, Steiner reminds us, was an extremely important country of exile for Austrians, especially after the occupation of Paris and the fall of France. For this reason, it is perhaps regrettable that until now histories of exile and exile literature have tended to focus on German individuals and German organisations in London, like the Free German League of Culture, although latterly Austrians in exile and Austrian or Czech exile organisations became more prominent and significant than their German equivalents. The present volume should help to correct the balance.

Because of the constraints of the series, Muchitsch, as editor, must largely follow the pattern set by previous volumes; nevertheless, the aim has remained the same, namely to allow the documents to speak for themselves, and it is precisely the consequent accessibility of sources otherwise only available in the specialist archives of London and Vienna which constitutes the value of such a book. In general terms, the nature of immigration into Britain is now well documented, but even so the sheer scale and scope of the numbers involved in a mass emigration of this kind only come across through the documents collected here, revealing the extent of all the personal tragedies, the governmental and charity organisations which sprang up to deal with the crisis, the 'Kindertransporte' rescuing at least the children if not the parents, and much more. The documents reproduced in the first section record the necessity for holders of German and Austrian passports to have the required visas for entry into the United Kingdom. Later, the documents record the debate over whether Austrians should be differentiated from Germans. Very interesting is the extent to which exceptions were made for famous refugees like Stefan Zweig (who was to spend some six years in England) or the Freud household, while others were destined to be admitted only on domestic service visas. Similarly, Oskar Kokoschka would end up in a flat in the West End of London; others in less salubrious households in less attractive regions of Great Britain. Not to be forgotten either is the part played by the Czech Refugee Fund from 1938 onwards. What is sometimes no longer apparent, fifty or so years after these events, is the general public's awareness of what was going on in Germany and Austria. Showing desperate appeals for help as they appeared in the 1930s in newspapers like the *Manchester Guardian* is a simple reminder that the normal newspaper-reader in Britain could not have failed to know what was happening.

Perhaps it is an essentially British method of responding to a crisis, but one is struck by the range of (at first sight amateurish) charity organisations which either sprang up, or were to some extent already in place, and which took it upon themselves to help the flood of refugees. Initially this may seem less than one would hope for, if it is assumed that Government policy and official agencies accomplish more. Then it becomes apparent that the Quakers, the German Jewish Aid Committee, the Church of England Committee for Non-Aryan Christians and all the other charities were capable of performing miracles. Despite the visa restrictions and despite restrictive Government policies, many thousands of desperate refugees were admitted to the safe haven of these shores through such help. Many would treat the British Isles as a brief respite in the quest for an even safer haven, for example in the United States; nevertheless, it would be hard to find a country which did more than Britain to alleviate the plight of the refugees.

In any history of the period, the British Government's mistaken policy of interning potentially dangerous 'enemy aliens' inevitably plays a major part and still divides opinions to this day. While from the Government point of view it is understandable how such a blunder could happen – the collapse of France, the spectre of a Fifth Column, the force of Vansittartism – it does seem incomprehensible that Jewish refugees, who had only just escaped from Nazi concentration camps, could be interned alongside real Nazis. Even more incomprehensible is the policy decision that resulted in the transportation of so called 'enemy aliens' to faraway colonies like Canada and Australia, again in some cases bundling Jewish refugees together with unrepentant Nazis. Equally distressing for many refugees were the tribunals which decided whether one was an enemy alien worthy of being interned or not, tribunals inevitably in many cases carried out by people with only the sketchiest knowledge either about real conditions in Germany or Austria, or the real reasons forcing Jews and non-Jews alike into exile. Pride of place among the real-life testimonies of the experience of internment is taken by the long poem by Theodor Kramer on the internees of Huyton. An even longer poem by Erich Fried, 'Ein Jahr Internierung', published in the London exile newspaper *Die Zeitung* in 1941, is not quite so impressive, because he was never himself an internee. Much of the discussion at the time, before, during and after internment, was clearly taken up by the question of work – what could refugees do in their land of exile, or rather, what were they allowed to do? Gradually, as the war progressed, the initial restrictions were relaxed and work did become available, in the sense of both keeping body and soul together and picking up the threads of broken careers and lost professions. No-one would wish to argue that exile meant an easy time for anyone, and there are countless tragic stories of lost careers and ruined lives. At the same time, there are also heartening stories of success. As far as the Austrians in wartime exile are concerned, they were also gradually allowed to play their part in the fight against National Socialism, at first in munitions work or civil defence, then in the army and also in other spheres.

In general terms, it has to be recognised that Austrians in exile in Great Britain could never be considered to be a cohesive, unified whole. As a result, there was never any question of the formation of an Austrian government in exile; indeed, because of the Anschluss, it was some time before Austrians could be officially recognised as different from voluntary members of the German Reich. Similarly, although exiles were not allowed to engage in active politics, it was recognised that Austrian exiles could in fact be Socialists, Communists, Royalists, Liberals and many other shades of political opinion. The Austrian Socialists in exile were soon as well organised as their German colleagues and had their own organisations, clubs and publications. The Monarchists, Conservative Catholics and Liberals, though not so numerous, were equally active. In fact, from the point of view of the British Government, too many organisations were established in Great Britain by émigrés for any one section to gain official recognition. Gradually, of course, conflicting groups were forced to come together and the People's Front movement did result in a unified Free Austrian Movement, but this never completely healed the divisions of the past.

What did emerge was an Austrian Centre as a 'cultural' club to compete with the Free German League of Culture. The Austrians also managed to produce their own newspaper, the *Zeitspiegel*, which was more than a match for the British-government-sponsored *Die Zeitung*. The cultural and political significance of this Austrian exile newspaper in London in wartime has yet to be written up. Looking at the achievements of the Austrian Centre as a whole, it becomes clear that these were truly remarkable. Between 1943 and 1944, its Musical Circle put on some fifty concerts; the Centre's theatre, the Laterndl, mounted some twenty-three plays and reviews, which were seen by thousands of people. The Centre's publishing facility, Free Austrian Books, brought out thousands of copies of books in English, as well as brochures and pamphlets in German. The Centre had a total of 3,500 members, around seventy employees and a yearly turnover of about £46,000. It was a large-scale operation, even though it did rely on a great deal of voluntary help and assistance. In every respect, it was bigger and better than the much more publicly recognised Free German League of Culture. Yet, at the same time, the two organisations do not need to be considered as competing with each other or as mutually exclusive. Both provided the essential German-language atmosphere and cultural services which all refugees and exiles desperately require. Most important for both organisations were the activities targeted at the young, who were most at risk from losing not only their language but also their cultural, political and national identity. Nor must it be thought that such activity was restricted to the London region. One of the revelations of the collections of documents in the *Österreicher im Exil in Großbritannien* volume is the extent to which such activities involved cities in the provinces, like Manchester, Birmingham, Edinburgh and Aberdeen, as well as Oxford and Cambridge.

It could be argued that, to date, excessive attention has perhaps been paid to the publishing and cultural activities of exile organisations. At the same time, this focus is understandable given the often famous names involved. The name of Erich Fried has been mentioned, and it is fascinating to follow his career, through the documents and other evidence, from young unknown to famous poet. Sadly, the opposite is also the case, and the same documents often reveal how once-famous personages suffered from the deprivations of exile and, in some cases, never recovered. Felix Braun, for example, clearly a prominent figure in the cultural life of British exile, is now known only to a handful of experts. Albert Fuchs, once so famous that he had a clubhouse in London named after him, is now hardly remembered. The Kulturelle Schriftenreihe of the Free Austrian Movement listed in one of its publications 'Austrian Writers in Exile'. Naturally the list includes the names of still famous writers, like Hilde Spiel, Stefan Zweig, Erich Fried and Theodor Kramer; but other names have only in recent years been emerging from the mists of the past as a result of the salvaging efforts of exile scholars. So Hermynia zur Mühlen is at last being rediscovered, which is to be welcomed. In the same list, Elisabeth von Janstein is also mentioned. She was once a prominent personality in the literary life of the Weimar Republic. Exile in Great Britain for her meant the end of a literary career and the lapse into silence and eventual death. Yet not all literary artists fell silent. Elias Canetti's struggles with the fundamental problem of language in exile are recorded here, while Erich Fried too came to terms with the problem of whether to change language or not. Both Canetti and Fried decided that, for them, German was the language of literary expression. Others like Hilde Spiel, Hermynia zur Mühlen, Anna Gmeyner, Anna Sebastian and Robert Neumann switched from German to English. On the whole, novelists and journalists obviously found it easier to change language than poets like Erich Fried, Theodor Kramer or Franz Baermann Steiner, who needed their own language.

Truly remarkable is the amount of German-language theatre which continued in London and elsewhere throughout the war years, especially but not only in the theatre clubs of the Free German League of Culture and the Austrian Centre. Here again, it is a great advantage to have scenes from satirical programmes of the Laterndl and other little theatres actually reproduced here. Also important are the contemporary review articles from English-language newspapers, like the *Times,* which show how great the impact of these highly professional performances was. Significantly, the programmes included real plays both classical and contemporary (the Austrian Centre often featured Jura Soyfer's work), as well as up-to-the-minute sketches based on the events of the time. Although Brecht and Friedrich Wolf did not loom large on any programmes, *The Eternal Schweijk* was a favourite, alongside a full-scale performance of *The Threepenny Opera* in German. Many of the artists from the exiles' little theatres successfully made the progression to the West End stage, film and radio. Regrettably, however, as the documents show, the one serious attempt to set up an 'Österreichische Bühne' to present full-scale theatre in German to London audiences failed after productions of *Nathan der Weise*, Friedrich Wolf's *Professor Mamlock*, and *Unentschuldigte Stunde*, a harmless comedy by Bekessy and Stella, which had been a success in English under the title *Little Ladyship*. Not even the directorial talents of Julius Hahlo and Hein Heckroth, nor the production talents of Arthur Hellmer, could save this venture. On a smaller scale, The Blue Danube, a theatre club under the artistic direction of Peter Herz and very professional administration of Heinz Saltenburg, proved capable of surviving until well after the end of hostilities.

Unlike their literary and theatrical colleagues, musicians had no language problems to contend with, and so it might be assumed that they had an easier time in finding outlets for their talents. At first, employment restrictions made life as difficult for them as for other professions. Later, however, an Anglo-Austrian Music Society was formed, and a Musicians' Refugee Committee came into being which instituted a survey and register of musicians. In time, leading figures like Hans Gal and Egon Wellesz were able to organise concerts and recitals. Artists and painters were also able to come together, break down the barriers of isolation (so common a feature of exile life), and organise exhibitions of their work. Kokoschka painted his 'political pictures' like 'Das rote Eil'; Georg Eisler got to know Kokoschka; Joseph Otto Flatter exhibited his cartoon series on 'The Life of Hitler'; and Georg Ehrlich put on an exhibition of his portraits, its centrepiece being his monument for the Coventry Crematorium with the title 'Peace'. Austrian artists from all spheres proved fully capable of reaching the general public and making clear their position as Austrians in the fight against National Socialism.

Not surprisingly, as the documents in this volume show, Austrian academics and scientists were as quick to organise as their musical, literary and artistic colleagues. By far the most famous name was that of Sigmund Freud, but he was by no means the only psychoanalyst to settle in Great Britain. Others soon established themselves, some 300 Austrian doctors were able to form their own association, and soon too there was also an Association of Austrian Chemists, Architects and Technicians. The two volumes published under the title *Vertriebene Vernunft*, already reviewed in *Austrian Studies 3*, show the full range of professions and academic subjects affected by emigration and exile. While some areas were clearly more affected than others – psychoanalysis was denounced by the Nazis as a Jewish science – no subject was immune, and scholars and academics from all faculties and all universities found themselves summarily dismissed and forced to leave the country. The final sections of *Österreicher im Exil in Großbritannien 1939–45* focus on two particular areas – service in the armed forces, and Austrians in the British propaganda war. At first, as in so many other spheres, British policy was divided. It was not possible to round up Austrians in exile and intern them as potentially dangerous enemy aliens on the one hand, and at the same time to enlist them in the British army to fight against the German army. Once the problem of internment had been solved, a solution to the military service issue was found by making it possible to serve in the non-combatant ranks of the Pioneer Corps. This was eagerly seized upon, and countless Austrian Jewish and non-Jewish intellectuals, academics, scientists, artists and writers found themselves engaged in hard manual work. The course of the war did, however, make it possible for those with technical, engineering and other skills to advance from the ranks to officer level. As the war progressed, it was also recognised that though special regiments of Austrians could not be formed into a fighting force (if captured, they were liable to be shot by the Germans as traitors), individuals could be accepted into the armed services after a change of name and provision of new identities. The documents in the present volume show that many Austrians were keen to play the most active part possible to bring down the hated National Socialist regime. Given the particular problems of Communists and Marxists, who followed the Moscow line that the war was an outcome of late-capitalist imperialism, it was not until after the invasion of Russia that the members of Young Austria in Great Britain were able to declare their own commitment to military service.

The propaganda war was another matter. Here, perhaps for the first time, detailed evidence is made generally available of the major role of the BBC in the propaganda war. Histories of the media are quick to point out how slow the British government was to respond to the propaganda bombardment of the Goebbels ministry, and how restricted everybody was by the official appeasement policy. Nevertheless, although hesitant in the beginning, and although clearly losing the propaganda battle at first, as the war progressed the BBC was encouraged to build up a German-language service and in the end its policies did prove more effective. The BBC decided to tell the truth, however painful it was. It also decided that the voice of the BBC would be a British voice, although the speakers, translators, editors and others were German or Austrian. This meant at first sight that exiles were engaged merely in secondary positions and were not the policymakers. In the end, this too proved to be the correct policy decision. The voice of the BBC could never simply be dismissed as that of aggrieved Jewish exiles, Marxists, Socialists, Royalists or minority groups. In time too, particularly as the war progressed in favour of the Allies, exiles came to assume very significant positions in BBC broadcasts, especially as these developed from mere news broadcasts and commentaries to features, satirical programmes, live jazz concerts with catchy (banned) songs and music. The Austrians engaged by the BBC almost outnumbered the Germans, and the quality and professionalism of this talent meant that around 1943 an Austrian section, broadcasting to Austria, had to be formed, quite distinct from the by then well-established German section.

Wolfgang Muchitsch, who has special expertise in this area, is to be congratulated on presenting extracts and evidence not only from the official BBC broadcasts, but also from the black propaganda units and special transmitters operative by the end of the war. The satirical material produced by the Viennese Robert Lucas in his Gefreite Hirnschal series, or by Bruno Adler for his Frau Wernicke programmes, is now generally available in popular paperbacks, but it is exceptional to have at last a sample from the BBC feature 'Der Alois in London' by the Viennese writer Richard Wiener.

As with all such surveys, the final section is devoted to the problem facing exiles at the end of the war: whether or not to return to Austria. Here, once again, the material presented is heart-rending, the personal dilemmas enormous. As far as literary figures in exile are concerned, whole volumes have already been devoted to the problem of the 'schwierige Heimkehr'. By now, it is clear that not nearly enough was done for the famous writers from the pre-Nazi period, for the man and woman in the street, or for the scientists, academics, intellectuals and others who had been forced out. Little or no effort was made to encourage them to return.

The subtitle of Wolfgang Muchitsch's second book, *Mit Spaten, Waffen und Worten*, gives the clearest idea of his concerns, namely the integration of the refugees in the war effort ('Die Einbindung österreichischer Flüchtlinge in die britischen Kriegsanstrengungen 1939–1945'). After a brisk but detailed treatment of Great Britain as a land of exile as far as immigration legislation and conditions were concerned, the treatment of 'enemy aliens', and the consequent internment policy, he moves on to the enlistment of Austrians (legally now to be distinguished from Germans) in the war effort. This entails an in-depth analysis of the Pioneer Corps and the part that Austrians played in it, in both Britain and other war zones. Austrians (including eventually Austrian women) were in the end admitted to other branches of the armed services, technical units, the Army, the RAF, the Royal Navy and special services. In the section of his book after 'Spaten', i.e. the Pioneer Corps, and 'Waffen', or the armed services, Muchitsch then moves on to 'Worten', with a detailed analysis of the part played by Austrians in the War of Words, dealing not only with the BBC but also with underground transmitters, black propaganda and broadcasting services aimed at Austria. This is without doubt the clearest. most detailed and accessible survey of such material yet published

While this volume by Muchitsch covers much the same ground as that presented through documents in *Österreicher im Exil in Großbritannien*, the exhibition catalogue *The Cultural Exodus from Austria* reproduces much of the material already published in the symposium volumes reviewed in *Austrian Studies 3*. Nevertheless, the Austrian authorities responsible for the present catalogue are to be congratulated, for it is further evidence that there is now support at the highest level – in this case the Bundesministerium für Unterricht und Kunst – for an international discussion of Austria's past and the forced emigration and exile of so many Austrians. The catalogue, which, like the exhibition it accompanied, demanded considerable resources and a dedicated team for its speedy production, was produced for the Biennale of

Venice 1993, running from 11 June until 10 October 1993. While a great deal of the material does derive from the earlier volumes, there is also much that is new. The main difference from earlier publications is that they were for the most part written in academic German for a specialist public, capable of digesting it in that form. The organisers of the exhibition have taken the major step of engaging a team of translators to convert all contributions into English. This immediately opens up these vital sources to a much wider public.

After a preliminary section covering in general terms the emigration of Austrian exiles, and the cultural exodus from Austria during the 'fascist' period, concentrating especially on exiled Austrians in the USA, the catalogue then deals with special areas of interest like philosophy and the emigration of the Vienna Circle, psychoanalysis and its exodus from Vienna, the social sciences, economics and law in exile. History and art history (including the Warburg Institute in London), Austrian literature in exile, architecture, music, film, journalism and communication studies then follow. Clearly, the translators have had to work at great speed, and their attempts at translating difficult German into readable English are not always successful. Konstantin Kaiser's essay on the exile concepts of 'culture' and 'nation' leaves them as impenetrable in English as they were in German, while many readers will be baffled by Wendelin Schmidt-Dengler's thoughts on 'Literature Studies and Exile'. Nevertheless, the volume as a whole is definitely more readable and more easily digestible as a result of the determined efforts of the translating team.

Fortunately too, the final section of the catalogue is taken up by the testimony of eye-witnesses in the form of I-was-there accounts, which are immediately more readable than in-depth intellectual analyses or statistical surveys. The final essay by Victor Matejka, who died in 1993, is a reminder of 'one of the first and the few, who at the beginning of the Second Republic invited back the Austrians who had been banished and exiled'. The volume is dedicated to his memory. In conclusion, it should perhaps be pointed out that the catalogue is not only richly illustrated: it also contains not one but two indexes, the first dedicated to Austrian 'Science in Exile' (the whole volume has difficulties over the word 'Wissenschaft'), and the second devoted to 'Austrian Literary Exile'. The first is extracted from the 2,000-plus biographies held in the data-bank assembled for the government-sponsored project 'Wissenschaft im Exil'; the second is extracted from another government-sponsored project for which Konstantin Kaiser, Siglinde Bolbecher and others are responsible, the aim being to produce a biobibliographical lexicon of Austrian literature by 1995. The second index is much more sparing in detail than the first, and the two computers have evidently not spoken to each other, because many names appear twice. Given the difficulties over 'Wissenschaft', Martina Wied, for example, appears once as an art-historian and again as a writer. Despite such minor discrepancies, both indexes make a wealth of valuable material easily accessible.

What the volume devoted to the cultural exodus from Austria makes clear among other things is that Exile Studies in Austria, as in Germany, have moved into the sphere of data-banks. To a certain extent, this means a change in perspective away from following the fates of the cultural elite to describing the lives of what has been called 'das Exil der kleinen Leute'.

A significant book with this title, edited by Wolfgang Benz, Director of the Institut für Antisemitismusforschung in Berlin, gives some idea of what this involves. But before the world of famous people is abandoned, note must be taken of two recent projects which have resulted in the rediscovery of much forgotten material and in both cases have produced lists of names and biographical details which will have to be added to the data-banks. The first, *London Calling*, is an excellent reminder of the international nature of the filmworld in the 1930s and charts the careers of German-language film people in the British film industry. After a final essay on Conrad Veidt and his British films, the last section – 'All Hands Abroad' – offers a 'kleines Lexikon deutschsprachiger Filmschaffender in Großbritannien 1925–1945'. Of the 100 and more names listed, many are Austrian, including Berthold Viertel, Oskar F. Werndorff and Friedrich Zelnik. Even fuller is the information supplied by the two volumes of *Aufbruch ins Ungewisse*, which lists no less than 550 Austrian exiles who worked in the world of film. From such a wealth of information, it is easy for the interested reader to extract those who worked in Britain (perhaps before Hollywood) and build up a picture of Austrian as distinct from German involvement in Elstree.

Coming back from the glamorous world of film to the 'exile of the little people', one striking difference emerges from the accounts gathered by Wolfgang Benz for his book, regarding German responses to Jewish refugees, compared with Austrian attitudes. Whereas many German cities have invited exiles to revisit their hometowns, Austria has preferred to avoid the whole area of 'Wiedergutmachung' and reconciliation. The Austrian way with such problems, according to the English historian Robert Knight, is to postpone them ('alles auf die lange Bank zu schieben'). For his book on the tricky question of the 'difficult return', Adi Wimmer has chosen to interview 'kleine Leute' rather than famous people, yet of his little people a remarkable number around the world have studied to university level and have become teachers of one kind or another, and not all famous names are excluded: the first illustration shows Anton Walter Freud, the grandson of Sigmund, in British army uniform. He made his way out of the Pioneer Corps into Special Services, trained as a commando and was parachuted into Austria in April 1945. The last picture in the book shows another successful Austrian – Lord Weidenfeld – in white tie and tails. Sir Ernst Gombrich figures twice in the book, and writers in exile are not completely shut out either. Stella Rotenberg, the poetess, shown in her picture as she was in 1938, still lives in 1995 in Leeds.

Austria between the Wars

Alan Bance

Donald G. Daviau (ed.), *Austrian Writers and the Anschluss: Understanding the Past – Overcoming the Past*, Studies in Austrian Literature, Culture, and Thought (Riverside, CA: Ariadne Press, 1991), xli + 364 pp., $42.00

Kenneth Segar and John Warren (eds), *Austria in the Thirties: Culture and Politics*, Studies in Austrian Literature, Culture, and Thought (Riverside, CA: Ariadne Press, 1991), iv + 391 pp., $39.95.

Walter Goldinger and Dieter A. Binder, *Geschichte der Republik Österreich 1918–1938* (Oldenburg: Verlag für Geschichte und Politik, 1992), 333 pp., 480 Sch.

Klaus Amann, *Die Dichter und die Politik. Essays zur österreichischen Literatur nach 1918* (Vienna: Edition Falter/Deuticke, 1992), 319 pp., 298 Sch./DM 43.

Klaus Amann's investigations into the inter-war period of Austrian literary life have had as explosive an effect on present-day perceptions of the cultural past as inquiries about Kurt Waldheim's personal history have had in the political sphere. Amann's books[1] used new sources such as police and government records to show the extent to which politics and literature were intertwined in the 1930s. His more recent book, *Die Dichter und die Politik*, is a collection of essays produced alongside work on the Anschluss which have for the most part already been published elsewhere, and thoroughly revised for republication. The appearance of Amann's work in the 1980s was perfectly timed to exert a major influence on all the research into the cultural history of the 1920s and 1930s which came together in 1988, when a number of symposia commemorated the fiftieth anniversary of the Anschluss. A Californian symposium generated a book edited and introduced by Donald G. Daviau, *Austrian Writers and the Anschluss*, while an Oxford gathering, for me slightly more impressive because of the breadth of coverage undertaken by most of the individual contributions, produced *Austria in the Thirties*, edited by Kenneth Segar and John Warren. The fact that one publisher was prepared to invest in two *Sammelbände* on the same topic in the same year is a sure sign that it is a subject whose time has come. As Donald Daviau reminds us in the Preface to his volume, the great impetus for an academic revision of Austria's claim to have been the first victim of Hitler, and consequent revision of her role in the Anschluss, was 'the placing of Austrian President Kurt Waldheim on the watchlist by the United States and the ensuing detailed investigation of his wartime military record' (p. i).

The 'revised' edition of a standard history of the First Republic, *Geschichte der Republik Österreich 1918–1938*, has been reprinted on the initiative of Dieter A. Binder, heir to the work of Walter Goldinger (d. 1990), who was the author of the first version, published as a free-standing book in 1962, although it had appeared in 1954 as part of a vast history of the First Republic edited by Heinrich Benedikt (also entitled *Geschichte der Republik Österreich*). In fact, Binder retains the original text almost unaltered,[2] and thereby takes us back to an earlier moment in Austrian political historiography. The reissue of this book precisely demonstrates why the revisionism of Amann and others is so necessary. Taken alongside the other recent volumes mentioned, Goldinger/Binder's work immediately conveys a salient point: political history is incomplete without cultural history. There is no lack of new work covering the attitude of the Corporate State towards culture as a political weapon (see John Warren, *Austria in the Thirties*, p. 289). But beyond cultural politics, the personal experience of cultural producers indispensably rounds out the picture of the period, and often contrasts with the somewhat bland results of the historian's search for balance and objectivity. I am thinking, for example, of James Shedel's account, 'A Question of Identity: Kokoschka, Austria and the Meaning of the Anschluss' (*Austrian Writers and the Anschluss*, p. 45), of Oskar Kokoschka's slow and reluctant evolution towards confronting Austrian reality in the 1930s: 'Finally, sometime after April [1934], ... Kokoschka condemned his country for being in effect a violent police state concealed by a touristic facade of tranquility behind which one could see men "in Kriegsgeschäfte, von denen sie nichts verstehen, verwickelt, vom Standgericht in die Gefängnisse und Konzentrationslager geworfen und mit dem Galgen bedroht"' (involved in war-deals about which they understand nothing, thrown into gaols and concentration camps by summary justice, and threatened with the gallows). Similarly, Goldinger/Binder's chronicle of anti-Semitism in Austria nowhere reproduces the bitterness of Kurt Rudolf Fischer's experiences in 'The Death of "Austrian Philosophy"' (*Austria in the Thirties*, pp. 292–308) as an émigré Jew who feels that Jews never had and still cannot have any real home in Austrian society. No amount of judicious weighing-up by the historian of the limited options available to the hard-pressed Austria of the 1930s, between the rock of Mussolini's Italy and the increasingly hard place of Hitlerian Germany, quite conveys the atmosphere of the time as well as the account which Fischer gives of the murder of the philosopher Professor Moritz Schlick (*not* a Jew, though his suspect first name, Moritz, gave rise to the belief that he was) by one of his students, Johann Nelböck. Especially telling is the reported statement of another student of Schlick's that 'Schlick had attempted to obtain police protection, which he thought he needed because of continued threats, but was informed that he would be asked to pay for the expense of having Nelböck interned in the local asylum, the *Steinhof* (p. 298). The affluent 'Jew' must pay for the protection of the State, which grudgingly sells him a citizen's rights.

If Goldinger/Binder's history tends to distance itself from the myth of Austria as the first victim of Hitler, there are distinct signs in this book of another version of the 'victim' narrative being established: Austria's freedom of choice and possibility of action on her own behalf is forfeit because of lack of support from other European countries (*Geschichte*, p. 272). This passive role contrasts with the active part played in their own enslavement by the Austrian people when the Anschluss was upon them, for, as Goldinger/ Binder reports, although after the Anschluss Hitler was not thinking of an immediate and complete incorporation of the 'Ostmark' into the Third Reich, one of the factors that swayed him in that direction was the enthusiasm of the Austrian response to his triumphant arrival in Vienna (*Geschichte*, p. 290).

This sober and understated account needs to be fleshed out, precisely the function of a very useful anthology of literary and historical documents assembled in the process of course development at the University of Salzburg, and published as *Vermittlungen. Texte und Kontexte österreichischer Literatur und Geschichte im 20. Jahrhundert*, edited by Walter Weiss and Ernst Hanisch (Salzburg and Vienna: Residenz Verlag, 1990). Their two separate introductions, written in full awareness of the problems of textual evaluation in the post-stucturalist era and since the 'linguistic turn', nicely weigh up the proper function for the historian of 'literary' and 'non-literary' texts. Not only will the reader find here a number of the key texts referred to in the other volumes under discussion in this article (for example, what John Warren means by 'playing the Prince Eugene card again' on page 277 of *Austria in the Thirties* is illustrated by the inclusion in the Weiss/Hanisch anthology of Hofmannsthal's essay of December 1914, 'Worte zum Gedächtnis des Prinzen Eugen', and of documentary 'Kontexte' to accompany it); she or he will also be brought up against the limits of historical explanation, and the enormously suggestive explanatory power of literature, in Hanisch's presentation of Ernst Jandl's poem 'wien: heldenplatz'. Hanisch is the social historian to Weiss's literary historian, and he confesses that:

Im Grunde steht der nachgeborene Historiker ratlos vor dem Massen-geschehen in den Märztagen des Jahres 1938. Massenpsychologische Theorien helfen gewiß einen Schritt weiter bei der Erklärung; aber sie stoßen rasch an ihre Grenzen. Ich kenne keinen Text, der auf einer halben Druckseite jene kollektive Flucht aus der Realität so präzise einfängt und so vielfältig, ironiegesättigt analysiert wie Ernst Jandls Gedicht.

[Basically, the historian born after the event is at a loss when confronted with the mass developments of March 1938. Theories of mass psychology help a little to explain these things, but soon come up against their limitations. I know of no text which so precisely encapsulates in half a page of print that collective flight from reality and analyses it so richly and with such a plenitude of irony as Ernst Jandl's poem.]

161

The poem captures a dimension that Goldinger/Binder's history does not even recognise: National Socialism as political religion,

> im Zentrum der Verehrung der 'gottelbock' [Hitler in the Heldenplatz in Vienna]: der Tanz um das Animalische, die Rasse, der Bock als Gott; die uralten Männlichkeits- und Weiblichkeitsrituale, der Mann als Jäger, als Krieger, als sexuell Potenter; die Frau als empfängnisbereit ... So ausgerüstet mit einem Paket von Fragestellungen und Interpretationshilfen kann der Historiker weitergehen, zu anderen Quellen und zu verfeinerten Erklärungen.

> [at the centre of adulation the 'god-goat': the dance around the animalistic idols, the race, the goat as god, the age-old rituals of masculinity and femininity, the man as hunter, as warrior, the potent male; the woman ready to conceive ... Thus equipped with a package of questions and aids to interpretation, the historian can proceed, to other sources and more refined explanations.]

The relationship of the sexual to the political is typically brought out only many years after the end of the Nazi era, not only in Jandl's poem (1962), but also by a new generation of writers like Peter Handke, for whom the personal is political, since he is literally a child of the Anschluss. In one of the most interesting essays among many in the books reviewed here, Thomas F. Barry almost rivals Jandl's poetic concentration in his description of the libidinous potential of Nazism as presented by Handke in *Wunschloses Unglück*: 'The seduction of the Nazi signs were indeed certainly that: an erotic affair. The need in his mother's life to escape the existential burden of her individuality became an ecstatic Dionysian merging of the self with the totality of "Volk" and "Gemeinschaft", a thanatotic loss of self, a political congress, an erotic Anschluss of a person and a nation. One was no longer isolated but part of the masses ...' ('Nazi Signs: Peter Handke's Reception of Austrian Fascism', *Austrian Writers and the Anschluss*, p. 305). In the work of another contemporary writer, Elfriede Jelinek, access to the reality of Austrian society past and present is sought by an interweaving of politics and sexual politics, and Jelinek achieves shock effects simultaneously in both spheres.[3] In her contribution to *Austrian Writers and the Anschluss*, Regina Kecht unravels the similar psycho-political knot which is the heroine's relationship with her Nazi father in Brigitte Schwaiger's novel *Lange Abwesenheit* (1980), with its central situation of the narrator's deliberately provocative affair with a Jewish man of her father's generation, survivor of the Holocaust ('Faschistische Familienidyllen – Schatten der Vergangenheit in Henisch, Schwaiger und Reichart', pp. 324–6).

The 'Erklärungen' to which Ernst Hanisch refers and to which literary achievements direct him will not, however, be found in a resolutely political history such as Goldinger/Binder's, which has several claims to make, none of them much helped by mass psychology or by Jandl's poem. One is that the failure of Austria between the wars was ultimately not of her own making, for the country was subject to irresistible pressures from all sides. The other (perhaps slightly contradictory of the first) is that the Austrian Social Democrats brought down destruction upon themselves in 1934 – and therefore indirectly upon Austria in 1938 – by their persistently alarming Austro-Marxist language and revolutionary perspective from 1918 onwards (see *Geschichte*, p. 142), abandoned only when it was too late and Schuschnigg fatally refused their help in fending off the threat from Germany. Another case where cultural history overlaps with political, and where the cultural history has simply been ignored, concerns the political use of 'law and order' forces. Goldinger/Binder suggests more than once that the right-wing bias of the judiciary in the 1920s and 1930s was a technical fault of the jury system as it operated in the First Republic. Nowhere is there a mention of Karl Kraus's long and honourable campaign to bring to account the Vienna Chief of Police, Schober, for his brutal treatment of protesting left-wingers during the riots following the burning-down of the Palace of Justice in July 1927 (the story is told by Edward Timms in 'Kraus's Shakespearean Politics', *Austria in the Thirties*, pp. 348–52), which was itself a response to blatant right-wing bias in the courtroom. The lenient treatment of the Nazi, Otto Rothstock, who in 1925 murdered Hugo Bettauer, author of the pro-Semitic novel *Die Stadt ohne Juden* (1922), is another legal scandal mentioned in the essays under review. The Austrian state certainly had ample opportunity to reform the jury system before 1931, when Pfrimer, leader of an abortive *Heimatschutz* coup in Styria, was let off scot-free by the jury at his trial (*Geschichte*, p. 187).

In his contribution to the Segar/Warren volume, 'The Corporate State versus National Socialism: Some Aspects of Austria's Resistance', Dieter Binder puts up such defence as can be made of the Corporate State's resistance to Hitler, but precisely here cultural history provides the best examples of the hopelessness of that resistance. The complete undermining of the Zsolnay Verlag by the Nazis well before the Anschluss is described by Murray G. Hall (*Austria in the Thirties*, pp. 204–18), while Gerhard Renner in the same volume shows that the Austrian film industry had *de facto* already been annexed by 1935 at the latest, when Austria effectively 'imported' Germany's Nazi film industry legislation ('The Anschluss of the Film Industry after 1934', p. 256). Klaus Amann was the first to drive home the very important point that economics and economic opportunism played a prominent part in the capitulation and annexation of Austria's culture industry, but Gerhard Renner makes the equally necessary observation that the success of Nazi film policy in Austria is not simply a matter of economics, but has a paradigmatic quality:

> Many there had for years nurtured hopes of an Anschluss, and the attempt by the Corporate State to propagate the concept of an 'Austrian nation' or of 'Austrian man' was in the context of the 1930s artificial and out of touch with realities. A large part of the Austrian bureaucracy saw no alternative to Anschluss, and this state of mind suggested to the Nazis that they could pursue their policy quite cold-bloodedly without fear of serious resistance. (p. 265)

Incidentally, nowhere in the works reviewed here is there any adequate attempt to define what is or was meant by a Corporate State or *Ständestaat*.

For those of us who work in what might loosely be called 'cultural politics', it is good and bad news that what happens in the cultural-political sphere is of decisive importance for the outcome in politics proper. This reduces our sense of impotence, but at the same time the story of Austria between the wars tells us how easily an evil ideology infiltrated one that was merely small-minded and oppressively nationalistic (this distinction between Austro-Fascism and Nazism is, incidentally, worth preserving, as Dieter Binder says: *Austria in the Thirties*, p. 79). Where cultural identity becomes a part of the definition of national identity, Austria's claim to a 'German' mission and tradition was a fatal paradigm for her later capitulation to German/Nazi hegemony, especially after the 'Verständigungsabkommen' between Austria and the Reich of July 1936 (see Amann, *Die Dichter und die Politik*, p. 84). Literature in particular was transformed into a Fifth Column movement, part of a softening-up process, 'ein Wandel in Lebensgefühl und Weltanschauung' whose champions were the leading 'Germanisten' Heinz Kindermann and Josef Nadler. As Nadler succinctly put it, 'die Dichtung hat ihn [den Wandel] bewegt und bezeugt. Der Staatsmann hat ihn vollstreckt' (quoted by Amann, *Die Dichter und die Politik*, p. 89). Edward Timms in *Austria in the Thirties* makes clear once more how exceptional Karl Kraus was in linking, as a life-and-death matter, the health of culture with the health of politics. That the two spheres cannot be kept apart is brought out by Amann in discussing Schuschnigg's attempts to do just that: to play upon familiar inter-war ideas of Austrians as 'the better Germans', and to insist upon their role in a so-called civilising mission – 'die deutsche Mission'. These were arguments completely unsuited to the founding of a separate Austrian identity and therefore an Austrian sovereignty. Schuschnigg was consciously playing with fire in propagating these concepts while trying to keep them within a 'Weltanschauung' context and claiming that they had nothing to do with politics. The practical result was that the Austrian-German frontier was inevitably perceived by many on both sides as permeable and provisional (see *Die Dichter und die Politik*, p. 96).

Amann's article on the supposedly apolitical writer Franz Nabl serves to bring out a lesson that perhaps needs to be spelt out so laboriously only in Austria: in the words of Max Frisch in 1948, 'Es gibt leider kein menschliches Wesen, das nur Kunst macht'. To claim to be apolitical is to serve the political *status quo*. A corollary of this startling truism is another – worth stating in the Austrian context because so many of the post-war debates familiar in Germany did not take place in Austria – which is that a book could be free from explicit propaganda and still serve Nazi purposes. (In fact, there was a considerable backlash in Nazi cultural politics against amateurish or blatant attempts at propaganda: see Amann, *Die Dichter und die Politik*, p. 124. One might think of Goebbels's resistance to direct Nazi propaganda in the German film industry, and his antipathy to Leni Riefenstahl's great projects for that reason.) This reads like a summary of one side of the argument in the very well-known debate between Thomas Mann and Walter von Molo in 1945 on the value of 'inner emigration' literature, subsequently taken up by a host of others. The same lesson, that writers neglect social and political responsibility only at a price, is spelled out in Donald G. Daviau's account in *Austria in the Thirties* of three authors who tried to avoid political engagement between the wars: Stefan Zweig, Raoul Auernheimer and Felix Braun. Heimito von Doderer presents the most stunning example of this wilful political blindness, able as he was to overlook Nazism, though living at the time precisely in Dachau (the town, not the concentration camp: see Hans Eichner, 'Heimito von Doderer, die Politik und die Juden', *Austrian Writers and the Anschluss*, p. 229). Blindness to the Nazi threat is a theme running through very many commentaries on the period, but good examples can be found especially in Jennifer E. Michaels's essay, 'The Anschluss remembered: Experiences of the Anschluss in the Autobiographies of Elisabeth Castonier, Gina Kaus, Alma Mahler-Werfel, and Hertha Pauli' (*Austrian Writers and the Anschluss*, p. 262). Leaving Doderer aside, the most astonishing blindness of all is that induced by the Austrians' complacency about their special place and mission within the 'German' world, which deluded them into believing that Anschluss would produce a union of equal partners (see *Geschichte*, p. 293).

Counter-examples can also be found: a writer like Horváth was impressively far-sighted in exposing the moral, political and cultural vacuum which was waiting to be filled by Nazism. He shows the very process by which 'fadenscheinige Gemütlichkeit', as Nestroy called it, turns into something sinister and vindictive, and ultimately deadly – the value, incidentally, which the term *Gemütlichkeit* now seems to have achieved in the currency of all critical commentators on Austria past and present.[4]

The hidden, or not-so-hidden, agenda of most of these critics is the relation of the Austrian present to the Austrian past. Dagmar Lorenz delineates the continuity of both popular culture and cultural bureaucracy from the 1930s to the 1950s ('1938 – die Stunde Null', *Austrian Writers and the Anschluss*, pp. 125-37), which can be followed at more length in Joseph McVeigh's *Kontinuität und Vergangenheitsbewältigung in der österreichischen Literatur nach 1945* (Vienna: Braumüller, 1988). In the important introductory essay to his *Die Dichter und die Politik,* 'Zum Begriff "Österreichische Literatur"', Klaus Amann isolates one of the main strategies that facilitated Austrian cultural continuity; the careful distinguishing of Austria from Germany, which immediately after the Second World War took up the old 'Austro-ideology' of Austro-Fascism and viewed the Nazi period retrospectively as an 'unösterreichisches Intermezzo' (p. 13). An outrageous but not untypical remark of this period is quoted here: '"In der Tat brauchen wir nur dort fortzusetzen," schrieb der spätere PEN-Club Präsident Alexander Lernet-Holenia im Jahre 1945, "wo uns die Träume eines Irren unterbrochen haben …"' (p. 3). 'Nadleritis', named after Josef Nadler, the notoriously 'braun' leading Germanist of the inter-war period, raged unabated among Germanists and critics in Austria for decades after the war (see also Donald G. Daviau, *Austrian Writers and the Anschluss*, p. xxx). Particularly shameful, especially in the light of its Nazi past, is the post-war behaviour of the Austrian PEN Club, which as Klaus Amann shows was totally unfaithful to the conditions of its refounding, and accepted back into its ranks writers like Max Mell and Friedrich Schreyvogl who had disgraced themselves under Nazism and earlier ('Wiederaufbau. Der österreichische PEN-Club 1945–1955', *Die Dichter und die Politik*, pp. 208–29). In 1972, the Austrian PEN Club protested at the awarding of the Nobel Prize for literature to Heinrich Böll. A positive outcome of this miserable gesture, however, was the formation of the 'Grazer Autoren-versammlung', which became the avant-garde 'Grazer Gruppe'. (See Allyson Fiddler, *Rewriting Reality*, pp. 22–3.) The Cold War, as in Germany, soon offered a welcome distraction from the immediate past and legitimised the suppression of uncomfortable memories. It enabled Hans Weigel (according to Donald Daviau, *Austrian Writers and the Anschluss*, p. xxx) to keep Brecht off the Austrian stage until 1966. On the other hand, it was to Weigel's credit that he it was, as Amann tells us, who in 1977 arranged for the republication of Karl Tschuppik's 1937 novel, *Ein Sohn aus gutem Haus*. But the very fact that such a talent as Tschuppik (born in Bohemia in 1876, he was one of the leading journalists of Vienna at a time when Viennese journalism was at its most brilliant, and his books were extravagantly praised by Max Brod and Joseph Roth; he died in Vienna in 1937) needed to be rediscovered – and there are parallels in West Germany, such as Horváth or even Heinrich Mann – is, as Amann says, evidence of the wall of silence and suppression of the past which has been in place since the 1930s in Austria to keep out inconvenient contemporaries (*Die Dichter und die Politik*, p. 32).

The depressing catalogue can easily be continued, as it is in a number of these essays; the awarding of post-war literary prizes to time-serving old Nationalists such as Max Mell or Franz Karl Ginzkey, even to writers who had been included in the notorious *Bekenntnisbuch* which joyously ushered in the 'Ostmark', is recorded in painful detail in the penultimate chapter of Amann's *Die Dichter und die Politik*. His book ends on a positive note, however, for while he (most effectively) writes on the 'pseudo-Vergangen-heitsbewältigung' of earlier documentary drama by Hochhuth and Weiss, his last essay puts forward Heimrad Bäcker's *nachschrift* (1986) as a genuine documentary work of engagement with the past.

Although there is some debate about when exactly 'Vienna 1900' can be said to have come to an end, 1938 being a favourite contender among possible dates, what is beyond dispute is an elegiac theme that runs through many of these essays; the end of cosmopolitan Austria, almost synonymous with Jewish-Austrian culture. Steven Beller makes the point very powerfully in his 'The Jewish Intellectual and Vienna in the 1930s' (*Austria in the Thirties*), where he links the anti-Semitism of Schönerer and Lueger with the death of liberal culture and ultimately of all that is signified by 'Vienna 1900'; for it was anti-Semitism that proved to be the key with which Karl Lueger unlocked anti-liberal feeling to overwhelm the liberal patriciate in the 1890s. 'As a result liberalism virtually disappeared as an effective political force, leaving the liberal bourgeoisie, but especially its Jewish contingent, politically impotent in a hostile environment' (p. 312). One could add that anti-Semitism was the cement that ultimately held together the anti-liberal front of Austro-Fascism and Nazism, despite the latter's hostility to Catholicism.

This takes us on to a phenomenon which has been known to puzzle onlookers, when Beller observes that these retreating Jewish/liberal elements 'were, ironically, forced to seek the protection of their old enemy, the Habsburg state, from the Viennese electorate', and explains how many Jews and Jewish intellectuals ended up supporting the Catholic conservatism of the *Ständestaat* (p. 321). Even Sigmund Freud was ensnared in the irony of this situation, for as Ritchie Robertson makes clear in 'Freud and the Catholic Church 1927–1939' (*Austria in the Thirties*), Freud withheld *Der Mann Moses* from publication because the Catholicism of the Austrian corporate (and anti-Semitic!) state was 'the last bulwark against the various barbarisms of Germany, Italy and Russia, and since Catholicism already viewed psycho-analysis with distrust he could not risk strengthening its suspicion' (p. 331).

For Joseph Roth there is, of course, something more positive in the turn to monarchism and Catholicism, the spiritual powers supposedly inherited by the *Ständestaat*; namely, nostalgia for the 'Austrian ideal' of a perfect liberal and pluralistic state which, on the evidence of *Radetzkymarsch* and *Die Kapuzinergruft*, Roth knew never to have existed 'except in the minds of many Jews and some Josephinist bureaucrats'.[5] It is therefore surprising that Klaus Amann makes such a clear distinction between Karl Tschuppik and Joseph Roth, when he denies that the former took the same direction as Roth in the 1930s, 'die Wandlung vom radikaldemokratischen Linken zum habsburg-treuen Monarchisten' (*Die Dichter und die Politik*, p. 41), while establishing the clearest possible parallel: 'so griff Tschuppik am Ende seines Lebens auf jene Welt des alten Europa vor 1914 zurück, deren Untergang er selbst einst mit den schärfsten Kommentaren begleitet hatte, eine Welt jedoch, die ihm angesichts der düsteren Gegenwart in immer freundlicheren Farben erschien' (p. 44) (so, at the end of his life, Tschuppik turned back to the world of the old pre-1914 Europe, whose decline he had himself attended with the most acerbic commentaries, but a world which in the light of the sinister present he now viewed ever more positively). The sad fact is that, in place of their former confident, cosmopolitan outlook, both writers felt obliged to put up a kind of parochialism masquerading as universalism, as a defensive shield against barbarity.

Equally sad is that, in the absence of writers like Roth and Tschuppik, modern Austria has since 1945 enthusiastically embraced provincialism, so that, as Steven Beller says, Hugo Bettauer's 1922 fantasy prediction of what would happen in a 'Stadt ohne Juden' is borne out: 'the provincialism which he is describing has gone on by leaps and bounds in postwar Vienna, right down to the astounding prevalence of loden cloth in the fancy stores on the Kärntnerstrasse and Am Graben' (p. 314). As dissidents like Elfriede Jelinek and Thomas Bernhard have been forced to proclaim in the most strident tones, Austria is the loser, the victim of her own short-sighted national introversion. This gives a new post-war twist to an appropriate epitaph for the whole inter-war period, supplied by Bruce F. Pauley in his 'Anti-Semitism and the Austrian Nazi Party' (*Austria in the Thirties*, p. 64): 'it was Austria's fate in these years to be both victim and perpetrator'.

Notes

1. PEN *Politik, Emigration, Nationalsozialismus* (Vienna, 1984) and above all *Der Anschluß österreichischer Schriftsteller an das Dritte Reich* (Frankfurt, 1988).
2. See the review by Charlie Jeffery, *German History*, 12 (1994), pp. 269–70: 'rather more through its omissions than through what it contains, it tells the reader a great deal about the early years of contemporary history in Austria' (p. 270).
3. See Allyson Fiddler, *Rewriting Reality: An Introduction to Elfriede Jelinek* (Oxford and Providence, RI, 1994), especially Chapter 1, 'Jelinek in Context'.
4. See Hans Eichner, *Austrian Writers and the Anschluss*, pp. 229 and 231–2, and in the same book Regina Kecht, p. 333, note 6; Horst Jarka, 'Everyday Life and Politics in the Literature of the Thirties: Horváth, Kramer, and Soyfer', *Austria in the Thirties*, p. 152.
5. Beller, p. 322. See the article 'Joseph Roth's *Kapuzinergruft* as a Document of 1938', in *Austrian Writers and the Anschluss*, where Geoffrey C. Howes makes again a point that I made in 1972 in an edition of the novel which is now, unfortunately, out of print: 'that Joseph Roth is much smarter politically than Franz Ferdinand Trotta and that Trotta's Austrian ideology is therefore suspect and cannot be identified with Roth's own' (Howes, p. 161). See also my forthcoming Introduction to a new Everyman Library edition of *The Radetzky March*.

The Reception of the Vienna School of Art History

Richard Woodfield

Margaret Olin, *Forms of Representation in Alois Riegl's Theory of Art* (University Park, PA: Pennsylvania State University Press, 1992), xxiv + 238 pp., $42.50.

Margaret Iversen, *Alois Riegl: Art History and Theory* (Cambridge, MA and London: MIT Press, 1993), ix + 223 pp., £22.50.

Erwin Panofsky once remarked that when he migrated to the USA he had to change the language of his thought;[1] later commentators have observed that it was not just his language which he changed but his thought as well.[2] He dropped his iconological ambitions in favour of iconographical analysis; only *Gothic Architecture and Scholasticism* attempted to reinstate his earlier, and thoroughgoing, 'neo-Hegelian' approach to art and culture.[3] Books migrate, as well as people. And when the second volume of Sedlmayr and Pächt's *Kunstwissenschaftliche Forschungen* arrived in America, it met an immediate hostile response from the young Meyer Schapiro. His long and densely-argued review 'The New Viennese School'[4] accused its authors, 'a group of very cultivated and sensitive young art-historians ... who follow in the tradition of Riegl', of strong anti-historical tendencies. This must have been deeply disappointing to scholars familiar with the work of the earlier members of the Vienna School, in particular Wickhoff and Riegl.

Wickhoff's *Wiener Genesis* was available in translation;[5] it was the most original and stimulating book on Roman art in its day, and remains so now. Riegl's work was known by repute, and we have yet to learn how many anglophone historians had actually struggled to read its densely-written text. From the late nineteenth century and prior to the Second World War, there was an intricate network of art-historians familiar with German scholarship extending from Vienna across Europe to the USA. Even Kenneth Clark, described by Cecil Gould as 'a Scotsman brought up in England' and not, by implication, party to 'the heady intellectual atmosphere of Vienna of the 1920s',[6] was part of that scene. The writers on philosophy and the history of art who had influenced him most deeply were 'Hegel, Schopenhauer, Jacob Burckhardt, Wölfflin, Riegl, Dvořák', and in his early years (as he recalls):

169

I had read, with immense difficulty, the works of Riegl and had formed the ambition to interpret every scrap of design as the revelation of a state of mind. I dreamed of a great book which would be the successor to Riegl's *Spätrömische Kunst-Industrie*, and would interpret in human terms the slow, heavy curve of Egyptian art or the restless, inward-turning line of Scythian gold, and would stand for hours looking at Anglo-Saxon ornament and try to describe how its rhythms differed from the decorations on a Chinese bronze.[7]

Clark was, of course, familiar with the work of Aby Warburg as well and so it is hardly surprising that he should have the felt the temptation to write a book on the subterranean mentality of Piero della Francesca.[8] How many more historians were caught in the Viennese net is a matter of great interest.[9]

The Vienna School was famous for its distinctive commitments to the idea of art-historical practice. Its two founders, Böhm and Eitelberger, had both stressed the importance of direct physical contact with the object, either in collections and museums, as *objets d'art,* or *in situ,* as buildings and monuments. Eitelberger founded the Austrian Museum for the Arts and Crafts in which he conducted lectures on practical exercises in the description and determination of works of art. With Heider, he edited a two-volume work on medieval monuments of the Austrian Empire, which Schlosser described as 'the first monumental achievement in the area of art topography in the German-speaking region'.[10] Furthermore, he edited the *Quellenschriften für Kunstgeschichte und Kunsttechnik des Mittelalters und der Renaissance,*[11] regarding direct contact with relevant critical source material as an important corollary to the study of the works themselves. The idea of a properly historical engagement with works of art was consolidated by an important institutional link with the Österreichisches Institut für Geschichtsforschung, where archival studies had been brought into the area of humanist scholarship. It was within this first state of the Vienna School that Riegl worked and it was the second state, following Riegl, that Schapiro attacked. Wherein lay the difference?

The two new books on Riegl by Olin and Iversen should help us to answer this question. Margaret Olin's book develops her doctoral dissertation of 1982, 'Alois Riegl and the Crisis of Representation in Art Theory, 1880–1905', and Margaret Iversen's is a reworking of her doctoral dissertation of 1979, 'Alois Riegl's Art Historiography', which Olin accurately described as a series of essays on Riegl's major works. Olin's is the better historical work, being based on archival research in Vienna, and Iversen has a greater interest in locking Riegl into current theoretical concerns, with the names of Fried and Foucault figuring prominently. The two books should complement each other, as between them they should answer the questions: out of what kinds of interest did Riegl's work emerge? How was his work constructed and how did its constituent elements relate to each other? How could his work be read by subsequent generations of historians, such as the second generation of the Vienna School, Kenneth Clark, Meyer Schapiro or ourselves? Of course, the last question is unanswerable in the sense that possible readings extend into the unforeseeable future, but at least we ought to have a grasp of the critical gap between Riegl and ourselves.

Iversen would have us believe that Riegl's 'fairly humble background and social awkwardness inform the range of his art-historical sympathies: the so-called minor arts, ornament, late Roman and Dutch art. Riegl turned from what were regarded as the pinnacles of artistic accomplishment, the art of classical antiquity and of the Renaissance, in order to champion these "others" of art history' (p. 18). This is, of course, completely misguided and underestimates the significance for Riegl of his profession and the institutional context within which he worked. According to Schlosser, the artistic interests of the Vienna School emerged out of Böhm's collection, which had its own distinctive physiognomy, a product of his being a 'man of the Vormärz', a member of the circle of the German Nazarenes and a Viennese bourgeois collector. Eitelberger, who was Böhm's pupil, established the Austrian Museum of Arts and Crafts within the context of the much wider Arts and Crafts movement. Wickhoff used objects from the Merovingian, Carolingian and Ottonian periods in his museum seminars. Riegl followed Wickhoff as Curator of Textiles, and his writing was integral to his employment at the museum.

Riegl's first major work, *Stilfragen,* can be understood as an answer to the question of how it is possible to write a history of ornament. Goodyear had handled the matter in terms of a theory of ornament as symbol; Semper would have found such an approach congenial. It was Riegl's bold choice to examine the developing morphology of a motif in terms of ideas of pure visual structure. This only occurred after he had written *Altorientalische Teppiche,* which was in the earlier Semperian mould; the connection with the Arts and Crafts movement is brought out clearly in Olin's chapter 'Style as Structural Symbolism'. But what motivated Riegl to adopt the formalist practice that he used? Certainly the language of analysis devised by the commentators on ornamental design. Furthermore, as Olin points out, 'Kunstwollen' was used in *Stilfragen* as a 'principle he wished to resurrect, rather than introduce' (p. 71). Olin's stress on the continuity between Riegl's work and his predecessors is much more useful than the idea of a radical break.

Olin's insight into the connection between Riegl's use of the term 'Kunstwollen' and that of his contemporaries provokes questions about his use of formalist techniques of analysis in *Spätrömische Kunstindustrie* (SK). Hildebrand's approach to visual analysis was influential, as we know, Wölfflin having famously declared that '"Problem der Form" fell like a refreshing shower on parched earth'.[12] Olin does discuss Hildebrand, but what were the other available options; what was the common currency of formalist criticism? The conditions which made SK possible were a commitment to the stylistic unity of the arts, for which the Arts and Crafts movement was responsible, and a language which made discussion of carvings, jewellery, architecture and painting equal on the same terms. But what were the habits of analysis of the Viennese scholars in their museum seminars when they were confronted with the immediate problems of talking about *objets d'art*? Drawing analogies with linguistics in this context,[13] as Iversen does, is not particularly useful because of the essential visuality of the objects under consideration.

When it comes to establishing connections between Riegl's ideas and those of the leading philosophers and psychologists, one is on very dangerous ground. Iversen suggests a connection with Herbart, Olin with Wundt: Riegl studied with Zimmerman who was a student of Herbart and reader of Wundt; Olin feels that Riegl was closer to Wundt than to Herbart. How precise can one be? Similar problems attach to the use of the label 'Hegelian', and did Riegl incline to Schopenhauer or to Kant? Arguments over influence are notoriously difficult to resolve, and it would actually make more sense to ask how adequate the ideas were to the tasks they had to perform. Analysis, as opposed to exposition, is not, unfortunately, one of Olin's strong points, particularly when it comes to complex philosophical ideas.

For Riegl's contemporary readers, two things seemed very likely: that he produced convincing analyses of points of visual continuity between visual artefacts, and that his conclusions were in accord with the overall purposes of the publications of the Austrian museums. Olin rightly points to the cosmopolitan ambitions of the Österreichisches Institut für Geschichtsforschung: in establishing the Late Roman Empire as an important connecting link between ancient and modern civilisation as Riegl did, there was a strong cultural argument against petty nationalisms which threatened to disrupt 'greater Austria' (pp. 18–19). Riegl's observations on the connections between art and culture, expressed in *Stilfragen* as 'Kunstweise' or 'Kunstgeist' (pp. 71–2), were hardly significant in *SK* in comparison to the achievement of diagnosing visual connections between a selected range of artefacts. The same is arguably true of his last major study, *Das holländische Gruppenporträt*.

Riegl's *Die historische Grammatik der bildenden Künste* would have made his reputation as a scholar of 'Kunstgeschichte als Geistesgeschichte', if it had ever been published.[14] But it was, actually, his successor Dvořák who attained that recognition. Riegl would be remembered as the scholar with the marvellous eye and gift for visual analysis, a person who established what the problems of a history of visual analysis might be; at that level, his work holds a fascination still today. The turning point in Riegl's posthumous career came in the 1920s when his work was republished and, one could argue, recuperated by Meyer Schapiro's Second Vienna School. Internationalism gave way to nationalism, and Nazism reared its ugly head in the precincts of the Österreichisches Institut für Geschichtsforschung and Vienna University's two institutes of art history.

It was in the summer of 1933 that Gombrich, then a student at Schlosser's 2nd Institute of Art History, drafted his attack on Riegl and Dvořák, subsequently published in the Vienna School's house journal *Kritische Berichte*.[15] At that time, he only accused them of ' [unreflexively assuming] the unity of the art concept, of the spiritual and social function of art within different spiritual/intellectual circles and constellations'. By asserting the unity of 'Kunstwollen', Riegl and Dvořák were able to assimilate the art of the past to that of the present, but they did so by adopting what Gombrich described as a thoroughly ahistorical aestheticism.

At the beginning of 1936, Gombrich took up residence at the Warburg Institute, which had been moved from Hamburg to London. Its Director, Fritz Saxl, had been trained in Vienna, under Dvořák, and was in contact with Gombrich's research colleague Ernst Kris, who recommended him as an amanuensis to Gertrud Bing. As we all know, Gombrich became Riegl's most effective critic. But, it must be stressed, it was Sedlmayr's essay 'Die Quintessenz der Lehren Riegls'[16] that he attacked in *Art and Illusion*, and it was Meyer Schapiro's criticism of Riegl for his invocation of 'racial dispositions' that he cited.[17] We know that both Sedlmayr and Schapiro had their own agendas as far as the use of Riegl was concerned. In the Preface to *The Sense of Order*, Gombrich later declared:

> I cannot but regret that my continued interest in the theories of one of the most original thinkers of our discipline has earned me the reputation of being hostile to this great man [Riegl]. It is quite true that I have not been able to accept all his findings, but I still believe that one can pay no greater tribute to a scholar or scientist than to take his theories seriously and examine them with all the care they deserve.[18]

It was Riegl's observational analyses and their theoretical underpinning in perceptual psychology which drew Gombrich's greatest attention. Sedlmayr had his own uses for Riegl's work, and Gombrich attacked Sedlmayr, Pächt and their colleagues again in the pages of *Art Bulletin* in 1964, echoing, though not mentioning, Schapiro's earlier arguments.[19] It is no exaggeration to say that in Gombrich's work we have the most fully-developed analytical rebuttal both of Riegl's theories and his rather dated, and context-dependent, historical assumptions. Many of Riegl's visual analyses still stand.

The question posed by Gombrich's work, and the fact that we have a massive intellectual apparatus to criticise Riegl, is again one of reception. What do we do with Riegl? As an answer to this question, Iversen's book is of little value. Perhaps if it had been brought out when she completed her dissertation in 1979, it would have been of some use. Although anglophones had Kayser's translation of an extract from *Das holländische Gruppenporträt*,[20] we had no translations of his other work. Times have changed. The work of the Vienna School has been making its way to us through translations into Italian, Spanish and French.[21] We now have Winkes's translation *The Late Roman Art Industry* (Rome, 1985) and Kain's *Problems of Style* (Princeton, 1992) and we can begin to make up our own minds about the value of Riegl's work. Iversen's attempt to update it by reference to Benveniste, Fried, Kemp and Foucault just makes me wonder whether she was happy writing about Riegl in the first place; it may be useful to the follower of fashion, but does nothing to build on Gombrich's critique and adds nothing to Podro's complex and demanding book *The Critical Historians of Art* (New Haven and London, 1982). The reason for reading Riegl must be that there is still a great deal to think and argue about: he offers not just another theory, but a complex body of analysis which creates an intriguing variety of problems.

Rather different problems are raised by Olin's book. It is a solid piece of historical scholarship, and she has made good use of the Riegl archives: she certainly knows her Riegl. But there are times when her writing becomes quite opaque. There are also times when she does not seem to have a perfectly clear grasp of the background philosophical, theoretical and psychological issue. On these occasions, I sense the yawning gulf which exists between Central European and Anglo-American art-historians. Whatever colleagues in Prague, Budapest and Vienna may make of Riegl's work, their work draws on an enormous treasure-house of knowledge of nineteenth-century intellectual history; it is that kind of intimacy that Olin lacks. This can only add to the excitement of reading Olin's book: one wants to know so much more.

We have lived with Riegl's legacy since Gombrich published *Art and Illusion*.[22] Perhaps some of our colleagues can begin to take Gombrich more seriously, to adopt a more rigorous attitude to the application of science to visual imagery and of logic to the analysis of arguments. That would be Gombrich's own version of what he is up to, in that he sees himself as living up to Wickhoff's founding ambitions for the Vienna School:

> What it aims at ... is to place Art History into the ranks of the other historical sciences by treating its subject scientifically. For this has by no means been achieved as yet. It can everywhere be observed that despite a number of scientific achievements the History of Art is not taken fully seriously by learned societies and colleagues in the neighbouring fields of history and philology. One must admit that this does not happen without reason for there are few disciplines in which it is still possible for empty verbiage and shallow reasoning to be tolerated and for publications to be launched which must be regarded as sheer mockery of all principles of scientific method.[23]

It could be argued that the Wickhoff's Vienna School of Art History left Vienna with Gombrich. Needless to say, the New Vienna School would not have felt too happy about that.[24]

Notes

1. 'Three Decades of Art History in the United States', in *Meaning in the Visual Arts* (New York, 1955), pp. 329–30.
2. See, for example, Yve-Alain Bois, 'Panofsky Early and Late', *Art in America* (July 1985), pp. 9–15.
3. I am conscious of the debate which has been provoked by Gombrich's use of the expression 'Hegelian' in *In Search of Cultural History* and aware that the use of the tempered expression 'neo-Hegelian' can do little more than mark a significant problem. That problem is too complex to be addressed here, however.
4. Published in *Art Bulletin*, 18 (1936), pp. 258–66.
5. *Die Wiener Genesis herausgegeben von Wilhelm Ritter von Härtel und Franz Wickhoff* (Vienna, 1895), translated into English as *Franz Wickhoff, Roman Art: Some of its principles and their application to early Christian painting*, ed. Mrs S. Arthur Strong (London, 1900).
6. In his review of Gombrich's *New Light on Old Masters*, *Apollo* (January 1987), p. 75.

7. *Another Part of the Wood* (London, 1974), pp. 114 and 108.
8. See 'Kenneth Clark's "Piero della Francesca"', in E. H. Gombrich, *Reflections on the History of Art*, ed. Richard Woodfield (Oxford, 1987).
9. There is a study available for Hungary: Ernö Marosi (ed.), *Die ungarische Kunstgeschichte und die Wiener Schule 1846-1930* (Budapest, 1983).
10. J. von Schlosser, 'Die Wiener Schule der Kunstgeschichte. Rückblick auf ein Säkulum deutscher Gelehrtenarbeit in Österreich', *Mitteilungen des Österreichischen Instituts für Geschichtsforschung*, Ergänzungsband XIII, Heft 2, p. 13. My account of the Vienna School is indebted to this work.
11. The series is conveniently listed in the catalogue of the library of the Victoria and Albert Museum.
12. *Classic Art*, tr. Peter and Linda Murray (London, 1952), p. xi.
13. The importance of linguistics does tend to get exaggerated. Schlosser worte: 'I also do not fail to recommend at every opportunity the study of the new philology to my students, and above all the romanic science of language [linguistics] which is especially fruitful for them ...' (op. cit., p. 62). This was not something that Gombrich experienced (response to a verbal question).
14. The text was not published until 1966 by Karl Swoboda and Otto Pächt (Graz, 1966).
15. 'J. Bodonyi, *Entstehung und Bedeutung des Goldgrundes in der spätantiken Bild-composition (Archaeologiai Értesitë, 46, 1932/3)*', *Kritische Berichte zur Kunstgeschicht-lichen Literatur*, 5 (1932/3), pp. 65-75. On which see my article 'Gombrich, Formalism and the Description of Works of Art', *British Journal of Aesthetics*, 34 (1994), pp. 134-45.
16. In Alois Riegl, *Gesammelte Aufsätze* (Augsburg and Vienna, 1929).
17. *Art and Illusion* (London, 1968), p. 16.
18. *The Sense of Order* (Oxford, 1979), p. viii.
19. Review of *Kunstgeschichte und Kunsttheorie im 19. Jahrundert (Probleme der Kunstwissenschaft, 1)* (Berlin, 1963), *Art Bulletin*, 46 (1964), pp. 418-20.
20. In W. Eugene Kleinbauer, *Modern Perspectives in Western Art History* (New York, 1971).
21. It is an indictment of our scholarship that we have not yet produced our own updated edition of Schlosser's *Die Kunstliteratur* (Vienna, 1924) as have the French: *La Littérature artistique* (Paris, 1984).
22. Having cited Clark on Riegl, it would be appropriate to cite his response to Gombrich: 'Eight of his volumes stand on my shelves. I have read them all, but owing to my inability to follow philosophical arguments, I cannot claim that I have always understood them': 'Stories of Art', *New York Review of Books* (24 November 1977), p. 36. The rest of the review is quite revelatory about Clark's lack of understanding (though it was he who was responsible for Gombrich's giving the Mellon Lectures, which became *Art and Illusion*).
23. *Kunstgeschichtliche Anzeigen. Beiblatt der 'Mittheilungen des Instituts für österreichische Geschichtsforschung'*, 1 (1904), p. 1; translation by E. H. Gombrich in a personal communication.
24. In this context, see Otto Pächt's article: 'Art Historians and Art Critics - vi: Alois Riegl', *Burlington Magazine*, 105 (1963), pp. 188-93. It is interesting to see that neither Olin nor Iversen comments on Pächt's reply to Gombrich's critique of Riegl.

Part Three
Reviews

John P. Spielman, *The City and the Crown: Vienna and the Imperial Court, 1600–1740* (West Lafayette, IN: Purdue University Press, 1993), xiv + 264 pp. $32.00.

John Spielman's study of the emergence of Vienna as a capital reveals a complex history which belies the later self-image of the city as the Austrian Habsburgs' loyal and proud 'Haupt- und Residenzstadt'. The city had been of only marginal significance for the medieval empire, and by the sixteenth century its economic foundations had been eroded. The arrival of the court therefore inaugurated a new phase in its development. The beginnings in the 1520s were far from promising: the Catholic Spanish court was viewed with suspicion and often hostility by the predominantly Lutheran urban community. It was only in the 1620s that the monarchy finally established a preference for Vienna over centres such as Prague, Linz or Graz and that the relationship between court and city evolved into one of mutual dependence fruitful to both sides. Two factors were crucial: the accommodation market and defence.

The need to accommodate a growing number of court officials, administrators and military personnel led to the development of a system whereby the city became to all intents and purposes occupied territory. By the 1670s, the quartering system had generated minutely detailed surveys of all urban property, and a carefully graduated scale of exemptions, as a sign of privilege, or as an inducement to rebuild on a larger and more ornate scale. The reality was inevitably more chaotic than the well-ordered system to which the court high marshals aspired. Demand for accommodation fluctuated sharply according to how many Habsburg relatives, each with a 'Hofstaat' of some 500, were in residence. Many courtiers complained of harassment by their reluctant landlords. The landlords in turn took vocal exception to abuses of the system, such as the illegal subletting of quarters by nobles who themselves disdained to live in often cramped and uncomfortable rooms. Above all, they resented the use of quarters, especially by the court guards, as illegal taprooms or sales premises for the thriving black economy in all manner of goods to which the resourceful military found access.

Despite the problems, however, the symbolic relationship between court and city was mutually beneficial. The court gained a forum for the theatrical display of majesty; the city prospered from its main economic activity; and the relationship was further underpinned by the increasingly important role of the city as banker and moneylender to the court. The complex web of overlapping interests also combined in initiatives such as the expulsion of the Jews in 1670. From the court point of view, it was a Counter-Reformation initiative. The city in turn was rid of an irksome and threatening minority in a move which also expanded its property base in the form of the Leopoldstadt.

At the same time, Vienna's military vulnerability both cemented the community of interests and hindered the city's development as a capital. From the 1520s to the 1680s, the spectre of Turkish aggression was a constant threat and, on occasion, a devastating reality. Ironically, the near-destruction of the city in 1683 laid the foundations for the emergence of the baroque capital. The quartering system with its complex exemption provisions proved a uniquely effective instrument in promoting rebuilding on a larger scale and in a more uniform ornate baroque style.

The rebuilding and expansion of the city between 1683 and about 1740 both created the external appearance that still survives today and reinforced the ties between city, court and administration. Indeed, when eighteenth-century cameralists conceived projects to promote local commerce and industry, they were frustrated by insurmountable problems. More important was what they took for granted: the reality of a city whose prime economic foundation was government.

Spielman's careful study represents a significant contribution to the history of European cities in the early modern period. At the same time, he illuminates an important facet of the making of the Habsburg monarchy. As Vienna prepares for the millennial celebrations of 1996, it is salutary to be reminded that the Imperial seat of government was constructed as little as two-and-a-half centuries ago.

JOACHIM WHALEY

Charles H. Sherman and T. Donley Thomas, *Johann Michael Haydn (1737–1806): A Chronological Thematic Catalogue of his Works*, Thematic Catalogues no. 17 (Stuyvesant, NY: Pendragon Press, 1993), xv + 385 pp., $64.00.

Big brothers cast hefty shadows. If it were not so, Michael Haydn would surely be far more widely performed, discussed, studied, enjoyed: he is a major composer in his own right, and I suppose we may have to wait until 2006 for a proper appreciation of his achievements. True, there was a faint flicker of recognition of his importance in 1987, on the occasion of the 250th anniversary of his birth (notably in the lavish pictorial biography by Gerhard Croll and Kurt Vössing), but for most musicians, and nearly all music-lovers, Joseph Haydn's younger brother is simply someone who was Mozart's colleague in Salzburg and wrote some symphonies and quite a lot of church music. A quick glance at the compact-disc catalogue might even suggest that Michael Haydn's two columns are just an appendage to the twenty-nine columns devoted to *the* Haydn.

Of course, there has been important pioneering research on Michael Haydn. As Charles Sherman points out in his useful if brief Preface to the volume under review, Nikolaus Lang may even have compiled the first thematic catalogue of Haydn's works while the composer was still alive; certainly there are no fewer than six in Lang's hand (which is deceptively like that of the composer himself), and Haydn's friend Werigand Rettensteiner compiled another in 1814.

Nearly a century passed before the next serious attempt was made to catalogue Michael Haydn's works. This was Lothar Herbert Perger's thematic listing of the instrumental music, printed as an invaluable preface to the publication in *Denkmäler der Tonkunst in Österreich* (Year XIV/2, vol. 29;

1907) of seven orchestral and chamber compositions. Perger's work was augmented in 1925 when Anton Maria Klafsky brought out a somewhat random and unreliable thematic catalogue of the compositions for the church, published in the same series (Year XXXII/1, vol. 62) in a volume including some of these works.

Sherman and Thomas thus had predecessors whose achievements had to be taken into account but were of variable quality. What makes their catalogue different from many is their decision to follow strict chronological order (Michael Haydn was a precise dater of almost all his autograph scores), rather than the pattern established most notably in Hoboken's three volumes devoted to the works of Joseph Haydn, which for very sound reasons favours grouping by type of work. Köchel, of course, was one who favoured the chronological approach in his monumental Mozart catalogue, and Deutsch with Schubert was another; the chief problem arising from this method is that, when datings and orderings are proven to be false, alternative numbers (often involving superscript letters and/or complex double numbers) have to be introduced with each new edition.

As the compilers are well aware, the 838 compositions which they number may with time be augmented or diminished, or require reordering (indeed, two last-minute insertions already use subspecies numbers). However, theirs is a notable achievement, likely to prove more durable than the first editions of Köchel and of Deutsch (thanks to the relative reliability of the composers in precise dating, rather than to any shortcomings of the earlier cataloguers). Apart from instances of clumsy word-spacing, the publishers have done a very good job: this is a solid and attractive large-format volume, easy to use, built to last.

The music incipits are limited to one stave, and do not include vocal entries unless the movement opens with them; brief descriptions follow, listing date, scoring, inclusion in previous catalogues, description of the autograph, and briefer notes on copies and editions. Apart from bibliography, index of titles/first lines of vocal works, and indexes of cross-references to the catalogues of Perger and Klafsky, the volume also includes no fewer than 162 figures of watermarks from the paper-types that occur in the autographs and authentic copies. Congratulations to everyone involved in the production of this fine addition to the stock in hand of music catalogues.

PETER BRANSCOMBE

Der Zauberflöte zweyter Theil, unter dem Titel: Das Labyrinth, oder Der Kampf mit den Elementen. Eine große heroisch-komische Oper in zwey Aufzügen von Emanuel Schikaneder. In Musik gesetzt von Herrn Peter Winter, Kapellmeister in Churpfalz-bayrischen Diensten. Vollständiges Textbuch, ed. Manuela Jahrmärker and Till Gerrit Waidelich, Wiener Stadt- und Landesbibliothek: Schriftenreihe zur Musik 7 (Tutzing: Hans Schneider, 1992), 175 pp., DM 98.00.

The feathered figures adorning the portico of the Theater an der Wien are no doubt assumed by most observers to represent some of the progeny who by the end of the original *Zauberflöte* are still only a twinkle in their parents' music. The editors of this volume suggest with some plausibility that they may more precisely represent some of Papageno's siblings, who actually turn out in force to help their brother resist the wiles of the Queen of the Night in Schikaneder's sequel. *Das Labyrinth*, with music by Peter Winter and stage machinery of almost unprecedented elaboration (and corresponding unreliability), was first staged at the Freihaustheater in June 1798, appearing in a revised version in 1803, and performed in Vienna over sixty times; it was played in a number of other German cities, including Berlin (see the account in Zelter's letter to Goethe, 10 August 1803), but was generally lambasted by the critics, and disappeared from the repertoire after about 1830. There have been a couple of revivals in the twentieth century, but, whatever the quality of Winter's music, it is hard to disagree radically with Zelter's verdict, prejudiced though it no doubt was, that the text is 'von der unbegreiflichsten Schlechtheit'.

The editors have produced the present version on the basis of the surviving manuscript text with its various revisions, supplemented with reference to other surviving manuscript and published sources; and they have included some interesting illustrative material. In their postscript, each contributing separately identified sections, they do what they can to bring out the work's historical interest. Manuela Jahrmärker argues that it can be seen as embodying the transition from a baroque form, allegorically embodying a conflict between clearly-defined good and evil forces, to a proto-Romantic one in which the forces involved are characterised more ambiguously. Waidelich, however, points out that good and evil are more ambiguously presented, at least initially, in the original *Zauberflöte*: in the sequel, the battle-lines are much more clearly drawn, at least in intention, though the behaviour of Sarastro and his party no longer suggests any definable humanitarian ideal. (Possible topical allusions are not very seriously discussed; and, incidentally, the word 'freemasonry' occurs here only in the title of one item in the brief bibliography.) Apart from this basic confrontation – as in Goethe's projected sequel, the plot essentially rests upon a counter-attack on the 'initiates' by the Queen of the Night – the details of motivation are confused and inconsequential in the extreme. The editors rightly point out that the title *Das Labyrinth* represents no real dependency, such as might be and has indeed generally been supposed, on Einsiedel's tale in Wieland's *Dschinnistan*: the labyrinth itself supplies only a very minor part of the protagonists' tribulations. Tamino's magic flute is heard on two or three occasions; but considerably more importance is assigned to Papageno's bells, whose assistance is invoked repeatedly in the second act and whose music furnishes the principal theme of Winter's overture. It is indeed the feathered frolics of Papageno and his associates which provide such limited attraction as the work still possesses.

F. J. LAMPORT

Sieglinde Klettenhammer (ed.), *Zwischen Weimar und Wien. Grillparzer – Ein Innsbrucker Symposion*, Innsbrucker Beiträge zur Kulturwissenschaft: Germanistische Reihe 45 (Innsbruck: Institut für Germanistik, 1992), 239 pp., 324 Sch./DM 52.00.

Grillparzer-Bilder 1991. Dokumentation und Bibliographie von Artikeln deutschsprachiger Zeitungen zum 200. Geburtstag des Dichters, ed. Monika and Michael Klein, Innsbrucker Beiträge zur Kulturwissenschaft: Germanistische Reihe 46 (Innsbruck: Institut für Germanistik, 1993), 129 pp., 288 Sch./DM 48.00.

In purely quantitative terms, the response to the bicentenary of Grillparzer's birth was initially rather disappointing after the large number of publications that had marked the 100th anniversary of the writer's birth in 1972. Throughout 1991, however, conferences and symposia were held in a variety of locations (including America and New Zealand, but not Germany), and the proceedings of the most important of these academic gatherings have gradually been appearing in print. The symposium in Innsbruck in April 1991 arguably presented the most structured approach in seeking to redefine Grillparzer's literary position between Weimar and Vienna. The majority of the essays reinforce the increasingly established picture of Grillparzer as a productive synthesis of earlier and contemporary ideas which in turn adumbrates subsequent literary developments, and the various contributions examine his relationship with the Enlightenment (Roger Bauer, Werner Bauer), with Classicism (Schaum), his views on German literature (Doppler, Bachmaier), or his position within literary history (Krolop). For Roger Bauer, Grillparzer was concerned to marry freedom to ideas of order, while according to Doppler's preface Grillparzer as a product of Josefinian philosophy was equally distant from the Baroque idea of *Ordo* and from German idealism or Romanticism, but tended instead towards the psychological realism of the fin de siècle. Both Doppler, in his main contribution, and Schaum emphasise that Grillparzer's characters lack the self-determination, the ability to control their own fate that is so central to Classicism, but that in a play such as *Ein Bruderzwist in Habsburg* Grillparzer is in any case more concerned with the wider contexts of empire, and human culture and justice, than with the individual fate of Rudolf.

The most original approach to the overall theme of the symposium is taken by Ulrich Fülleborn in his study of temporality. Fülleborn argues that Grillparzer's dramas reveal an increasing awareness of time, both in contrasting scenes that express a different concept of time (a scene of relative calm in which time almost stands still, followed by a scene of rapid action) and in the juxtaposition of time as a feature of human life and destiny with time in a pure, almost mythical sense. Not least as a consequence of the French Revolution, Grillparzer sees the fates of individuals and nations very much as temporal processes with beginning, changes and an ending. For Fülleborn, all these features contrast with the apparently timeless action in Schiller's plays and point forward to the modern scientific idea of complementarity.

An important aim of the symposium was to focus on Grillparzer's epigrams, diaries and other autobiographical writings. W. E. Yates rightly complains (p. 160) that the diaries have received scant attention and sets out to consider their importance for Grillparzer's self-awareness in matters of literary production. Yates also underlines Grillparzer's desire to be alone on his travels, his refusal to meet people even when he had letters of introduction, while Lengauer evaluates the diaries as an indication of 'Publizitätsverweigerung'. Bachmaier examines the understanding of literature revealed in the epigrams, as Grillparzer highlights the aesthetic faults of all new developments, although in what might be seen as an excess of academic zeal Bachmaier feels constrained to provide a lengthy semantic explanation of the concept 'new'.

Günther Nenning is clearly not restrained by such niceties, whether in the cause of accuracy or pedantry. The lament *(Grillparzer-Bilder,* p. 84) that the bicentenary of Grillparzer's birth was in danger of being swamped by the media hype generated by the celebration of the 200th anniversary of Mozart's death is well founded, but in seeking to redress the balance Nenning claims Grillparzer as the undiscovered hero of postmodernism, someone of political insight with a fear of the new. The fanatics of progress whom Grillparzer feared in his own day resemble those who would now take Austria into an EU dominated by the Germans. Nenning's conclusion that 'im Grillparzer-Jahr wird die Welt Grillparzerisch' (p. 88) may be far-fetched, but the articles in *Grillparzer-Bilder* at least indicate that in January 1991 attention was briefly deflected from Vienna's adopted son to its legitimate son.

The volume is a selection of articles from Austrian, German and Swiss newspapers and magazines, written partly by journalists and columnists, but also by Grillparzer scholars such as Helmut Bachmaier, Dieter Borchmeyer and Ulrich Fülleborn. Not surprisingly on such an occasion, a recurring theme is the insistence on Grillparzer's modernity as a complex and contradictory figure who, according to Fülleborn, combined an emphasis on moral responsibility with the depiction of man's instincts and drives, richness of life with artistic content. Borchmeyer underlines the self-criticism verging on self-hatred that was a central theme of his diaries and which is a further characteristic anticipating twentieth-century writers such as Kafka. Adalbert Schmidt writes of the psychological complexity of Grillparzer's character that is reflected in the dramatic constellations of the sexes in his plays, and the convincing depiction of women is similarly underlined elsewhere, by Bachmaier, Borchmeyer and in particular by Renate Wagner. Borchmeyer presents Grillparzer as perhaps the most theatre-conscious of great German dramatists, always aware of the demands of the stage and increasingly undermining the autonomy of verbal language as the medium of the theatre. Yet ultimately he was 'ein Moderner wider Willen' (p. 27) seeking to force his modernity into pre-modern, classically-composed artistic forms.

One dissenting voice is that of Detlef Felken, for whom Grillparzer was a Viennese bureaucrat still adhering to Baroque ideas of divinely-sanctioned *Ordo* and creating characters that lack real presence for today's audiences. Not surprisingly, however, the picture of Grillparzer in the press on the occasion of a bicentenary was generally positive, and, as the editor points out (p. 8), the articles in the collection seek to summarise Grillparzer's significance for the educated layperson rather than offering new critical insights. Whether the Innsbruck papers achieve that latter aim must be a matter of debate (what do we mean by 'new'?), but W. E. Yates sensibly draws our attention to two obvious gaps in Grillparzer scholarship: a complete edition of contemporary reviews, and a concordance to the dramatist's works. It remains to be seen whether those gaps will have been filled in time for the next anniversary in 2022.

IAN F. ROE

Susan Doering, *Der wienerische Europäer. Johann Nestroy und die Vorlagen seiner Stücke* (Munich: Ludwig, 1992), 327 pp., DM 48.00

Inside this rather thin book there are two much more substantial ones waiting to get out. Susan Doering's study of Nestroy's source material falls somewhat oddly into two halves: the first half presents on overview of relations between the theatres in four major European cities, Vienna, Paris, London and Berlin, showing how rapidly news of theatrical success travelled, and how readily material was transferred from one stage to another. The second half of the book is taken up with a transcription from manuscript of Nestroy's own translation of the Kock-Varin vaudeville *La Jolie Fille du Faubourg*, which formed the basis for Nestroy's own comedy, *Das Mädl aus der Vorstadt*. Both of these are, in themselves excellent enterprises; but to cram them both into one relatively short book was surely misguided.

The first section, 'Literarische Vorlagen auf den Wiener Theaterbühnen', makes a valuable contribution to our understanding of the commercial and cosmopolitan nature of Viennese popular theatre. Against the sentimental – and deeply entrenched – notion of an ethnically pure theatrical tradition (the rosy vision of Alt-Wien and the 'Backhendlzeit'), Dr Doering sets a wealth of information which demonstrates how extensively the Viennese turned to other literatures for inspiration, whether individually, from the lending libraries, or collectively, on the stage. She discusses the rise of the vaudeville in the late 1830s and the network of foreign correspondents, theatrical agencies, translators and publishers which brought such works to the attention of playwrights like Nestroy; she also shows how the conditions prevailing in the Viennese theatre – copyright regulations, economic pressures, the need to tailor a work to existing ensembles and exacting audiences, and finally the requirements of the censor – combined to affect the choice of source material and the way in which it was treated. A shorter section, 'Literarische Vorlagenbearbeitung am Beispiel Johann Nestroys', deals more specifically with Nestroy's own practice, as a prelude to the manuscript transcription which takes up the rest of the book.

Interesting though all this undoubtedly is, there is just not enough room to do justice to the material, and the result is patchy and superficial. Confusion is caused by the fact that the information is not always as well organised and presented as it might be (there are some basic slips in layout, choice of font, etc., too, which could have been obviated by careful proof-reading). Some illuminating insights into Nestroy's alteration of his source material in the interests of character, structure, or satiric observation of society, would have benefited from a more comprehensive treatment of the topic.

The same goes for the manuscript transcription, which surely deserves more detailed attention than it receives here; indeed, it could have furnished material for an entire book on its own. An unfortunate choice of layout obscures the value of what has been transcribed: why did the author not opt for parallel texts, which would have shown clearly where Nestroy summarises, paraphrases or omits text? It might also have been helpful to adhere to the editing conventions of the new historical-critical edition (Vienna: Jugend und Volk), to which this material forms an important supplement. The short critical commentary which concludes the transcription could have appeared either at the foot of each page or, perhaps more helpfully, in extended form as an introduction to Nestroy's procedure.

Dr Doering's knowledge of her subject is extensive, and the object of her inquiry a valuable one; yet the treatment of the topic is ultimately disappointing. On this occasion, perhaps, 'two for the price of one' was not such a strong selling point after all.

LOUISE ADEY HUISH

F. R. Bridge, *The Habsburg Monarchy among the Great Powers, 1815–1918* (New York and Oxford: Berg, 1990), viii + 417 pp., £39.95.

István Deák, *Beyond Nationalism. A Political and Social History of the Habsburg Officer Corps, 1848–1918* (New York: Oxford University Press, 1990), xiii + 273 pp.

Mark Cornwall (ed.), *The Last Years of Austria-Hungary* (Exeter: University of Exeter Press, 1990), 155 pp., £7.50

Samuel R. Williamson Jr, *Austria-Hungary and the Origins of the First World War* (London Macmillan, 1991), xviii + 272 pp., £35.00

Three institutions are commonly credited with upholding the Habsburg Monarchy in its final phase: the army, the civil service and above all the monarchy. These were the powers that kept the centrifugal forces of the various nationalisms from pulling the empire apart. F. R. Bridge's study is essentially an account of Habsburg diplomacy as it evolved from the Congress of Vienna to the military defeats of 1918. It is also an account of the men who shaped foreign policy, who interpreted the wishes of the Emperors and on occasion pursued their own agenda. Bridge's approach is based on a range of sources but draws most effectively on unpublished archive material. The private papers of Aehrenthal, for example, feature prominently in chapters 6 and 7 on Austro-Russian relations between 1897 and 1914. Presenting the complexities of Austria's foreign policy following the annexation of Bosnia-

Hercegovina in 1908 is no easy task, and it is one that Bridge accomplishes with an admirable eye for the ins and outs of Imperial power politics. This is history of the grand diplomatic sweep, the kind of history that summarises the interests of nationalist movements, indeed nations themselves in order to explain the dynamics behind the chain of events that led to the First World War.

The sociological detail that is of necessity lacking in a book like *The Habsburg Monarchy among the Great Powers* is to be found in abundance in István Deák's *Beyond Nationalism*. Since the publication in 1976 of Gunther Rothenberg's *The Army of Francis Joseph*, the last major study on the Royal and Imperial Army in English, the Habsburg Army and its officer corps in particular have continued to exert a fascination far beyond the borders of the old monarchy. In the past fifteen years, a number of detailed monographs, among them doctoral dissertations at the University of Vienna, have added considerably to our knowledge. Sadly, little of this material has been available in a more readily accessible form outside Austria. It is to Deák's credit that he integrates many of the findings of this newer research successfully into his general account. Yet his work is much more than a synthesis of its author's evidently extensive research on the subject.

Probably the most important departure from the accepted view of the Habsburg officer corps contained in this book is the intriguing suggestion that it may be an oversimplification to describe the overwhelming majority of Habsburg officers as 'German' (a figure of over 70 per cent is typically cited). The situation as normally presented is of a predominantly 'German-Austrian' officer corps leading a polyglot army that contained a representative proportion of every group in the Empire. The Habsburg officer often had to learn the language(s) of the men under his command. In theory, he could lose his job for failing to do so within a specified time. In practice, this rarely happened. In retrospect, such linguistic enterprise and the frequently reiterated 'apolitical' status of the officer were used to portray the officer corps as the faithful servant of the dynasty, loyal only to the supranational black-and-yellow idea. Deák's persuasive account of the statistics reminds us that while many officers would have given their mother tongue as 'German', this alone does not imply that they could all be counted as 'ethnic' Germans. A cursory study of the surnames of Habsburg officers would back up this view. Deák surmises on the basis of his detailed survey of two sample cohorts of career officers that only around half of the regular officer corps were German-speaking and of German-Austrian descent. Indeed, he concludes that 'if the Joint Army displayed any bias in its promotions, it was in favor of its Magyar officers' (p. 187). This was a bias that resulted from the peculiar arrangements for a Hungarian *honvéd* or reserve army of 1868. The *honvéd*, as an embryonic Hungarian national army, was a powerful attraction to Hungarian-speaking potential officers. In order to counteract its popularity, it would seem that the Habsburg state was forced into a kind of positive discrimination. For his scepticism towards the zealously collected and beautifully preserved records of the Habsburg bureaucracy, Deák is to be praised. He observes pointedly that the 'military did not know how to handle ethnic statistics' (p. 184).

186

A further bonus is Deák's epilogue on 'Habsburg Officers in the Successor States and in the Second World War', where the author traces some remarkable career paths. Former Habsburg officers were frequently to be found on opposing sides in the civil conflicts in the aftermath of the First World War. While it is true that more of them died for one fascist regime or another than were killed for opposing the Axis powers, it also remains true that some fought on the Allied side in the Second World War. Most welcoming to former black-and-yellow officers was the Polish Army, half of whose officers in 1922 were former soldiers of Franz Joseph. Puzzling over the vastly differing fates of former Imperial soldiers, Deák summarises: 'professionalism had a greater influence on these individuals than ideology. ... At war's end Habsburg officers found that gone forever was their sense of purpose in a professionalism directed chiefly toward preserving peace. Beyond this ... no political ideology could claim them as an indissoluble fraternity in the far-flung region that was once the Habsburg monarchy' (p. 212). The fact that professionalism itself could be and often was ideological in character does nothing to detract from the fairness of this judgement.

It should perhaps come as no surprise that the serious and thorough reappraisal of the role of the Habsburg officer corps that István Deák is able to give should come from the perspective of an American professor of Hungarian origin. His preface, for example, refers to Imperial echoes in the Hungary he knew in the 1930s. If anything has beset the writing of good general historical accounts of the Habsburg Empire, then it has been the fact that, of the successor states, only Austria laid claim to the Habsburg legacy in full measure. For good reason, of course; but as a result there has been an over-concentration on the German-speaking minority in the Austro-Hungarian Empire, at least as far as material written in German and English is concerned. And on this point I must take issue with Mark Cornwall's preface to his volume *The Last Years of Austria-Hungary*. He writes: 'The intricate linguistic composition of the Monarchy has undoubtedly thwarted many a prospective western historian, inducing him or her to seek refuge in calmer, usually western European, linguistic waters' (p. 3). While this is certainly true, it is problematic to go on to assert that 'Modern Austria, in viewing itself as something of an heir to the Habsburg Empire, has arguably been most capable of producing relatively impartial accounts of the Monarchy's last years' (p. 4). Most capable perhaps, but that does not mean that 'Modern Austria' has always done so. For one thing, the sheer scale of the physical legacy of the Habsburg era has made the task of Austrian archivists, librarians and academics an arduous one. Furthermore, presenting a positive image of the Habsburg era in the immediate post-1945 period had immense ideological significance in burying the all-too-recent Nazi past. While individual Austrian historians have made considerable contributions to a reassessment of the final years of the Habsburg Monarchy, the official version has often had more to do with the demands of the tourist trade and nostalgia for a vanished noble and civilised age.

Nevertheless, *The Last Years of Austria-Hungary* is to be recommended for the way in which it includes the perspectives of historical research from the other successor states in one volume. It bears the subtitle 'Essays in Political and Military History 1908–1918' and contains seven short pieces, principally on the former rather than the latter aspect. Contributions vary in length and quality, but all fulfil the blurb's promise of stimulating discussion and acting as a potential springboard for further research. F. R. Bridge, author of the work mentioned above, offers a view of 'The Foreign Policy of the Monarchy 1908–1918' that makes plain the way in which Austrian diplomats sealed the fate of the monarchy by making Habsburg foreign policy appear so absolutely dependent on Germany. He writes: 'The dynasty might be able to take a supranational, open-minded view: but the elite that controlled the machinery of the state had by 1918 become just as infected by the virus of nationalism, and just as narrowly inflexible, as the subject nationalities' (p. 29).

A brief essay by Z. A. B. Zeman on the four Austrian censuses between 1880 and 1910 provides precisely the kind of sceptical review of Habsburg statistics that has generally been lacking. He reminds the reader that the figures obtained were not in any sense neutral. By 'nationalism' he understands the patterns created by the evolving relationship between the nation and the state, and notes: 'In Eastern Europe this process was marked by an awareness, on the part of the politicians especially, of the vulnerability and fluidity of national groups and by their attempts to dam such fluidity' (p. 38).

The three essays which follow are devoted to surveys of the political interests and experiences of respectively the German-speaking Austrians, the Hungarians and the South Slavs. Lothar Höbelt's 'Austrian Pre-War Domestic Politics' covers well-trodden ground in a survey of political parties in the half of the monarchy run from Vienna, concluding that the administration 'was more or less successfully engaged in muddling through in time-honoured fashion in its last years of peace' (p. 58). Reading Höbelt's piece against the contributions from Tibor Zsuppán and Janko Pleterski provides exactly the kind of contrast that the editor was presumably hoping for when he arranged the collection.

The collection is rounded off by an essay on 'The Eastern Front 1914–1918' by Rudolf Jeřábek and one by Cornwall himself on 'The Dissolution of Austria-Hungary'. A final bibliographical essay will be of great assistance to students new to the field and can be recommended without reservation.

A more general work which also reflects the shifting emphasis in research on the Habsburg Monarchy is Samuel R. Williamson's *Austria-Hungary and the Origins of the First World War*. The text appears in the Macmillan series 'The Making of the 20th Century'. As such, it aims to provide sufficient narrative and explanation to ensure that the newcomer can follow the argument and at the same time offer source references and reassessments that will be of interest to the specialist. To this end, a helpful glossary of names and an outline chronology are provided, as well as a detailed bibliography. The centre of gravity of the book is firmly in the Balkans in the years 1908 to 1914 and the successes and failures of Habsburg policy in that region. Williamson considers Austro-Hungarian foreign policy in the international system and in the context of domestic politics. He provides separate chapters on Aehrenthal's legacy, the enemies and the allies of the monarchy and the diplomatic offensives conducted in the face of the First and Second Balkan Wars of 1912–13. At every stage he points out the intricacy and complexity of the Habsburg state, how very different it was from its German neighbour. He emphasises, for example, that Austria-Hungary's civilian leaders were not subordinate to its military ones but stood alongside them in the decision-making process. Indeed, reading Williamson after the specialised work of Deák and the essays edited by Cornwall, one begins to appreciate that a reconsideration of the significance of the army and of the evolving relations between language, nationality and culture in the Dual Monarchy has begun to produce a far less 'Western' view of the origins of the First World War than we have been accustomed to reading in English. The final years of Austria-Hungary continue to offer a challenge to our easy assumptions regarding national, political and ethnic identity. As Williamson puts it in his introduction, the problems that worried policymakers in Vienna and Budapest from 1908 to 1914 continue to trouble the leaders in Bonn, London and Washington.

IAN FOSTER

Juliane Vogel, *Elisabeth von Österreich: Momente aus dem Leben einer Kunstfigur*, mit einem kunstgeschichtlichen Exkurs von Gabriela Christen (Vienna: Brandstätter, 1992), 224 pp., DM 56.00.

'So many legends were inspired by the life of Empress Elisabeth, that it is difficult to assess her influence on events', says William M. Johnston in *The Austrian Mind* (1972). It is these legends, their sources and effects that Juliane Vogel sets out to trace and untangle. Proceeding from the polarised images of Valhalla, where maternal figures send their sons out to seek fame and ethereal ones point them to heaven, and all female figures lack individuality, she charts the specific images that make Elisabeth into a legend. She shows the willed, almost systematic construction of a public identity based on biographical material, on illusion and myth, and Elisabeth's own collusion with these. The first chapter deals with the markedly subjective and partisan biographical and literary sources. The next five focus on specific topoi: Elisabeth's passion for solitary travel; distaste for public ceremonies; her legendary beauty; the sorrow of her failed marriage and her son's death; and her own death. The author sets these in the context of Elisabeth's life, of the lives of other royal women, and of nineteenth-century history, showing how complex and fantastic legends gather around biographical facts. She makes the point that the life of a royal woman endows an average female biography – childhood, engagement, marriage, motherhood – with public, even historical significance, and it is this conjunction that attracts the makers of images and legends, and the historian who would ignore the average woman's life.

From the moment she becomes a public figure, on her engagement to Franz Joseph, Elisabeth is implicated in the process of image-making, first as an unwitting, relatively passive object, then later in her attempts to evade the deadly rituals of life at the Imperial Court, as an active, even compulsive participant. She invents alternative rituals to those of the Court; hers are self-absorbed parodies of the originals, carried out with an obsessional drive that exhausted and bewildered those around her. Her reclusiveness, her beauty and her fate attract comparison with literary, mythological and religious figures. Her sorrow when her son dies turns her into a *mater dolorosa*, her own death into a martyr. All this image-making, and her own part in it, is set against the declining influence of the monarchy in Europe and the replacement of royal women as public models by other public figures such as actresses. A final chapter by Gabriela Christen elucidates the many representations of Elisabeth in painting and sculpture. The book is generously provided with illustrations, showing Elisabeth at different stages of her life, as well as some of the historical or imaginary figures whose stories shape the complex image of her. One of the most interesting for feminist criticism is a 'Schriftbild' of Elisabeth (p. 17) by Heinrich Spitzer, a drawing of her head and shoulders formed from lines of writing from her biography, a literal example of 'writing the body'. This is a complex and fascinating study, in which diverse and copious material is moulded skilfully into a persuasive argument. The author and her collaborator make apparent the neurotic processes of image-making – the arbitrary associations and projections, the need to perfect and then to destroy a legend – but Elisabeth's involvement in these never makes her an unsympathetic figure. Perhaps it was the only option for a woman of undoubted spirit in her situation.

PATRICIA HOWE

Karlheinz Rossbacher, *Literatur und Liberalismus. Zur Kultur der Ringstraßenzeit in Wien* (Vienna: Jugend & Volk, 1992), 580 pp., 598 Sch.

Karlheinz Rossbacher's study of the literature and culture of the so-called 'Ringstraße' epoch is surely the most substantial publication of the year 1992 in the field of Austrian literary studies. It has the particular merit of redirecting critical attention to the literary life of a period which, unlike the fin de siècle, has not attracted synthetic treatment by scholars, and one with which citizens of the late twentieth century, perhaps overly influenced by Broch's judgemental comment on the period's lack of moral values, 'Wertvakuum der Epoche', have difficulty in empathising.

The author is well known for his work as editor and interpreter of late nineteenth-century prose fiction, notably Ebner, Saar and Anzengruber. Analysis of the exemplary character of their work in the context of the liberal era, together with that of Ada Christen and the feuilletonists Friedrich Kürnberger and Daniel Spitzer, forms the backbone of his book. Indeed, *Literatur und Liberalismus* offers the most sophisticated and authoritative study to date of the work of Saar and Ebner, while the – relatively brief – analysis of the literary phenomenon of Ada Christen, drawing widely on her unpublished work and exemplifying the economic situation of the writer in contemporary Vienna, is an original feature of the book.

It was one of the paradoxes of Viennese liberalism that in the immediate aftermath of Austria's defeat at the hands of Prussia, German cultural hegemony over Austria was greatest. This hegemony was expressed most forcibly in the theatre, the opera and in the monumental style of public art and architecture, which might seem inappropriate for Austria's historical situation. However, Viennese liberals not only accepted that hegemony but also actually went some way towards identifying themselves with the German 'Kulturnation', seeing its artistic manifestations as appropriate forms of the self-representation of an increasingly affluent section of modern society. They had, after all, much in common with their German counterparts in the 1870s. Both erroneously tended to suppose a future convergence between their sectional interest and that of society as a whole, just as they fallaciously anticipated a similar convergence between their own political policies and the future evolution of their state. One of the consequences of the preference of liberal patrons of the arts and arbiters of public taste in the 'Ringstraße' epoch for 'representational art' was to marginalise those whose dramatic talents would or could not conform. These included many of the major writers of the day and one of the epoch's most original talents, Ludwig Anzengruber. Their voices function as key witnesses in *Literatur und Liberalismus* to the ambiguities and paradoxes of the age; their texts, Rossbacher argues, compel the initiated to read them against the grain. All ultimately favoured prose or lyric poetry, and even Anzengruber, whom the censorship prevented from capitalising on his dramatic gifts after the great success of his timely *Pfarrer von Kirchfeld* (1870), turned a decade later, almost in despair, to prose fiction.

The book opens with a brilliant and sustained close reading of Saar's *Schloß Kostenitz* (pp. 33–42), in which temporal indicators, spatial and human relationships are made to reveal the social and political dynamic of the age; it is but the first and most accomplished of countless such exemplary textual analyses effectively employed by the author to signify broad trends. Rossbacher has clearly benefited from a characteristic feature of modern Austrian studies, which, incidentally, in this respect are rather different from the practice of 'Germanistik' in the Federal Republic, namely the collaborative nature of the work of the younger generation of Austrian Germanists. This collaboration embraces the work of Austrian social historians, such as Ernst Bruckmüller, Moritz Csáky, Wolfgang Häusler and Hannes Stekl; the author has drawn on Csáky's authoritative study of the operetta and Stekl's important work on Viennese architectural history and autobiography to contextualise the literary texts of the epoch. In their turn, Austria's historians have integrated literary texts into their own teaching and writing, something that is not common, except at an overly abstract level, among German historians. It seems to me a fact of very great significance and a singular achievement of the present study that, on the one hand, Rossbacher is able to convey a sense of someone who is writing *within* his nation's history and, on the other, that the liberal era in Vienna is clearly seen to form part of the continuity of Austrian history, across the paradoxes and self-contradictions which informed it and in spite of the hostile forces which it ultimately empowered to destroy it.

Rossbacher's approach affords the reader insight into the concerns and the self-understanding of representative figures of the age. From the opening pages of the introductory section on the Liberal era, its literary market and the position of the writer, which span some 100 pages, through the 360-page section on literary responses to the concerns of the age, Rossbacher engages his reader in a sustained conversation. Within the compass of each section, as for example on women, the Jews, the social question, the 'Kulturkampf' or the nationalities, he offers his reader a variety of perspectives on his subject, in terms of the production, distribution, consumption and impact of particular texts and genres, and with reference to sociological, philosophical and psychological theorists, among them Freud, Weber, Mannheim, Elias, Veblen and Habermas. The text moves fluently through easily-absorbed short subsections which provide a multiplicity of interlocking themes; both for the characterisation of the epoch and the exploration of the literary text, his use of the same text in different contextual perspective proves effective.

The public domain of the liberals was above all the modern capitalistic press, which diminished the moral authority of the creative writer of prose fiction at the same time as it afforded him, and her, the realistic opportunity of a career. *Literatur und Liberalismus* offers a substantial discussion and something of a rehabilitation of that most characteristic feature of the Viennese liberal press, the feuilleton. There are over seventy references in the index of proper names to the leading feuilletonists of the day, to Kürnberger, Schlögl, Speidel and Spitzer, and several more in the index of works cited (there is, alas, no subject index). These writers were perfectly aware of how much they were products of the 'culture industry' of their day, yet they used the genre to expose the inner contradictions of Viennese liberalism. Posterity, not least in the shape of such disparate figures as Karl Kraus, Hermann Broch and Stefan Zweig, tended to judge the feuilleton by reference to its weaker practitioners, those freewheelers, as it were, on the journalistic bandwagon. In the hand of a master, Rossbacher argues, following his own acutely formulated survey of the genre's salient characteristics on page 82, it is a work of art meriting sophisticated critical interpretation. In his finest work, such as *Mündlich und Schriftlich* of 1872 or *Ich suche im Nebel meinen Weg* of 1875, Kürnberger is in Rossbacher's view a pioneer of the critique of ideology via critique of language; he offers, as Hubert Lengauer, editor of the planned critical edition of Kürnberger's feuilletons, puts it, 'an aesthetic of resistance' to contemporary culture.

The discussion on the feuilleton reminds an English-speaking reader of the absence in liberal Vienna of the moral authority and power of consensus of the great British journals of the mid-Victorian era. Despite their long-lasting influence, they too were the work of a relatively small educated elite, who however managed, even while each represented a specific sociological group or spectrum of opinion, collectively to engage in genuinely public discourse.

What was the difference? To Kürnberger and Spitzer, the dialogue between author and reader, which appeared to be the hallmark of the feuilleton, was a fiction. 'It is a monologue with myself', wrote Kürnberger, comparing himself to Robinson Crusoe 'conversing with wind and wave'. By contrast, as Rossbacher exemplifies in the case of the 'Kulturkampf', while the rhetoric of the liberals, based on book culture, failed to create a genuine community, the oral culture of their opponents was based on a genuine dialogue, from the pulpit or the portals of the church, between priest and people.

Beyond doubt, Rossbacher, drawing creatively on the work of other Austrian colleagues, has produced a work full of arresting perspectives, and one which is a pleasure to read. He has succeeded in what he credits Daniel Spitzer as having achieved in his feuilletons: 'aus kleinen Zeichen einen großen Zusammenhang zu machen' (p. 84). As in the case of Spitzer and other great feuilletonists, the disparate nature of Rossbacher's material, as well as his chosen approach to his theme, results in a mosaic. But as in all great mosaics, art and craft are married in splendid harmony, and the grateful reader delights as much in the detail as in the grand design.

EDA SAGARRA

Maria Klanska, *Problemfeld Galizien in deutschsprachiger Prosa 1846–1914* (Vienna, Cologne, Weimar: Böhlau, 1991), 231 pp., 392 Sch./DM 56.00.

Galizien. Fotographien von Guido Baselgia, mit einem Essay von Verena Dohrn (Frankfurt: Jüdischer Verlag, 1993), 95 pp., DM 36.00.

The large number of publications on the culture and literatures of the easternmost provinces of the Habsburg Empire, Galicia and the Bukovina, testifies to the increasing interest in an area on the fringes of the old Europe which was hidden behind the Iron Curtain for so long.[1] The two volumes under review here deal with the Galicia of a bygone era, and, interestingly, with specific and seemingly contradictory aspects of the same phenomenon which still determine the prevalent view of this region in the public's eye: the very concrete 'Problemfeld' and the almost unreal 'myth' of Galicia (the latter forms the title of Verena Dohrn's introductory essay to Guido Baselgia's photographs).

Galicia appears as a problematic area in so far as ethnic, political, social and

---

1. To name but a few: M. Pollack, *Nach Galizien. Von Chassiden, Huzulen, Polen und Ruthenen. Eine imaginäre Reise durch die verschwundene Welt Ostgaliziens und der Bukowina* (Vienna/Munich, 1984); S. H. Kaszynski (ed.), *Galizien. Eine literarische Heimat* (Poznan, 1987); R. Rinner/K. Zerinschek (eds), *Galizien als gemeinsame Literaturlandschaft* (Innsbruck, 1988); D. Goltschnigg/A. Schwob (eds), *Die Bukowina. Studien zu einer versunkenen Literaturlandschaft* (Tübingen, 1990); A. Corbea/M. Astner (eds), *Kulturlandschaft Bukowina. Studien zur deutschsprachigen Literatur des Buchenlandes nach 1918* (Iasi, 1990); V. Dohrn, *Reise nach Galizien. Grenzlandschaften des alten Europa* (Frankfurt, 1991).

religious conflicts dominate the literary portrayal of this multinational region. Consequently, Maria Klanska's book is divided into three main chapters on the 'national', the social and the Judaeo-Christian conflicts in Galicia between the Polish uprising in 1846 and the First World War, which saw the end of Habsburg rule and hence marks the most decisive watershed in modern Galician history. These chapters are preceded by a long introduction which, to benefit the reader without access to Polish historiography, could have offered still more of the fruits of Klanska's historical background reading – as it is, important historical facts are all too often hidden in scattered footnotes. Klanska's corpus of texts, however, is very impressive: apart from those authors who have recently enjoyed renewed popularity, like Karl Emil Franzos, Leopold von Sacher-Masoch, and Leo Herzberg-Fränkel, Klanska draws attention to previously unknown books which helped to shape Western judgements on this strange region or contributed to the political debates in Galicia itself – books which future investigations of the subjects will no longer be able to neglect. Klanska's first chapter (on 'national' conflict, especially during and in the aftermath of the events of 1846) is the most convincing, mainly because of the yardstick which Klanska so consistently applies: the attitude of the authors whom she treats towards the various ethnic groups in Galicia, the Poles, the Ruthenes and the Germans. By contrasting the authors' views with the historical facts, she arrives at a better understanding of their prejudices, vested interests and biases. However, when the same works (or works of the same authors) are discussed in different contexts in the following chapters, it becomes obvious that Klanska's strict thematic distinction does justice neither to the complexity of the texts in referring to non-literary reality nor to reality itself, of which the historian can only ever give an incomplete account. Statements like 'in his work Herzberg-Fränkel chooses the method of faithful depiction of reality' ('die Methode der wahrheitsgetreuen Abbildung der Wirklichkeit'), so that gloomy colours prevail in the portrayed structure of his texts ('in der dargestellten Struktur seiner Texte')' (p. 160), reveal a strikingly naive concept of 'Realism' as a 'direct' depiction of an allegedly identifiable 'reality', as well as a certain lack of precision in her critical language. Klanska's study is thus not an entirely convincing book; it is, though – a rare thing in scholarly writing today – a passionate book, offering a welcome counterweight to the still largely Austrocentric perspective of most critical surveys because it is written from a clear and distinctly concerned Polish standpoint. However, in spite of its weaknesses, or even because of them, Maria Klanska's book will remain compulsory reading for all those trying to come to a deeper understanding of the 'half-Asian' legacy on the eastern fringes of Europe.

In her introductory essay to Guido Baselgia's volume of photographs, a very personal but still tremendously informative sketch of Galicia as a multinational and multicultural frontier region, Verena Dohrn reminds her readers that two World Wars, Hitler's and Stalin's regimes, and several decades of Soviet rule have left these areas ravaged, and that 'German history played the major part in this devastation' (p. 7). In her juxtaposition of old names with contemporary ones, impressions from literature with those from recent visits, she arrives at the ambivalent conclusion that 'the whole of Galicia seems such an unreal, unexplored world' (p. 16). Guido Baselgia's photos speak a similar language. It seems as if the photographer's eye could not help capturing the scenes which convey the feeling that time had stood still there; and for the viewer the few Lada cars parked in front of the Railway Station and the Hotel George in Lemberg (p. 30ff.) cannot spoil the impression of Imperial splendour. Even the portraits of contemporary life – for instance, the market in Buczacz (p. 62ff.), the Thanksgiving Procession in the Carpathian mountains (p. 83) and others – blend together with the photographically captured relics of the past to form the myth of unreality so strongly prevalent in this book. The fact that many photos show aspects of Jewish life – for example, the crumbling synagogue and Jewish graveyard in Brody (p. 42ff.), the synagogue and congregation in Czernowitz (p. 69ff.) – contributes, at least for the German reader, to the impression of a vanished world. The sixty-five black and white photos assembled in the book – most of them depicting buildings, fewer portraying people, fewer still showing land-scapes – seem unremarkable at first glance, but viewed in context and with time for reflection, they prove just how aesthetically and atmospherically powerful they really are.

FLORIAN KROBB

The Vienna Coffeehouse Wits 1890–1938, tr. and ed. Harold B. Segel (West Lafayette, IN: Purdue University Press, 1993), xiii + 390 pp., $40.00.

The editor, a professor of Slavic literatures at Columbia University, has provided both the general reader and the student of fin-de-siècle Vienna with what, at first glance, looks like a useful source book for an alternative approach to a period more conventionally represented by Hofmannsthal, Schnitzler, Beer-Hofmann, etc. The book consists of an introduction; selections of varying length and depth from Hermann Bahr, Karl Kraus, Peter Altenberg, Felix Salten, Egon Friedell, Alfred Polgar, Anton Kuh and Edmund Wengraf; and biographical sketches of each author. Unfortunately, the translations themselves quickly weaken the initial impulse of gratitude toward a translator willing not only to introduce writers such as Altenberg, Polgar and Kuh to English-speaking readers, but also to tackle Kraus's first independent publication, the satirical pamphlet *A Literature Demolished*, as well as Kuh's brilliant polemic against the satirist, *The Ape of Zarathustra*.

What are we to make of the rendering of 'Ansichten vom Wurstelprater', with which Kraus, parodying Hermann Bahr, characterises the lower-class inflections of a popular actor, as 'faces stuffed with sausages at the amusement park' (p. 67); or of the equally incomprehensible translation of 'dieses "Deutsche Volkstheater" mit den Anführungszeichen um jeden Preis' as 'this Deutsches Volkstheater – where quotation marks surround every price' (p. 67)? The answer can only be: a lack of familiarity with Vienna's topography and the city's cultural politics, as well as an extremely shaky grasp of German. A comparably flagrant misunderstanding of things Austrian occurs when Segel translates the phrase 'Kaiserfleisch des Naturalismus' as 'imperial flesh of Naturalism' (p. 66). Even a Germanicised rendering as 'the smoked pork chop of Naturalism' would have captured at least one comic effect of this satirical quotation of Bahr's self-destructing metaphor.

While it is wise to remain both humble and indulgent when judging efforts to translate Kraus, it seems reasonable to expect more success with the delicate yet simpler texts of a writer such as Peter Altenberg. Here, too, however, the translator makes basic mistakes, such as misunderstanding 'die kleine Monatsrente' as 'rent' (p. 130) or settling on the literal equivalent 'a rudimentary' (p. 12) for 'Ein Rudimentär'. Such elementary errors occur throughout the book, making the director of the 'General Administrative Archives' in Vienna, who on the dust jacket praises the translations as 'outstanding', look seriously misinformed.

The lack of care extended to the primary texts does not bode well for the reliability of the introduction and the biographical sketches. While both convey much useful basic information and contain helpful references and bibliographies, the latter particularly are also peppered with clichés and misinformation. It is psychologically improbable, for example, that Karl Kraus, whose own published work runs to some fifty volumes, envied Hermann Bahr for being 'immensely prolific' (p. 42). Alexander Girardi, the great comic actor and operetta star, is called a 'nineteenth-century Viennese actor' (p. 242) even though he died in 1918 and had a successful late phase of his career in Berlin. Egon Friedell's study of the modern poet, inspired by Peter Altenberg's eccentric self-stylisation, is called *Ecce poeta*, not '*Ecce homo*' (p. 194); and, given extensive evidence to the contrary, it would not be prudent to suppose that Altenberg 'good-naturedly submitted to serving as the butt of humorous stories about him[self]' (ibid.). Although Friedell may have produced an edition of Lichtenberg's works, it is unlikely that he would have identified their author as 'the eighteenth-century Jewish Freemason Georg Christoph Lichtenberg' (p. 198).

Even the conception of this book must be called into question. Not everyone, for instance, will agree with the inclusion of Hermann Bahr, who was called many things in his own day, but never mistaken for a 'wit', however defined. As subversive as the decision to make these mostly non-canonical writers available in English may be, the actual choice of texts reflects little interest in darker, but scarcely hidden, perspectives on coffeehouse culture. Why not include, for example, Altenberg's portrayals of the seamy side of nocturnal café life or the virtually surrealistic coffeehouse scenes in *The Last Days of Mankind*? Theodor Herzl, who was considered one of the period's most accomplished writers of feuilletons, might have been represented by an excerpt from *Altneuland*, his novel of Zionist awakening that begins in the stultifying atmosphere of a coffeehouse in Vienna's ninth district. Ultimately, it is painful to report so negatively on this oversized, elegantly-designed volume that does, after all, contain some very fine, practically unknown texts. A good example is Peter Altenberg's letter to the famous dancer Grete Wiesenthal in which he suggests that they celebrate the sixtieth birthday (9 March 1919) which he did not live to see by combining her solo numbers with his renditions of Ashanti dances in a 'Lido' costume or bathing suit. A more unwittingly comic *danse macabre* commemorating the end of the multinational Habsburg Empire is hard to imagine. Regrettably, such textual jewels cannot compensate for the deficiencies of this amateurish undertaking. What is advertised as a 'much needed text on one of the most important institutions of Viennese culture' turns out to be a ponderous tome more suitable for the coffee-table than the coffeehouse.

LEO A. LENSING

Maurice Godé, Ingrid Haag and Jacques Le Rider (eds), *Deux sites de la modernité –
Zwei Metropolen der Moderne (1900–1930)*, Cahiers d'Etudes Germaniques. Revue
semestrielle 1993, no. 24, 203 pp., 90 FF.

To investigate Vienna and Berlin as contrasting and complementary sites of modernism and the avant-garde must have seemed an enticing project for the organisers of the colloquium which took place in Montpellier between 2 and 4 April 1992; to describe this same colloquium as 'international' is, however, the kind of slight exaggeration that one has come to expect when representatives from more than two countries come together. Understandably, academic members of staff from various departments of the University of Montpellier did take part, plus various French colleagues from other universities. Germany and Austria also provided good support, although, strangely, comparatively few Germanists from Vienna or Berlin seem to have been involved. The wider international perspective was provided by a paper from the Hungarian Endre Kiss on the intellectuals of Central Europe between Vienna and Berin. The conference papers as presented in this volume are divided into five separate sections: relations between the avant-gardes; Berlin and Vienna in literary fiction; the theatrical arts; philosophy and the history of ideas; and finally sociology, social sciences and history. The papers are published in the language in which they were delivered, French by the French and German by the German-speaking participants. Modestly, however, the editors have chosen to abridge some of the French contributions, sometimes cutting them down to extremely short versions, on occasion even of just over two pages, a process designed no doubt to leave greater space for the German-language contributions.

Some of the French papers too are of a tentative, even introductory nature. So, for example, Andrea Allerkamp in the very first article in this volume confesses that her two chosen authors, Carl Einstein and Robert Müller, are little-known and hardly read in France, while even Maurice Godé writes: 'Jusqu'à ces dernières années, seuls quelques érudits et amateurs éclairés se souvenaient encore d'Albert Ehrenstein' (p. 59). The very next paper, by Sigrid Schmidt-Bortenschlager, reveals that things are very different in Germany, where Müller's *Tropen* has been republished and has been exposed to intense critical examination, while Ehrenstein has had a critical edition devoted to him and has also been the subject of doctoral dissertations. Even Hanns Eisler, in an essay on the composer 'entre Vienne et Berlin', is described as 'peu connu, surtout en France' (p. 51). Clearly there was much groundwork to be covered at the colloquium before the relationship between the avant-gardes in Vienna and Berlin could be compared and contrasted.

The section of the book on Vienna and Berlin in literary fiction is short, and the opening paper by Alain Blayac, on Vienna and Berlin between the wars, cannot compare in scope or coverage with the paper by J. J. White, on 'The Pattern of English, Irish and American Reactions to the Berlin of the Interwar Years', in *Berlin – Literary Images of a City* (London, 1989), pp. 124–45. The other papers in this section deal with Berlin as an imaginary setting in Broch's *Die Schlafwandler* and with Musil between Vienna and Berlin. The section on the theatrical arts ranges from the Max Ophüls film version of *Liebelei* through the contrasting impact of Josephine Baker on Berlin and Vienna, to the Bronnen/Brecht encounter, Polgar's theatre criticism in the two cities, and back to Schnitzler again. The fourth section is also comparatively short, though it does expand the range to embrace the world of science in the two great cities. Without doubt, however, the outstanding essay in this volume is that in the final section by Jacques Le Rider, whose major work has now been translated into English as *Modernity and Crises of Identity* (Cambridge, 1993), on anti-Semitism and anti-Semites in Vienna and Berlin around the turn of the century. This essay alone makes the colloquium and the volume of essays which has emerged from it worth while.

J. M. RITCHIE

Iris Paetzke, *Erzählen in der Wiener Moderne* (Tübingen: Francke, 1992), 208 pp., DM 68.00.

A quintet of prose works spanning roughly a decade from 1895 to 1906 (Andrian's *Der Garten der Erkenntnis*, Hofmannsthal's *Reitergeschichte*, Beer-Hofmann's *Der Tod Georgs*, Schnitzler's *Frau Berta Garlan*, Musil's *Die Verwirrungen des Zöglings Törless*) provides Iris Paetzke with the material for a searching examination of perspectival narrative techniques of the Austrian fin de siècle.

Hermann Bahr had already demanded a new method of narration – deterministic, dialectical and 'decompositive'. The third term referred to the aim of excluding as far as possible authorial comment on and explanation of a character's mental states and processes. The result, he hoped, would be a narrative approach able to show the subject's entanglement in his emotions, fantasies and so forth, without providing the reader with a clear, independent corrective, such as that of the traditional omniscient narrator, or the reflective, mature first-person narrator reviewing his experience from a safe vantage point. Bahr felt that this alone would do justice to the distinctively modern predicament of isolation, spiritual disintegration and profound uncertainty.

In her study, Paetzke shows in detail how each of these writers develops this perspectivism ('konsequent personales Erzählen'). The contribution of other literatures, in the shape of Dostoyevsky, Chekhov and Flaubert, is not overlooked, nor is the persistence, in these avant-garde German works, of older, traditional tecnniques. Thus in her discussion of *Törless* she shows convincingly how the narrator, while acknowledging a realm beyond the rational, does nevertheless comment on the cadet's perplexity from a more informed, assured standpoint (p. 123f.). In fact, she views this as a contradiction which compromises the novel's unity (p. 140). This is usefully contrasted with the two styles of narration in *Reitergeschichte* (rapid, factual reporting versus Lerch's self-absorbed and self-indulgent perspective). Here, the discrepancy of styles is a reflection of that unbridgeable gulf between inner and outer worlds which proves fatal to Lerch (p. 70).

For each of the five works, Paetzke shows a different relationship between authorial and subjective elements. Sensitivity to this is essential in view of the undoubted fact that all the central figures are presented without an antagonist or 'Gegenspieler'. This does not mean that the author endorses his central figure, only that criticism of the figure's own perspective is unlikely to come in the form of direct comment from a narrator. Schnitzler's Leutnant Gustl contrives to condemn himself and his caste out of his own mouth; this piece of interior monologue is a limiting case of the kind of tension between perspectives which Paetzke is examining. Readers are spared yet another discussion of that work, however, and are given instead a valuable study of *Frau Berta Garlan*, which is interpreted as virtually a third-person equivalent of *Leutnant Gustl* (i.e. there is no superior narrative standpoint articulated at any stage: p. 95). The prevalence of clichés from 'Trivialliteratur', which Paetzke documents here, is just one way of suggesting the extent of Berta's self-deception, as well as her conventional outlook. This chapter and the chapter on *Der Tod Georgs* are probably those currently most needed by students of the Wiener Moderne.

There is a useful bibliography of work on these authors up to 1989, but unfortunately no index. The notes, which occupy almost forty pages, are well written and often illuminating on matters such as the visual arts, literary 'Jugendstil', or the intricacies of 'erlebte Rede'. They contain many suggestions for further exploration in this field.

MICHAEL LEVENE

W. E. Yates, *Schnitzler, Hofmannsthal, and the Austrian Theatre* (New Haven and London: Yale University Press, 1992), 286 pp., £25.00.

Focusing on the relationship of Schnitzler and Hofmannsthal as 'complementary opposites', this study in fact reflects the Janus face of a whole epoch. The title is somewhat ironic, however, given that both men relied upon German theatres to disseminate plays which, for all their differences, had common roots in the Viennese 'Konversationsstück'. For Hofmannsthal, failure to become established at the Burgtheater remained a constant concern: even his most 'Viennese' drama *Der Schwierige* was first performed in Munich.

Using the extensive Schnitzler documentation in Exeter University Library, the author's approach is to unite cultural history, biography and literary criticism. Thus the uneven quality of both authors is freely admitted, and they are presented selectively, to exclude the 'turgid obscurity' of the weaker Hofmannsthal and the 'lifeless triviality' of redundant Schnitzler. Few will quibble at the choice of texts, even though *Der Turm* attracts merely passing mention.

The work opens with an examination of fin-de-siècle culture under the twin headings of Irrationalism and Renaissance. Yates has to admit, however, that, although important for the period in general, the Renaissance made little impact upon Viennese theatre. It is nevertheless germane to Hofmannsthal's early lyrical dramas, but they are not discussed because of their essentially untheatrical nature. In compensation, we get a stimulating reading of the 'Chandos-Brief', indicating the difficulty of restricting such multi-genre authors to the confines of the theatre.

Chapter 2 presents biographies of Hofmannsthal and Schnitzler based upon their letters and diaries, encouraged by each man's concern 'to define the character of his own development; each of them ... endeavoured to impose a coherent form on life and work, in defence of identity itself' (p. 58). In Chapter 3, attention shifts to the theatre. Here, Yates's erudite love of minutiae can be delightfully revealing, as when he points out that the Theater in der Josefstadt still awaited Reinhardt's transformation when *Liebelei* was written. Weiring's job there would thus have been lowly indeed, his status instantly fixed for the Viennese audience. With a dual-author focus and wide remit, this book cannot have been easy to organise, and sometimes the strains show. The unavoidable issue of Schnitzler and anti-Semitism, not directly connected with the theatre and unparalleled by anything in Hofmannsthal's experience, appears rather unexpectedly in this chapter. The ensuing discussion of *Professor Bernhardi*, the first extended dramatic criticism in the book, is particularly enriched by Yates's awareness of contemporary critical reception. The chapter ends by discussing Hofmannsthal and theatrical comedy, exposing Hofmannsthal's Nadler-inspired misconception that his work flowed directly from the Baroque.

At the outset of the chapter 'Eros', dealing with that most central of Viennese themes, Yates modestly claims to present no more than a brief summary of well-worn issues. He does himself an injustice, for he demonstrates that major divergences between Hofmannsthal and Schnitzler were predicated not just on different experiences in life but also on 'the extent to which each is willing to shape the world recreated in dramatic fashion to a specific view '(p. 123). Analyses of *Anatol*, *Liebelei* and *Reigen* are balanced by one of Hofmannsthal's *Elektra*, showing how deeply he was affected by Freudian psychology when producing a tragic counterpoint to *Reigen*. Both plays are about the dissolution of the concept of individuality and the impact of instinctual drives. We again are shown how valuable early critics can be in helping modern commentators assess works which today epitomise the spirit of 'Vienna 1900'. *Elektra* brought not only Hofmannsthal's belated first theatrical success but also his collaboration with Richard Strauss. Their most celebrated work remains *Der Rosenkavalier* of 1910, the same year as Schnitzler's *Das weite Land*. Both works were successful, but they marked a parting of the ways artistically and personally as their long friendship cooled. Ironically, in *Der Rosenkavalier* Hofmannsthal comes closest to Schnitzler in reflecting feminist issues, but whereas in Hofmannsthal's comedies moral imperatives govern events, in Schnitzler chaotic and irrational instincts provide the motive power. However, where Hofmannsthal lets *Der Rosenkavalier* end happily, Hofreiter is isolated when *Das weite Land* closes: 'Happy ends are the stuff of myth-making, not of sceptical realism' (p. 156).

This book occasionally strays instructively from its specific subject, as when examining the monarchy's demise. Yates maps out the divergent paths of his subjects in 1914 – the sceptical Schnitzler, the mythopoeic Hofmannsthal – placing them in the artistic and political landscape of the Great War. Schnitzler's moral outrage, so like Kraus's yet unspoken publicly, is set alongside Hofmannsthal's conservative notion of the 'Austrian idea'. This is not specific to the theatre, but provides such a wealth of historical, geopolitical and cultural insights that to point out its marginality may seem churlish. Moreover, this chapter prepares the ground for Hofmannsthal's post-war return to drama and the founding of the Salzburg Festival, a 'first practical step in the "conservative revolution"' (p. 204), grounded in a consistent falsification of Salzburg's cultural history.

As Schnitzler's post-war plays were of minor significance, Hofmannsthal dominates the book's later stages. Perceived as a mirror image of a Schnitzler play because of its advocacy of marriage over philandering, *Der Schwierige* lies close to Yates's heart, but he does not conceal such imperfections as its unclear setting (pre- or post-war?) or contradictions in Hans Karl. A similar clarity informs the assessment of *Jedermann* and the 'black and white unsublety' (p. 214) of *Das Salzburger große Welttheater*. Yates on 'Cultural Conservatism in the Theatre' provides the best critique that I know of the 'ideological muddle and historical error' (p. 217) behind the Salzburg Festival. At the same time, however, Hofmannsthal provides a 'striking demonstration of the inspirational power of misunderstanding' (p. 217).

In 'Post mortem', the alienation of Schnitzler and Hofmannsthal in the 1920s is stressed, but they now shared little else as their problematic friendship foundered on the 'inequality in their assessment of each other's gifts' (p. 222). Schnitzler failed to meet Hofmannsthal's standards of greatness and was alienated from what he saw as Hofmannsthal's snobbery and artistic pretentiousness. Yet Hofmannsthal's death hit him hard, and his eulogy was gracious and heartfelt. Schnitzler was lucky to die before National Socialism consigned both men to obloquy and temporary oblivion. The book ends with their post-war rehabilitation, but, impartial to the end, Yates reveals no preference which would promote one above the other in his esteem. He does point out, however, that by the early 1980s Schnitzler, not Hofmannsthal, had become the most-performed Burgtheater author after Grillparzer and Nestroy.

Claudio Magris observes in *Danube* that 'a true literary critic is a detective, and perhaps the fascination of this debatable activity does not consist in making sophisticated interpretations but in having the bloodhound scent'. In this work of rich scholarship, presented with modesty and integrity, Yates proves that having the nose of a bloodhound can heighten the interpretative sense. Not for the first time, a British scholar and the Yale University Press have produced a handsome and reasonably-priced book on a major Austrian topic.

ANDREW BARKER

Alfred Pfoser, Kristina Pfoser-Schewig and Gerhard Renner, *Schnitzlers* Reigen. *Zehn Dialoge und ihre Skandalgeschichte. Analysen und Dokumente*, 2 vols (Volume I: *Der Skandal*; Volume II: *Die Prozesse*) (Frankfurt: Fischer Taschenbuch Verlag, 1993), 421 + 374 pp., DM 29.80 per volume.

The protracted furore occasioned by the first productions of *Reigen* was never entirely about the play itself. Among those who raised vociferous objections, both in Berlin and in Vienna, were many who had neither read it nor seen it. In their survey of the scandal, Alfred Pfoser, Kristina Pfoser-Schewig and Gerhard Renner wisely devote only one introductory chapter (by Pfoser) to the main lines of interpretation. The rest is given to a detailed account, in the form of a commentary and over 400 contemporary documents, of the publication history, the Viennese production in February 1921 in the Kammerspiele (which then belonged to the Deutsches Volkstheater), and the trial which was prompted by the Berlin production and in which the entire cast together with the theatre directors, Gertrud Eysoldt and Maximilian Sladek, appeared as defendants. Echoes of the affair elsewhere are treated only cursorily.

Most of the first volume is devoted to the events surrounding the Vienna production, which are treated by Pfoser; the second volume concentrates mainly on the Berlin trial, which is treated by his two co-authors. The picture that emerges in both capitals is of a scandal that was at every stage politically motivated, driven by anti-Semitism; its consequences in Vienna included a hardening of the anti-clericalism of the Social Democrats. In this sense, the book confirms and fills out the picture given in Helmut Gruber, *Red Vienna: Experiment in Working-Class Culture 1919–1934* (New York and Oxford, 1991), one of the more useful background books to have escaped the bibliography.

Schnitzler was predictably scornful of the half-hearted support that he received from the 'liberal' press. He must have found Auernheimer's reviews in the *Neue Freie Presse* on 31 January and 2 February, which are reproduced, thoroughly unhelpful. Few commentators emerged with credit; two who succeeded in seeing the affair in a wider perspective were Berta Zuckerkandl, whose article 'Reigen-Epilog' in the *Wiener Allgemeine Zeitung* of 14 February criticises its 'Jesuitical' inflation (Pfoser quotes from this article, but it is not reproduced in full), and Musil, whose comically barbed account in the *Prager Presse* on 30 March (which is reproduced) ends with a firm statement of principle that the responsibility of the state towards art consists in providing institutions capable of guaranteeing its existence.

The three compilers have unearthed material in numerous archives, at a time when this is still not always easy in Berlin. The book is well illustrated, with photographs and a number of contemporary cartoons, mainly anti-Semitic. The most entertaining section of the book is the excerpts from the transcript of the trial, which was issued by defence lawyer Wolfgang Heine in 1922 under the title *Der Kampf um den 'Reigen'*, and from which over half the documents in Volume II are drawn. (Perhaps it would have been better to list them in strictly chronological order, preserving the rhythm of the trial, rather than in the order of references in the commentary.) The book's most substantial impact, however, will no doubt be its contribution to Austrian cultural history. When Schnitzler finished reading *Der Kampf um den 'Reigen'*, he noted in his diary (2 July 1922), in laconic approval, 'A document'. This new survey, too, is a rich source of material on the political culture and cultural politics of the First Republic.

W. E. YATES

Douglas A. Joyce, *Hugo von Hofmannsthal's* Der Schwierige: *A Fifty-Year Theater History*, Studies in German Literature, Linguistics, and Culture (Columbia, SC: Camden House, 1993), xvi + 395 pp., $65.00.

This collection of annotated theatre reviews is a welcome addition to Hofmannsthal literature. It enables us to follow in detail the uneven fortunes of *Der Schwierige* between 1921 and 1974 and offers a fascinating insight into the interaction of aesthetic taste, social and political context, and downright prejudice. The work is divided into three parts: an introduction, the body of reviews, and three appendices. The introduction contains a helpful survey of the 'indescribable hostility' (p. 2), as Hofmannsthal called it, to which the press subjected him in the decade before the first production of *Der Schwierige*. As Dr Joyce rightly stresses, it is essential that we appreciate the origins, depth and tenacity of this animosity if we are to understand the overwhelmingly unfavourable response that greeted the first productions in Munich, Berlin and Vienna.

Half the volume is devoted to the selection of reviews. Out of almost 600 reviews and preview articles located by Dr Joyce, he has reproduced 114; these were selected 'first, for their well-reasoned opinion and the quality of the writing, second, for the distinction of the critics ...; and, third, to ensure a range of opinion, factors were considered such as critics' political and social orientation and the geographic distribution of newspapers'. To learn of the critical wrong-headedness of most early reviews and the personal hostility of several reviewers is a sobering experience. Critics were for the most part unable or unwilling to abandon their stereotype image of Hofmannsthal, 'the myth of Loris': 'aestheticism, artistic impotence, and divorce from reality' (Preface, p. i). Worse, such critical prejudice was often accompanied by anti-Semitism, veiled or overt.

More than many twentieth-century works, *Der Schwierige* fell in and out of favour. The last documented pre-war performance was in Munich in 1932, the first post-war production in Vienna in 1945, a hiatus of thirteen years, only seven of which can be ascribed to the Anschluss. Curiously, a second hiatus followed; there was no further German-language production until 1954, when five new productions commemorated the eightieth anniversary of Hofmannsthal's birth, to be greeted by reviewers as 'an astonishing discovery' (p. 77). Thereafter, *Der Schwierige* was firmly established in the repertoire, with nineteen stage productions in as many years.

The appendices (a catalogue of all known reviews, tabulated details of some forty productions between 1921 and 1974, and a catalogue of the directors, set designers, and actors involved in all the productions listed) enable the reader to gain a sound overview. A couple of criticisms should, however, be registered. First, it is a pity that the selection of reviews ends with the centenary of Hofmannsthal's birth; it would have been instructive to follow the play's fortunes during the following sixteen years. The second, a quibble, concerns the intended readership. Dr Joyce helpfully documents the reception outside the German-speaking world, including two reviews of the 1956 *Gastspiel* in Paris (the 1954 Josefstadt production), and two of a Dutch-language production in 1954. While readers of this specialist publication may reasonably be expected to cope with reviews in French, few are likely to be familiar with Dutch; a translation of this material would have been useful. Finally, one would like to have learnt more about the 480 reviews that Dr Joyce has not reproduced here: do they simply reflect the concerns and prejudices of the leading reviews, or do they display critical independence?

JOHN MCKENZIE

Silvina Milstein, *Arnold Schoenberg: Notes, Sets, Forms* (Cambridge: Cambridge University Press, 1992), xix + 210 pp., £50.00.

Silvina Milstein has already distinguished herself among the younger generation of Schoenberg scholars in this country, and this book should do much to consolidate her reputation in a wider circle. This is a volume for the musical specialist: it consists largely of technical discussion, necessarily conducted with the vocabulary, and accompanying graphic work, of musical analysis. It should be snapped up eagerly by the serious student of Schoenberg who wishes to encounter and absorb brilliant analytical interpretations of (in particular) the Suite op. 29, the Fourth String Quartet and the *Ode to Napoleon*, during a comprehensive examination of all Schoenberg's leading twelve-note works. Musical analysts sometimes forget (Dr Milstein much less than most) that the hermetic nature of their somewhat arcane pursuit largely precludes its detailed perusal, never mind its appreciation, by the general reader, even the musically well-disposed one. Also, musical analysts, especially American ones, tend to write extremely badly, in a kind of horrific sub-English. It should be said at once that Dr Milstein writes very well indeed, with great clarity, precision and a good sense of rhythm.

Dr Milstein is quite single-minded in her intention. This is neither a biographical nor a historical work. The issue of 'comprehensibility' – so often relentlessly chewed over in discussions of Schoenberg – she explicitly, and quite rightly, dismisses as 'psychology' which 'therefore lie(s) beyond the scope of my inquiry'. When one recollects the footling nature of aestheticians' worrying of this subject, one counts Dr Milstein's decision to leave it well alone as a double blessing.

Now a scholarly work of any stature will – almost involuntarily, it sometimes seems – send out longer rays of illumination, set in motion wider vibrations and evoke deeper resonances than its actual subject matter and focused approach would presuppose. So it is here. Nevertheless, there is still mediation to be performed between the author and the educated but general reader. Just for once, the cliché of 'relevance' is itself relevant here. What are these wider connotations? To find out, it is necessary to build a few bridges by placing Dr Milstein's work in a wider cultural context.

Schoenberg – and it is sometimes difficult to remember this today – is central to the whole cultural history of our century – and not merely in music, but in the more general world of ideas about art. Any musician worthy of the name must by now have realised that Schoenberg left behind a body of work which long ago earned at least our respect. For many of us, it also impels our devoted love and is the inspiration behind all our compositional activities. Beside these affirmations, the equally undoubted fact that he changed the whole face of Western music seems almost like a side-issue. But it is true. In a fiery, tragic whirlwind of a lifespan, whose adult portion fitted almost exactly into the first half of this century, Schoenberg sent out, like some intellectual catherine wheel, sparks into many far corners of the cultural world. But now that the tides of modernism have receded, leaving behind a dull and desolate beach, strewn with the flotsam of postmodernism, the jetsam of neo-Romanticism, and the odd minimalist jellyfish – it is difficult to recapture (and for the younger generation to believe in) the ardour of fighting for the New, the bold, fearless intellectual exploration which for Schoenberg's generation was as natural as breathing, but as ruinously self-sacrificing as the quest of any dedicated life must be.

The story has been told many times, and has mostly been told wrongly. It is important not to forget that all over-simplification is a form of white lying. The young Schoenberg eagerly seized on the most radical implications of all that was most advanced in his early years – Wagner, Brahms, Liszt, Strauss. He soon developed his own music to the point that the functions of tonality, and therefore its *raison d'être*, found themselves, after 200 years, called into serious question. With a problem raised, a solution was eventually found, but only after many years' search: the twelve-note method was formulated round about 1921. The extreme originality and inconceivable potential of this new way of composing, and of thinking about music, seems not at first to have been fully grasped by Schoenberg himself. With a knowledge of the man, it is difficult to divine whether the remark of 1923 that Dr Milstein uses as her starting point – 'You use the row and compose as you had done it previously' – was yet another of those ambiguous, paradoxical, ironic remarks – to put off the stupid, or even to tease the faithful, and always salted with Jewish wit – which were entirely characteristic of him; or whether, more startlingly, he in this instance meant exactly what he said.

A superficial acquaintanceship with the works that immediately followed has in the past been thought to bear out the simpler interpretation of this remark. The very young Pierre Boulez wrote off all later Schoenberg as new but soured wine in old bottles. Dr Milstein disposes of this impertinence once and for all, and is altogether more subtle in doing so:

> to view Schoenberg's post-World-War-I works as archaic shells filled with twelve-tone content would be to misunderstand their motivation and position in history; for, on the contrary, they represent an organic response to an urge for rational and disciplined musical discourse, an attempt at reconstructing a syntax in a state of dissolution.

How could these works have been otherwise? For Schoenberg felt enshrined within himself the whole continuity of the Austro-German musical tradition, of which he had an incomparable knowledge and understanding: he regarded it as a sacred duty to prolong this tradition in his own work as well as in his teaching. He was never out to create a new heaven and a new earth. At the same time, he was, inescapably, a man of extremely original mind. He realised that, for the new language to establish its identity, there had also to be certain exclusions – triads, octave doublings, cadential formulae, to name some of the more obvious small-scale tonal features. Some of these (it has been half-understood) over the course of time crept back in. This is where mainly hostile commentators use the *naturam expelles furca* ... argument, which confers on tonality a sort of divinity which it does not possess. The truth is otherwise. Nature never went away.

It is Dr Milstein's outstanding achievement to examine and precisely to document not only the nature of what Schoenberg took – and transformed – from his and music's past, but also to chart the extent of these recoveries – both how early they began to happen and how pervasive and truly functional they were. The answer to these last two points is almost startling: very early (almost at once); and all-pervasive. How far did single pitch-levels or pitch-classes act as tonal centres? In what manner did Schoenberg continue to use formal prototypes and the idioms that went with them? Just how did he integrate tonally evasive material with the use of historical forms? I simply paraphrase here some of her chapter headings, realising that such questions may appear obscure, even incomprehensible, to anyone not looking out from within the stockade of an inescapably technical art. But the results – a detailed and discriminating series of insights, new in their probity and depth – do add up to something which all cultured people can readily appreciate. Properly read, this book will give the attentive reader an unprecedentedly truthful and profound picture of how Schoenberg's music really works. It demonstrates what relation it bears to the tradition of which he was so important a part, and therefore awakens new thoughts about the relationships of tradition and innovation. Finally, it most powerfully reminds us of the centrality of Schoenberg's position, as a great mind and a consummate musician.

HUGH WOOD

Margarita Pazi, *Ernst Weiß. Schicksal und Werk eines jüdischen mitteleuropäischen Autors in der ersten Hälfte des 20. Jahrhunderts*, Würzburger Hochschulschriften zur neueren deutschen Literaturgeschichte, 14 (Frankfurt: Peter Lang, 1993), 143 pp., SFr 45/DM 49.00.

The Moravian Ernst Weiss (1882–1940), one of the many doctor-writers in twentieth-century literature, has still to establish himself in the modern Austrian canon. In the early 1980s, the appearance of a sixteen-volume 'Werkausgabe' in the Suhrkamp Taschenbuch series suggested that the breakthrough was imminent, but it has yet to happen. Among the reasons for his comparative neglect may be the stylistic eclecticism of his fiction (the Suhrkamp edition failed to include either his dramas or his verse), coupled with a certain thematic monotony. In his early Expressionist phase, during which time he enjoyed (if that is the correct term) a rather tense friendship with Kafka, he reveals an obsession with a demonised world to which human beings are helplessly exposed. The later work mirrors that of Joseph Roth in moving towards 'Neue Sachlichkeit'. This is followed in the 1930s with evocations of the lost world of the Habsburg Monarchy in such novels as *Der arme Verschwender* and *Der Verführer*. A frequent device in the later fictions is the use of a first-person narrator, often a doctor, telling his life-story. Dominant in these fictional autobiographies is the depiction of idealised father-son relationships, which Margarita Pazi regards as a legacy of his fascination with Kafka.

Pazi has long shown an interest in the German-language literature of her native Czechoslovakia, and is known for her work on Max Brod as well as the writers of what Brod dubbed the 'Prager Kreis'. Although he spent relatively little time in Prague, Pazi includes a long section on Weiss in her *Fünf Autoren des Prager Kreises* (1978), and the present study is evidently a continuation of that chapter. It is cast in the form of a continuous extended essay, structured around the chronological appearance of his works between *Die Galeere* in 1913 and the posthumous (and acrimonious) publication of Weiss's best-known work, the 'Hitler-Roman' *Der Augenzeuge*, in 1963.

Although the book's subtitle suggests a biographical and critical study, the story of Weiss's life does not loom large. For example, Pazi fails to investigate the vexed question of Weiss's possible contacts with Freud in Vienna before the First World War, nor is his problematic regard for both Stefan Zweig and Joseph Roth examined. To describe Roth simply as Weiss's friend does scant justice to a relationship which culminated in an exchange in a Parisian café in the 1930s during which Roth said to Weiss: 'Je vous estime comme écrivain, mais je ne vous aime pas', to which Weiss retorted: 'Je vous aime, Roth, mais je ne vous estime pas'. However, an examination of Weiss's lonely exile in France, where he was plagued by ill-health and poverty, barely figures in this study. Such as it is, the biographical focus is essentially on the relationship between Weiss and Kafka (much of the material was published by Pazi in an article of 1973), and the extensive quotations from the unpublished correspondence between Weiss and his lover of many years, the actress and writer Rachel Sanzara. These shed considerable light upon Weiss's creative processes and represent the most original and rewarding aspect of the book.

Surprisingly, given the work's long and detailed title, the question of Weiss's Jewishness is by no means central to the discussion, nor is his literary fate (i.e. reception) discussed. Pazi is, nevertheless, an informed and sympathetic reader of Weiss's oeuvre, though the examination of individual works generally presupposes detailed knowledge of the texts on the part of the reader. Although not afraid to criticise what she sees as shortcomings in individual works, Pazi is somewhat limited in her vision of the texts, this being most obvious in her failure (or disinclination) to tackle the misogynistic, Weininger-inspired portrayal of many female characters. This, however, may be symptomatic of the book's most telling failure: to take into consideration the most wide-reaching examination to date of Weiss's work, Franz Haas's *Ernst Weiß: Der Dichter von der traurigen Gestalt* (1986). Haas is not especially sympathetic to Weiss, but far more than Pazi he contextualises the works besides providing detailed interpretations of individual texts and a more comprehensive scholarly apparatus. For the author to state in her introduction that she has not stinted with the 'korrigierender oder bestätigender Blick auf die Sekundärliteratur' ('correcting or confirming glance at the secondary literature') strikes this reviewer as possibly disingenuous.

Although this book in no way supersedes that of Haas, Pazi's generous responses to Weiss are a useful correlative to his occasional waspishness. However, her work is repeatedly undermined by the shoddy production standards which convey the impression of a book in a pre-publication state. Inconsistencies of presentation abound, grammatical solecisms and typos are far too frequent to list. This study may have its shortcomings, but it deserved better than the desultory editing of Anneliese Kuchinke-Bach, whose name figures on the cover in letters almost as large as those of Margarita Pazi herself.

ANDREW BARKER

Klaus-Dieter Krohn (ed.), *Frauen und Exil, zwischen Anpassung und Selbstbehauptung* (Exilforschung, Ein internationales Jahrbuch, Bd 11, Munich, 1993).

> The burden that lies on the shoulders of the emigrant family is a heavy one. It is not always equally distributed and very often the greater part of it lies on the shoulders of the women. The fate of a family in emigration very often depends more on the wife and her psychic energy than on that of the husband. If she succeeds in overcoming the difficulties that arise, the family as a whole will profit, if she fails she will draw the family down into the abyss with her. (*Aufbau*, 1 March 1940)

It seems high time both to acknowledge and to question this conception of the importance of women in exile. To acknowledge it would entail a detailed study of the precise conditions imposed on women in exile, their spheres of action and their reflections on this experience. To question it, and indeed there is ample reason for doing so, generates a whole series of new questions. Why was this conception of woman as the saviour of the family in times of crisis so tempting that even otherwise very critical and independent women like Anna Seghers and Erika Mann contribute to this picture of the heroic woman developing her full potential only in the extreme situation of exile? What, in other words, were the psychological and sociological factors that encouraged a reactivation of this conservative role-model for women in exile – and in what way did it succeed? Did it initiate a creative outburst of energy which seems to have allowed women to be more inventive and adaptable than men? Does this conception of women in exile correspond with the biographical and fictional statements of women in exile? Or does the very conventional equation of women with familial life perhaps conceal more than it reveals about the actual conditions under which women lived and fought for their survival?

The collection of essays in this volume is in part an attempt to find answers to these questions, posed in the first article by Heike Klapdor from which the above quotation is taken. It thus permits a more differentiated analysis of gender-specific conditions of exile and of reactions to it. By focusing on the lives and works of those women who continued their careers as writers and artists in exile and after re-emigration, the volume illuminates the conditions which confronted women writers in various countries of exile, their active participation in exile communities and the influence that exile had on the development of their work.

As a fine example of an author originally highly esteemed but not acknowledged in contemporary studies on exile, Hermynia zur Mühlen seems particularly equipped to analyse the condition of exile. As a 'Russian emigrant' in Austria, she was already accustomed to life in exile before the Nazis made it a common form of existence. Eva-Maria Siegel calls attention to zur Mühlen's explicit criticism of the 'ideal of a German heroic woman and mother' in various novels and unpublished short stories and essays. She emphasises zur Mühlen's success in devising alternative role-models for women which take into account the changing demands imposed on them by the political events of the period. The value of this achievement becomes obvious when contrasted with the results of Lutz Winckler's study of Louise Strauss-Ernst's novel *Zauberkreis Berlin*. Winckler interprets the protagonist's development as a regression to conservative role-models in the face of the demands of exile, and concludes that Strauss-Ernst failed both thematically and aesthetically in her analysis of specific gender problems. Both articles emphasise the importance of these writers for exile studies in general. Siegel points to the sociopolitical and historical relevance of zur Mühlen's novels and unpublished short stories as studies of the causes of the rise of fascism and as a depiction of the attitudes of ordinary people in Austria and Germany. Her argument is supported convincingly by a documentation of the difficulties that zur Mühlen had in publishing *Unsere Töchter, die Nazinen* and other short stories. Winckler draws attention to Strauss-Ernst's detailed description of everyday life of both men and women in exile in Paris and shows that it contains important comments on the sociological structure of the exile community in Paris.

Irmela von der Lühe, who has recently published the first biography of Erika Mann, gives a good account of Erika's successful adaptation to the demands of exile and of her intellectual and political achievements in America. Compared with her brother Klaus, she is pictured as politically more realistic and active in her fight against fascism and as a major moral support to her brother. Possible gender-specific attitudes of women to their autobiographies that might have contributed to their initial neglect are examined in Gabriele Mittag's paper on 'memory, writing and written records'. She suggests that women's autobiographical writing tends to take less public forms (for example, memoirs) and that the tendency to underestimate the value of their personal opinions manifests itself on the structural level of the texts.

Further essays explore a variety of relevant issues in exile studies in the writings of Grete Weil, Christa Winsloe and Nelly Sachs, among others. Thematic and aesthetic reactions to fascism and the experience of exile are analysed by Anne Stürzer in the dramatic writings of various playwrights. Hilde Rubenstein, for example, is shown to transform her style in a successful attempt at finding new forms of expression to capture the experience of a radically changed world. Her writing becomes a kind of scientific experiment, constructed to explore different reactions of people in times of crisis. The main section of the volume is brought to a close by drawing attention to another rather neglected category of texts written in exile: Dirk Krüger's excellent paper on Ruth Rewald's books written for children in exile shows the central importance of this genre for research concerned with productive models for life in exile and the conception of exile as a temporary condition combined with the hope of a possible return to Germany after fascism.

In a second section, the picture of professional women in exile is extended by German information on art-historians in exile, the Jewish historian Selma Stern and the dancer Lotte Goslar. The volume concludes with a recent interview with Lisa Fittko and a select bibliography on women in exile. One of the collection's great merits lies in the inclusion of a wide range of unpublished autobiographical, documentary and fictional material; another in its successful attempt to emphasise the importance of authors who have so far been neglected in exile studies (apart from zur Mühlen, writers from Austria receive little attention). In doing so, it provides inspiration for further research – especially on those authors hitherto exiled from exile studies.

CAROLINE WELSH

Joseph Strelka (ed.), *George Saikos magischer Realismus – zum Werk eines unbekannten großen Autors* (Berne, Frankfurt, New York, Paris: Peter Lang, 1990), 165 pp., SFr 27.00.

Who was George Saiko? It is not easy to find out. None of his works is currently in print, except in the expensive edition brought out by the Residenz Verlag under the editorship of Adolf Haslinger, which is normally accessible only in libraries. Anyone who consults the most obvious source, Johann Sonnleitner's article on Saiko (1892–1962) in Walther Killy's *Literaturlexikon*, will be discouraged to learn that although most of his stories and his two novels *Auf dem Floß* (1948) and *Der Mann im Schilf* (1955) were published after 1945, they belong thematically and formally to the inter-war period, and are heavily indebted to Broch and Musil. *Der Mann im Schilf*, a historical novel set in a provincial town near Salzburg during the attempted Nazi putsch of 1934, may sound promising, but though Sonnleitner grants it 'einige geglückte Porträts alpenländ. Niedertracht' ('some successful portraits of Alpine vileness'), he decides that it collapses under the weight of its own symbolism.

An inferior epigone of Broch does not sound inviting. If, however, you actually read *Der Mann im Schilf*, you will find a different and much more readable and engrossing novel. It begins with the arrival in Salzburg of three archaeologists, the Viennese Robert and an English couple whose sexual relationship is obscure. The atmosphere of uncertainty, perplexity and fear is compellingly conveyed, especially in the shockingly sudden incident when Robert is beaten up by people who take him for a foreigner. The machinations of the army, the police, the Heimwehr, government and Nazi agents and double agents, pervade the book. Latterly the focus shifts from the archaeologists to the brutal Ministerialrat Mostbaumer, who assassinates a used-up agent, and to the man hiding in the reeds, who is thought to be a Putschist on the run. At the book's centre is an episode of sexual violence that took place during archaeological work on Crete; archaeology is also a metaphor for recovering the past, and primitive violence on Crete is related to similar practices, laced with sexuality and superstition, in the Salzkammergut.

Focusing on the discomfort of a Viennese amid a frighteningly alien provincial society, this novel deserves comparison with Broch's *Die Verzauberung* and Bernhard's *Frost*. But its stature also requires international analogies. Saiko excels at describing confrontations, often erotic, where the unsaid bulks larger than the said: here he resembles Lawrence more than Broch. As a political thriller, *Der Mann im Schilf* recalls the tension achieved by Greene (*The Comedians*) or Naipaul (*In a Free State*), though Saiko takes greater compositional risks and his network of symbols, far from being gratuitous, gives the novel its unity.

Joseph Strelka deserves thanks for assembling eleven distinguished Germanists who take Saiko seriously and describe his achievement convincingly. I shall single out three outstanding contributions. Dietmar Goldschnigg, who has written more fully about Saiko's novels in *Modern Austrian Literature* (1988) and elsewhere, cogently illuminates their narrative technique and political context. Donald Daviau provides a persuasive introduction to the shorter fiction. And Hartmut Steinecke offers sensitive reflections on Saiko's treatment of the irrational and the crucial differences between him and Broch. In the absence of a monograph, this collection is an indispensable stopgap. Biographical and bibliographical data are lacking, but these may be found in the Saiko chapter by Friedrich Achberger in Daviau's *Major Figures of Modern Austrian Literature* (1988), also a valuable introduction to an author who would surely have found the fame he deserves if he had been German instead of Austrian.

RITCHIE ROBERTSON

Henriette Mandl, *Cabaret und Courage: Stella Kadmon – eine Biographie* (Vienna: WUV Universitätsverlag, 1993), 257 pp., 250 Sch.

The 'Klein- und Kellerbühnen' of Vienna have not been well served by theatre historians, and this lively and very readable biography of one who might well be called the 'Mother Courage' of Vienna's alternative theatre is most welcome. Based on a series of conversations which Henriette Mandl held with Stella Kadmon shortly before her death in 1989, the volume, which is attractively presented and illustrated, takes us through Kadmon's career from young aspiring actress of the 1920s to founder of the pre-war cabaret *Der Liebe Augustin*, émigrée in what was then Palestine, and finally founder and director of the Theater der Courage. It is an inspiring tale which, in spite of a lack of any scholarly apparatus (list of productions and index of names apart), tells us much about both the political cabaret of the years of clerical fascism and the important contribution made by Kadmon to a post-war theatrical scene too heavily dominated by the state theatres (Burgtheater and Akademie) and the Theater in der Josefstadt.

Stella Kadmon's early career was typical of many a young actress. She worked in Linz, in Mährisch-Ostrau (Ostrava) and then at the 'Neue Wiener Bühne'. She was discovered as a putative cabaret star by no less a person than Fritz Grünbaum (although plans for her to appear in Vienna in cabaret as an *ersatz* Josephine Baker with Karl Farkas came to naught). Touring through Germany, she was so impressed by Wemer Finck's Berlin cabaret *Die*

Katakombe that she determined to open a similar cabaret in Vienna. The story of the founding and running of *Der Liebe Augustin*, together with details of her talented colleagues, is an important contribution to the history of Viennese 'Kleinkunst', amplifying as it does the account given in Rudolf Wey's *Cabaret und Kabarett in Wien* (Vienna, 1970). Among the talented youngsters of the *Augustin* were Fritz Spielmann (better known in the USA as Fred Spielmann), Gerhart Mostar, H. F. Königsgarten (H. F. Garten), the young Manfred Inger and Fritz Muliar. They opened on 7 November 1931, but despite some imaginative personal advertising on the Ringstraße and at a 'masked ball' (there was no money for newspaper adverts and no mention in the papers without them) they were soon suffering from what we term today 'cash-flow' problems. Stella Kadmon had to beg Hugo Breitner to be relieved from the obligatory concession fee. At one point the audience was down to two, but one of the two was Dr Hans Nüchtern, head of the literary section of RAVAG, who was so impressed that he gave them a live broadcast from the cellars of the Café Prückel. From then on, they became established as one of Vienna's leading 'Kleinkunstbühnen', their programme changing after 1933 to attack political events in Germany (including an attack on Gerhart Hauptmann and on the removal of Jewish names from German war cemeteries). As for the form of their programme, which was based on songs, sketches and even an artist, it was the *Liebe Augustin* which introduced the 'Mittelstück' (the major, more literary section of the programme). Indeed, Gerhart Mostar's adaptation of *Lysistrata* (with Gusti Wolf) so enchanted the Greek ambassador that he saw it four times, and later provided the Kadmon family with the transit visas which were effectively to save their lives. The personal story of Kadmon at the Anschluss shows a strain of good fortune and optimism: two brothers temporarily arrested by the Gestapo, flight (and marriage of convenience) through Yugoslavia and Greece to Palestine where, after learning Hebrew in six months, she was soon organising cabaret evenings and dramatic readings in a mixture of both languages.

Back in Vienna, showing (and needing) a determination born of experience, Stella Kadmon returned to the Café Prückel where, after one attempt at reviving cabaret, she turned to drama. From October 1948 until May 1960 in her original home, and then from November of that year until 1981 in her new small theatre on the Franz-Josefs-Kai, Kadmon directed one of the most adventurous of Vienna's small companies. The range of dramatists, from Kaiser, O'Casey and Sartre to Wesker, Fugard, Kipphardt and Kroetz, greatly extended the relatively narrow repertoires of the major theatres. Productions of Brecht's *Furcht und Elend im Dritten Reich* and Bruckner's *Die Rassen* were poignant reminders of recent history, but despite the loss of family and colleagues in the Holocaust there seems to have been little bitterness. Of interest to theatre practitioners will be the off-stage details of negotiations with authority and problems overcome. Her last production was a Peter Turrini adaptation. The Theater der Courage also proved a starting point for many actors later to achieve fame: Elizabeth Orth, Karlheinz Hackl and Joachim Bissmeier, to name the three best known at present.

Two stories are told here with verve and humour (owing much, one feels, to their basis in the taped conversations, excerpts from which are sometimes quoted verbatim). The one is Stella Kadmon's life, and the other that of a small but vital part of Vienna's theatre history. The latter is an important contribution to the history of the satirical and political cabaret in Vienna, *Der Kleine Augustin*, which along with the *Literature am Naschmarkt*, *Die Stachelbeer* and *Das ABC* led that little group of independent cabarets which kept the Viennese laughing in troubled times and also provided creative employment for Austrians returning from Nazi Germany. We then have (the Palestinian interlude providing an interesting artistic bridge) a major contribution to the history of Vienna's small independent theatres after the war. Both stories, the personal and the theatrical, are well worth reading, but it is the detail provided by the second which makes this book a necessary purchase for any institution or individual with a serious interest in the history of the Viennese theatre from the 1930s to the 1980s.

JOHN WARREN

Amy Colin, *Paul Celan: Holograms of Darkness* (Bloomington and Indianapolis, IN: Indiana University Press, 1991), 202 pp., £25.50.

Anyone attempting to introduce a primarily non-German-speaking readership to a German poet is faced with the immense task of recovering what is lost in the translations. In the case of poetry of such legendary density as Paul Celan's, the task becomes nearly impossible; how does one communicate the intricacies of Celan's etymological neologisms, the multiple layers of meaning, to students without the wherewithal to appreciate them? This is what Amy Colin's study attempts to do; she also tackles the equally daunting problem of rendering accessible a subject of sometimes quite extraordinary blackness, such that no Hollywood treatment could alleviate it.

Colin, like Celan born in the Bukovina, evokes the cultural, historical and social complexity found in the Czernowitz of the 1930s, which she describes as being 'at the crossroads of traditions'. Her 'postmodern' approach, which reflects this diversity, is expressed in the Celanian oxymoron that forms her title: 'holograms of darkness'. She uses this image only at the beginning and end of the book, yet the impression of multiple facets is conveyed by the intervening chapters, which demonstrate an almost Joycean approach to literary criticism; the mode shifts from the historical to the anecdotal to the analytical with remarkable ease.

She divides her study into three main sections. The first deals primarily with Celan's literary beginnings and the circumstances he faced under occupation during the Second World War (and incidentally corrects one or two remarks made by his first biographer, Israel Chalfen). This contains a critical portrait gallery of Bukovinan poets, including especially an important sketch of Celan's friend Immanuel Weissglas, whose images reflect the same enthusiasm for Surrealism and for Rilke that is evident in Celan's early

214

poetry. Colin also reflects on the poets who most deeply influenced Celan and his contemporaries, among whom she lists Alfred Margul-Sperber and Karl Kraus. The second section deals partly with the visual aspect of Celan's fascination with Surrealism, in a study of his essay on Edgar Jené, and partly with the stylistically experimental poems which he wrote in Romanian. The third, beginning with the chapter 'Innovation and Repetition', is analysis of a far more philological nature, somewhat over-peppered with anxious references to other critics, but nonetheless containing lucid commentary on poems such as 'Huhediblu', 'In der Luft' and 'Osterqualm'. She does what many others have been tempted to do, picking up images used by Celan in later poems and referring back to early work, but she does so in order to emphasise the power and significance of memory for Celan. This is another way of underlining Celan's own denial that his poetry was impenetrable: 'ganz und gar nicht hermetisch'.

In some respects, Colin overcompensates for Celan's difficulty. Given that the study is intended for those with little knowledge of other languages, her translation of even the simplest German phrases is comprehensible, if irritating to those used to reading Celan in the original. But she does not translate all the French quotations, and one would like to know why not. There are also actual mistakes that should never have occurred with more thorough checking: a cedilla on 'voici', stanzas miscounted, 'Jahrtausend' translated as 'century', and a rogue apostrophe on the word 'weint' in a quotation of Celan's 'Espenbaum' – which changes the tense from present to past. Celan once said of his poetry: 'dieser Sprache geht es um Präzision', and Colin, who has sat on the editorial board of the Historical-Critical Celan Edition, certainly conveys this in her discussion of the different versions of his mature poems. It is a pity that, in this lively and diverse introduction to Celan's work, such details have been missed.

CAROLINE DOBSON

Margarete Lamb-Faffelberger, *Valie Export und Elfriede Jelinek im Spiegel der Presse: Zur Rezeption der feministischen Avantgarde Österreichs* (New York: Peter Lang, 1992), 224 pp., \$39.95.

Reviewing a book which is about reviews and the conduct of those involved in the 'Institution Kunst-Kritik' is a self-reflexive challenge, and one which gave this reviewer plenty of food for thought. In her documentation of the reception of the writer Elfriede Jelinek and artist and film-maker Valie Export by the German-speaking press, Margarete Lamb-Faffelberger charts the tortuous history of the Feuilleton's relationship to the Austrian, feminist avant-garde. It is a shame that it is beyond the brief of this particular publication to ask how far this reception is different to that of male Austrian avant-garde artists, or of 'mainstream' women artists and writers, but *Valie Export und Elfriede Jelinek im Spiegel der Presse* does provide the reader with valuable and interesting information from sources which should not be ignored.

The book is structured clearly and crisply into sections covering ten of Jelinek's novels and plays and four of Export's films, and is prefaced by brief introductions on the state and function of art criticism via the Feuilleton, and on feminism in Austria. In the first section, Lamb-Faffelberger enumerates a number of important questions regarding the nature of writing reviews, who reads them (they have a very small readership indeed), the institutional character of the critics which may be determined by the 'politics' of the paper for which they are writing, and so on. The book would have been greatly enriched had some of these questions been brought to bear in a more openly interpretative way on the reviews of Jelinek's and Export's work which the author uses to characterise their reception. An appendix gives some information about political affiliations and circulation statistics which readers can call on if they too are interested in this line of inquiry.

By letting her many quotations from the press in large part speak for themselves, however, Lamb-Faffelberger avoids becoming sucked into the personalised and often vituperative moments in these two artists' reception – in Austria in particular. She reports these facts, but refuses to replicate the voyeurism and insensitivity of many of their critics and interviewers by over-emphasising these in her account. The author's own interviews with Export and Jelinek which complete her book (in the former she is mysteriously joined by another participant, Margret Eifler, her 'geistige[r] Mentor' – see the preface) are refreshing, academically useful and focused (in stark contrast to the mass of journalistic offerings on Elfriede Jelinek, for example).

In the section on Export, Lamb-Faffelberger provides short plot descriptions and some comment in order to characterise the aesthetics of Export's work. Perhaps such information is less necessary in dealing with the better-known Elfriede Jelinek; the book is in any case structured to allow readers to use it for reference on the text(s)/film(s) with which they are familiar and are perhaps researching. This is an important quality, since the book, which is published in the relatively new Peter Lang series 'Austrian Culture', does not have an index. In both parts, the author takes care to cover important comparisons when there is evidence to do so: she considers differences between reception in Austria and in the Federal Republic of Germany – the last work covered is *Lust* (1989); in Vienna as compared to the other Austrian Bundesländer; between male and female critics. In Jelinek's case, reference is made to the different reception of productions of plays and their published versions, indeed of different productions of one play, and to the reception of a film version and its original text (*Die Ausgesperrten*).

One cannot help wondering if the avant-garde status of Export's and Jelinek's art has already been superseded. The term is obviously a slippery one, and Export makes a telling point: 'Die Avantgarde – wie das Wort ja auch sagt – hat den Anspruch etwas vorzubereiten. Dann soll es im traditionellen Bereich übernommen werden. Was einmal Avantgarde war, geht dann in das Kino ein' (p. 176) ('The avant-garde, as the word implies, claims to be preparing something which is then to be adopted by the sphere of tradition. What used to be avant-garde ends up in the cinema'). Lamb-

Faffelberger and Export share an optimism that there are at least *some* positive developments in the highly patriarchal business of cultural politics in Austria. Jelinek, on the other hand, remains ever the pessimist. On the basis of the convincing evidence amassed here, Lamb-Faffelberger is probably in a better position to know. Jelinek's alleged disregard for her critics is, after all, a self-avowed survival strategy and one which should amuse *any* critic with a sense of irony (especially critics of Jelinek, like Lamb-Faffelberger and myself). For, as she has said in an interview with Donna Hoffmeister: 'Wir Schriftsteller produzieren sozusagen Dinge, über die wir irgendwelche Idioten urteilen lassen' ('We writers produce things, as it were, and let any old idiots pass judgement on them!').

ALLYSON FIDDLER

Notes on Contributors

EVELYN ADUNKA, Doctor of Philosophy of the University of Vienna, is a historian of Austrian Jewry who is writing a history of the Jewish community of Vienna.

ALAN BANCE is Professor of German at Southampton University and author of *Theodor Fontane* (Cambridge University Press, 1982). He has recently written the introduction to the Everyman edition of Joseph Roth's *Radetzky March*.

ANDREW BARKER is Senior Lecturer in German at Edinburgh University. He is working on a book on Peter Altenberg.

JEFFREY B. BERLIN is an Academic Dean and Professor of Humanities at Holy Family College, Philadelphia. He is editor of *Approaches to Teaching Mann's 'Death in Venice' and Other Short Fiction* (Modern Language Association, 1992) and co-editor of Stefan Zweig, *Briefwechsel mit Hermann Bahr, Sigmund Freud, Rainer Maria Rilke und Arthur Schnitzler* (Fischer Verlag, 1987), and is currently helping to prepare a four-volume edition of Stefan Zweig's correspondence.

PETER BRANSCOMBE is Professor of Austrian Studies at the University of St Andrews. His most recent book is *Mozart: Die Zauberflöte* in the Cambridge Opera Handbooks series (1991), and he is one of the editors of the new critical edition of Nestroy.

CAROLINE DOBSON teaches German at Oxford and is the author of a doctoral thesis on Celan's poetry; she is also a painter and print-maker.

ALLYSON FIDDLER is a Lecturer in German at Nottingham University and author of *Rewriting Reality: An Introduction to Elfriede Jelinek* (Berg, 1994).

KONSTANZE FLIEDL is Assistant Professor in the German Department at Vienna University. Her edition of the correspondence between Arthur Schnitzler and Richard Beer-Hofmann was published by Europa-Verlag in 1992, and she is preparing a 'Habilitationsschrift' on Schnitzler.

219

IAN FOSTER is a Lecturer in German at Salford University and author of *The Habsburg Army in Austrian Fiction* (Lang, 1992).

PATRICIA M. HOWE is Senior Lecturer in German at Queen Mary and Westfield College London and author of numerous studies of Fontane, Saar, Droste-Hülshoff and others.

LOUISE ADEY HUISH teaches German at Oxford. She has published numerous articles on Nestroy, Keller, Horváth and others, and is one of the editors of the new critical edition of Nestroy.

FLORIAN KROBB is Lecturer in German at St Patrick's College, Maynooth, and author of *Die schöne Jüdin* in the 'Conditio Judaica' series (Niemeyer, 1993).

F. J. LAMPORT is Fellow in German at Worcester College, Oxford. His books include *German Classical Drama* (Cambridge University Press, 1991) and an edition of Schiller's *Die Räuber: Ein Schauspiel* (Bristol Classical Press, 1993).

STEVEN W. LAWRIE is a Lecturer in German at the University of Aberdeen. His doctoral thesis 'Erich Fried: A Writer without a Country' (Aberdeen, 1993) is to be published by Berg.

LEO A. LENSING is Professor of German at Wesleyan University, Middletown, Connecticut, and author of a study of Wilhelm Raabe and many articles on Kraus, Altenberg and the visual arts.

MICHAEL LEVENE is a Lecturer in German at Bristol University and has written a number of articles on Schnitzler and fin-de-siècle Vienna.

DOROTHEA MCEWAN has a research post as archivist at the Warburg Institute in London. In addition to her interests in the visual arts, she works in the field of feminist cultural theory and is also researching the history of the Goldschmidt banking family.

JOHN MCKENZIE is Senior Lecturer in German at Exeter University, and author of *Social Comedy in Austria and Germany 1890–1930*, in the series 'British and Irish Studies in German Language and Literature' (Lang, 1992). He is one of the editors of the new critical edition of Nestroy.

GREGORY MASON is Professor of English and Director of the Peace Education Program at Gustavus Adolphus College in Saint Peter, Minnesota. He has published numerous articles in the USA, Canada and Japan, and is currently starting work on an edition of the correspondence of Felix Pollak and Anais Nin.

WOLFGANG MUCHITSCH is management assistant to the Vice-Chancellor of the University of Graz. He is a member of the exile research group of the Dokumentationsarchiv des österreichischen Widerstandes and editor of the volume dealing with Britain, *Österreicher im Exil: Großbritannien 1938-1945* (Österreichischer Bundesverlag, 1992)

HARRIET MURPHY is a Lecturer in German at Warwick University. She has published *The Rhetoric of the Spoken Word in* Die Wahlverwandtschaften

(Lang, 1990) and is now working on a book on Canetti's *Die Blendung*, to be published by the State University of New York Press.

J. M. RITCHIE was until recently the Director of the Centre for Exile Studies at Aberdeen University, where he was Professor of German. He has published numerous studies and translations, mostly of twentieth-century German literature, including *German Literature under National Socialism* (Croom Helm, 1983).

RITCHIE ROBERTSON is Fellow and Tutor in German at St John's College, Oxford, and author of *Kafka: Judaism, Politics, and Literature* (Oxford University Press, 1985 German translation published by Metzler, 1988).

IAN F. ROE is Senior Lecturer in German at Reading University and author of a study of Grillparzer (Edwin Mellen, 1991).

EDA SAGARRA is Professor of Germanic Studies at Trinity College, Dublin. Her many books include *A Social History of Germany* (1977).

JÖRG THUNECKE is Senior Lecturer in German at Nottingham Trent University and has published many articles on National Socialism and exile literature.

EDWARD TIMMS is Professor of German and Director of the Centre for German–Jewish Studies at the University of Sussex. His publications include *Karl Kraus: Apocalyptic Satirist* (Yale, 1986), to be published in German by Deuticke in autumn 1995.

JOHN WARREN, who was for many years Head of German and Austrian Studies at Oxford Polytechnic, is co-editor of *Austria in the Thirties: Culture and Politics* (Ariadne Press, 1991).

CAROLINE WELSH, who is DAAD Lektorin at the University of Sussex, is writing a doctoral thesis on migrant literature.

JOACHIM WHALEY is a University Lecturer in German and Fellow of Gonville and Caius College, Cambridge. His book *Religious Tolerance and Social Change in Hamburg 1522–1819* (Cambridge University Press, 1985) has recently been translated into German (Wittig, 1992).

HUGH WOOD is a University Lecturer in Music and Fellow of Churchill College, Cambridge. He studied composition with Iain Hamilton and Mátyás Seiber and has written a symphony, concertos for cello, violin and piano, and numerous chamber works.

RICHARD WOODFIELD teaches art theory at Nottingham Trent University. He is currently at work on a book on E. H. Gombrich and a collection of essays on Semper and Riegl.

W. E. YATES is Professor of German at Exeter University. His most recent book is *Schnitzler, Hofmannsthal, and the Austrian Theatre* (Yale, 1992), and he is one of the editors of the new critical edition of Nestroy.

Austrian Studies

Acknowledgements: The Editors gratefully acknowledge the support of the Austrian Institute in London. Thanks are also due to the colleagues listed below for their willingness to serve on the Advisory Board.

Advisory Board: Andrew Barker (Edinburgh), Peter Branscombe (St Andrews), Amy D. Colin (Pittsburgh), R. J. W. Evans (Oxford), Sander L. Gilman (Cornell), Murray G. Hall (Vienna), Leo A. Lensing (Wesleyan), Jacques Le Rider (Paris), Eda Sagarra (Dublin), W. G. Sebald (East Anglia), Joseph Peter Strelka (New York), Robert Wistrich (Jerusalem), W. E. Yates (Exeter).

Books for review should be sent to Ritchie Robertson, St John's College, Oxford OX1 3JP, England.

Manuscripts for publication should be submitted in duplicate to Edward Timms, Arts Building, University of Sussex, Brighton BN1 9QN, England.

Guidelines: Articles should be written in English and should not exceed 7,500 words. They should be typed double-spaced, using endnotes (not a numbered bibliography) to identify the source of quotations. Quotations should normally be given in the original language, followed by an English translation. A detailed style sheet is available from either of the Editors, on request.

Austrian Studies may be ordered through any bookshop. Since it is an annual publication, it may also be obtained by subscription direct from the publishers, Edinburgh University Press, 22 George Square, Edinburgh EH8 9LF, Scotland.